READY FOR REVISED RICA

A TEST PREPARATION GUIDE FOR CALIFORNIA'S READING INSTRUCTION COMPETENCE ASSESSMENT

Third Edition

READY FOR REVISED RICA

A TEST PREPARATION GUIDE FOR CALIFORNIA'S READING INSTRUCTION COMPETENCE ASSESSMENT

James J. Zarrillo
California State University, East Bay

Boston Columbus Indianapolis New York San Francisco Upper Saddle River
Amsterdam Cape Town Dubai London Madrid Milan Munich Paris Montreal Toronto
Delhi Mexico City Sao Paulo Sydney Hong Kong Seoul Singapore Taipei Tokyo

Editor in Chief: Aurora Martinez-Ramos
Editorial Assistant: Meagan French
Vice President, Director of Marketing: Quinn Perkson
Marketing Coordinator: Kate Romano
Executive Marketing Manager: Krista Clark
Marketing Assistant: Elizabeth Mackenzie-Lamb
Senior Managing Editor: Pearson Central Publishing
Production Editor: Cynthia Parsons
Project Manager: Laura Messerly
Operations Supervisor: Pearson Central Publishing
Cover Art Director: Jayne Conte
Cover Designer: Central Design
Full-Service Project Management: Karpagam Jagadeesan, GGS Higher Education Resources, A Division of PreMedia Global, Inc.
Composition: GGS Higher Education Resources, A Division of PreMedia Global, Inc.
Printer/Binder: Bind-Rite Graphics/Robbinsville
Cover Printer: Lehigh-Phoenix Color/Hagerstown
Text Font: Garamond 10/12

Library of Congress Cataloging-in-Publication Data

Zarrillo, James.
    Ready for revised RICA : a test preparation guide for California's reading instruction competence assessment / James J. Zarrillo.—3rd ed.
       p. cm.
    ISBN-13: 978-0-13-700868-1 (alk. paper)
    ISBN-10: 0-13-700868-6 (alk. paper)
    1. Reading (Elementary)—California—Examinations—Study guides. I. Title.

LB1573.Z315 2011
372.48'2'09794—dc22

                                                   2009049203

10 9 8 7 6 5 4 3 2 1

www.pearsonhighered.com

ISBN 13: 978-0-13-700868-1
ISBN 10:   0-13-700868-6

BRIEF CONTENTS

Preface   xi

Introduction   xiii

Chapter 1   Competency 1
Planning, Organizing, and Managing Reading Instruction   1

Chapter 2   Competency 2
Reading Assessment   14

Chapter 3   Competency 3
Phonological and Phonemic Awareness   24

Chapter 4   Competency 4
Concepts About Print, Letter Recognition, and the Alphabetic Principle   31

Chapter 5   Competency 5
Phonics and Sight Words: Terminology and Concepts   41

Chapter 6   Competency 6
Phonics and Sight Words: Instruction and Assessment   47

Chapter 7   Competency 7
Syllabic Analysis, Structural Analysis, and Orthographic Knowledge   57

Chapter 8   Competency 8
Fluency: Role in Reading Development and Factors That Affect the Development of Fluency   65

Chapter 9   Competency 9
Fluency: Instruction and Assessment   69

Chapter 10   Competency 10
Vocabulary, Academic Language, and Background Knowledge: Role in Reading Development and Factors That Affect Development   75

Chapter 11   Competency 11
Vocabulary, Academic Language, and Background Knowledge: Instruction and Assessment   79

Chapter 12   Competency 12
Comprehension: Concepts and Factors Affecting Reading Comprehension   90

Chapter 13   Competency 13
Comprehension: Instruction and Assessment—Before Children Read, While Children Read, and After Children Read   95

Chapter 14   Competency 14
Comprehension: Instruction and Assessment—Understanding and Analyzing Narrative/Literary Texts   104

Chapter 15   Competency 15
Comprehension: Instruction and Assessment—Expository/Informational Texts and Study Skills   114

Chapter 16   Study Guide: Key Points to Remember   125

Chapter 17   The Case Study   130

Chapter 18   Working With the Practice Test on the RICA Website   135

Appendices   138

Reference Notes   149

Index   151

CONTENTS

Preface   New to This Edition   xi

Introduction   The Test, Test-Taking Strategies, and Common Strategies for Meeting the Needs of All Learners   xiii

Chapter 1   Competency 1
Planning, Organizing, and Managing Reading Instruction   1
Introduction   1
Principles of Standards-Based Reading Instruction   1
Key Factors in Differentiated Reading Instruction   4
Organizing Instruction to Meet the Needs of All Students   5
Components of Effective Instructional Delivery in the *California Reading/Language Arts Framework*   6
Engaging and Motivating Students   7
Strategies for Promoting and Monitoring Independent Reading   8
Support Systems to Promote the Skillful Teaching of Reading   12

Chapter 2   Competency 2
Reading Assessment   14
Introduction   14
The Three Primary Purposes of Reading Assessment   14
Alternative Assessments for Students With an Individualized Education Program (IEP) or a Section 504 Plan   15
Quality Indicators That Apply to Standardized Assessments   16
Interpretation and Use of Assessment Results   17
Students' Independent, Instructional, and Frustration Reading Levels   20
Communicating Assessment Results   22

Chapter 3   Competency 3
Phonological and Phonemic Awareness   24
Introduction   24
The Role of Phonological and Phonemic Awareness in Reading Development   25
How to Teach Phonological Awareness, Including Phonemic Awareness   25
The Relationship Between Phonemic Awareness and Development of Phonics Knowledge and Skills   27
Meeting the Needs of All Learners   28
Assessment of Phonological Awareness, Including Phonemic Awareness   29

Chapter 4   Competency 4
Concepts About Print, Letter Recognition, and the Alphabetic Principle   31
Introduction   31
Concepts About Print: Their Role in Early Reading Development and Instructional Strategies   32
The Importance of Letter Recognition in Reading Development and Instructional Strategies   34

The Alphabetic Principle   35

Writing and Students' Understanding of the Alphabetic Principle
and Letter–Sound Correspondence   36

Meeting the Needs of All Learners   36

Assessment of Concepts About Print, Letter Recognition,
and the Alphabetic Principle   38

Chapter 5   **Competency 5**
Phonics and Sight Words: Terminology and Concepts   41

Introduction   41

The Role of Phonics and Sight Words in Word Identification   42

The Sequence of Phonics and Sight Word Instruction   42

The Interrelationships Between Phonics Development and Stages
of Spelling Development   45

Chapter 6   **Competency 6**
Phonics and Sight Words: Instruction and Assessment   47

Introduction   47

The Fundamentals of Teaching Phonics   47

Systematic, Explicit Instruction in Phonics at the Beginning Stage   49

Systematic, Explicit Instruction in Phonics at More Advanced Stages   50

Systematic, Explicit Instruction in Sight Words   51

Meeting the Needs of All Learners   52

Assessment of Phonics and Sight Words   54

Chapter 7   **Competency 7**
**Syllabic Analysis, Structural Analysis, and Orthographic
Knowledge   57**

Introduction   57

How Phonics, Sight Word Knowledge, Structural Analysis, Syllabic
Analysis, and Orthographic Knowledge Work Together   58

How to Teach Structural Analysis and Syllabic Analysis of
Multisyllabic Words   58

How to Teach Spelling   60

Opportunities to Use Structural Analysis Skills, Syllabic Analysis Skills,
and Orthographic Knowledge in Reading and Writing   61

Meeting the Needs of All Learners   61

Assessment of Structural Analysis Skills, Syllabic Analysis Skills,
and Orthographic Knowledge   62

Chapter 8   **Competency 8**
**Fluency: Role in Reading Development and Factors That
Affect the Development of Fluency   65**

Introduction   65

The Key Indicators of Reading Fluency   65

The Role of Fluency in All Stages of Reading Development   66

Interrelationships Among Fluency and Word Analysis Skills,
Background Knowledge, and Comprehension   66

Factors That Can Disrupt Fluency   66

The Role of Decodable Text in Fluent Reading   67

The Role of Systematic, Explicit Instruction in Promoting Fluency
Development   67

Independent Silent Reading and the Development of Fluency   68

Chapter 9   **Competency 9**
Fluency: Instruction and Assessment   69

Introduction   69

Instructional Strategies That Will Improve All Components of Fluency:
Accuracy, Rate, and Prosody   69

Specific Strategies for Building Accuracy   70

Specific Strategies for Building Reading Rate   71

Specific Strategies for Building Prosody   71

Meeting the Needs of All Learners   71

Assessment of Fluency   72

Chapter 10   **Competency 10**
**Vocabulary, Academic Language, and Background
Knowledge: Role in Reading Development
and Factors That Affect Development   75**

Introduction   75

The Role of Vocabulary, Academic Language, and Background
Knowledge in Reading Development   76

Important Issues Related to the Development of Vocabulary, Academic
Language, and Background Knowledge   77

Factors to Consider in Developing Students' Vocabulary, Academic
Language, and Background Knowledge   78

Chapter 11   **Competency 11**
**Vocabulary, Academic Language, and Background
Knowledge: Instruction and Assessment   79**

Introduction   79

Research-Based Principles of Vocabulary Instruction   79

Direct Teaching of Specific Words   80

Independent Word-Learning Strategies   81

Developing Word Consciousness in Students   83

How to Use Wide Reading to Increase Vocabulary, Academic
Language, and Background Knowledge   84

Instructional Activities to Support What Students Have Learned   84

Meeting the Needs of All Learners   85

Assessment of Vocabulary, Academic Language, and Background
Knowledge   87

Chapter 12   **Competency 12**
**Comprehension: Concepts and Factors Affecting Reading
Comprehension   90**

Introduction   90

How Word Analysis, Fluency, Vocabulary, Academic Language, and
Background Knowledge Affect Comprehension   90

Literal Comprehension   91

Inferential Comprehension   91

Evaluative Comprehension   92

The Role of Sentence Structure and Text Structures in Facilitating
Comprehension   92

The Role of Oral Language, Listening Comprehension, Text-Based
Discussions, Writing Activities, and Independent Reading
in Facilitating Comprehension   93

Chapter 13   Competency 13
Comprehension: Instruction and Assessment—Before Children Read, While Children Read, and After Children Read   95

Introduction   95

Instruction Before Children Read   95

While Children Read: Question Classification/Answer Verification   97

While Children Read: Strategic Reading   97

Instruction After Children Read   99

Meeting the Needs of All Learners   99

Assessment of Comprehension   101

Chapter 14   Competency 14
Comprehension: Instruction and Assessment—Understanding and Analyzing Narrative/Literary Texts   104

Introduction   104

Strategies to Help Students Recognize the Structure and Characteristics of Major Genres   104

Instruction in the Elements of Story Grammar   106

Instruction in Narrative Analysis and Literary Criticism   108

Oral Language Activities With Literature   109

Writing Activities With Literature   110

Meeting the Needs of All Learners   110

Assessment of Comprehension of Literary Texts and Literary Response Skills   111

Chapter 15   Competency 15
Comprehension: Instruction and Assessment—Expository/Informational Texts and Study Skills   114

Introduction   114

Characteristics of Expository Texts   114

Using Text Structures   115

Using Text Features   115

Other Instructional Strategies for Content-Area Textbooks   116

Oral and Written Activities for Expository Texts   119

Promoting Study and Research Skills   119

Meeting the Needs of All Learners   121

Assessment of Comprehension of Expository Texts and Research/Study Skills   123

Chapter 16   Study Guide: Key Points to Remember   125

Chapter 17   The Case Study   130

Chapter 18   Working With the Practice Test on the RICA Website   135

Appendices   138

Reference Notes   149

Index   151

PREFACE

NEW TO THIS EDITION

The purpose of this book is to help you pass the revised California Reading Instruction Competence Assessment (RICA), administered for the first time in August 2009. There are two formats for the RICA: a written test and video performance assessment. This book will prepare you to take the written examination.

This third edition includes significant changes from previous editions because the content of the revised RICA is very different from the original test. Over 50% of the content in this third edition is new. Do not prepare to take the RICA by using the first or second editions of this book. The text of *Ready for Revised RICA* (third edition) is new and different because of each of the following factors:

1. This book must have considerable new content because the revised RICA is based on two documents that were completed in 2007, well after the first two editions were written: (a) the new *California Reading/Language Arts Framework* and (b) the revised *RICA Content Specifications*.

2. The original RICA was a test of material organized into 13 "content areas." The revised RICA has a different structure; material is organized into 15 "competencies."

3. This edition must reflect a change in emphasis in the *Content Specifications* for the revised RICA. Some competencies that were content areas in the original RICA now have a greater emphasis. These competences include: (a) Phonemic Awareness, (b) Phonics and Sight Words, (c) Vocabulary, and (d) Comprehension. In the area of Phonemic Awareness, the competency has been retitled to incorporate the broader concept of "Phonological Awareness." In the original RICA, Vocabulary and Phonics/Sight Words were each single content areas. In the *Content Specifications* for the revised RICA, Vocabulary and Phonics/Sight Words each are covered in two competencies (total of four). The changes are most significant for Comprehension. In the revised RICA, 4 of the 15 competencies are about Comprehension.

4. The important topic of Fluency has been given far greater coverage. In the original RICA, Fluency was not even a separate content area; it was buried in the content area on Comprehension. Now, material related to Fluency is covered in two competencies.

5. The role of Academic Language and Background Knowledge in reading development is acknowledged in the revised RICA. There was little mention of these two topics in the original RICA.

6. Finally, this third edition, like the *Content Specifications* for the revised RICA, gives considerable coverage to the topic of Universal Access in reading instruction. For all topics covered in this book, from Letter Recognition to Comprehension of Expository Texts, there is a section on how teachers differentiate instruction to meet the needs of all learners. Specific teaching ideas are provided for (a) struggling readers and students with reading difficulties or disabilities, (b) English learners and speakers of nonstandard English, and (c) advanced learners.

OTHER THINGS TO KEEP IN MIND WHILE USING THIS BOOK TO PREPARE FOR THE RICA

Please note that in comparison to the RICA Content Specifications for the revised test, this book is modified to include the 15 competencies and the names of major topics within each competency. This seemed necessary to achieve both brevity and clarity.

There are a few considerations you should keep in mind while you study from this book. It was written for credential candidates who have taken (or who are taking) reading methods courses. This book is *not* a substitute for coursework or a more comprehensive methodology text on how to teach reading. This book should be read as a review for RICA. It is streamlined, containing essential information you should know before you take the test. You can find out more about the topics covered in this book, including references to journal articles and books, in your reading methods textbook. My purpose is not to analyze elementary reading instruction; my purpose is to help you pass the RICA.

The RICA is a "high-stakes, exit exam." The good news is that *with proper preparation* the chances are very good that you will pass the test.

We would like to thank the following reviewers for their insight and comments: Paul Boyd-Bastone, California State University, Long Beach; Margot Kinberg, National University; Connie Petit, California State University, Bakersfield; and Alice M.L. Quiocho, California State University, San Marcos.

INTRODUCTION:
THE TEST, TEST-TAKING STRATEGIES,
AND COMMON STRATEGIES FOR MEETING
THE NEEDS OF ALL LEARNERS

AN OVERVIEW OF THE TEST

Domains, Competencies, and Test Format

The content of the revised RICA is organized into 15 competencies, which are, in turn, organized under five domains. Again, I have modified the titles of the competencies for brevity and clarity:

Domain 1: Planning, Organizing, and Managing Reading Instruction Based on Ongoing Assessment

> *Competency 1:* Planning, Organizing, and Managing Reading Instruction
>
> *Competency 2:* Reading Assessment

Domain 2: Word Analysis

> *Competency 3:* Phonological and Phonemic Awareness
>
> *Competency 4:* Concepts About Print, Letter Recognition, and the Alphabetic Principle
>
> *Competency 5:* Phonics and Sight Words: Terminology and Concepts
>
> *Competency 6:* Phonics and Sight Words: Instruction and Assessment
>
> *Competency 7:* Syllabic Analysis, Structural Analysis, and Orthographic Knowledge

Domain 3: Fluency

> *Competency 8:* Fluency: Role in Reading Development and Factors That Affect the Development of Fluency
>
> *Competency 9:* Fluency: Instruction and Assessment

Domain 4: Vocabulary, Academic Language, and Background Knowledge

> *Competency 10:* Vocabulary, Academic Language, and Background Knowledge: Role in Reading Development and Factors That Affect Their Development
>
> *Competency 11:* Vocabulary, Academic Language, and Background Knowledge: Instruction and Assessment

Domain 5: Comprehension

> *Competency 12:* Comprehension: Concepts and Factors Affecting Reading Comprehension
>
> *Competency 13:* Comprehension: Instruction and Assessment—Before Children Read, While Children Read, and After Children Read
>
> *Competency 14:* Comprehension: Instruction and Assessment—Understanding and Analyzing Narrative/Literary Texts
>
> *Competency 15:* Comprehension: Instruction and Assessment—Expository/Informational Texts and Study Skills

The format of the revised RICA is the same as the original test. There are three parts to the RICA:

- Multiple Choice Questions
- Short and Long Response Essays (called "Open-Ended Assignments" or "Focused Educational Problems and Instructional Tasks")
- Essay Based on a Case Study

Multiple Choice Questions

The RICA includes 70 multiple choice questions. Ten of the questions are "experimental" and are being tested for future RICAs. You will not know which ten are experimental, so you must try to get every question correct.

Essays (or Open-Ended Assignments)

You will have four essay questions to answer. Two of the questions will require a short answer that must fit on one page—about 75 to 125 words. The other two questions will require a longer answer that must fit on two pages—about 150 to 300 words.

The Case Study

The case study is another essay question. You will be presented with test data about a student and challenged to describe instructional strategies that will help the student become a better reader. The answer must fit on four pages—about 300 to 600 words.

TEST-TAKING STRATEGIES

(1) Don't Waste Time "Self-Assessing" Because You Don't Have to Get Every Answer Right to Pass the Test

One advantage you have with the RICA is that you don't have to answer every question right to pass the test. At the time this book went to press, the minimum passing score for the revised RICA had not been established. It should be close to the minimum passing score on the original RICA. Then, there were 120 points possible on the test. A score of 81 was passing. That was 67.5%! Thus, the following two thoughts should not enter your head: "Hey, I'm doing great on this test," or "Oh my gosh, I'm going to fail." *Don't waste your time evaluating your performance*. Your attitude when you take the test should be business-like. Just answer the questions.

(2) Budget Your Time

On most timed, high-stress tests like the RICA, the most common reason people fail is NOT a lack of knowledge. Rather, it is from not budgeting the time you spend on each question. The more questions you answer, the better your chances for passing the test. Here is more good news about the RICA. You have four hours to complete the test, and you can spend the time however you want. Some students work on the case study first, others take the test in the order it is presented. That is up to you, but what is absolutely essential is that you follow these time allotments:

Multiple Choice Section: 90 minutes

Short Essays: 30 minutes (15 minutes each)

Long Essays: 50 minutes (25 minutes each)

Case Study: 60 minutes

So, be sure you have a watch when you take the RICA and budget your time. If you follow my time guidelines, you will have 10 extra minutes to use however you wish.

(3) Develop a Strategy for Completing the Multiple Choice Section

I am of the opinion that on most tests like the RICA the multiple choice questions are more difficult than the essay questions. So, don't get bogged down or frustrated on the multiple choice section of the RICA. Expect difficult questions. *The biggest mistake you can make when completing the RICA multiple choice section is to spend too much time on this section of the test.*

Answer every question; there is no penalty for guessing.

All multiple choice questions have two parts: (1) a "stem," which is a phrase, a sentence, or a paragraph that leads to the (2) "options." The stems of the multiple choice questions on the RICA will be very long. You probably are used to multiple choice questions with short stems (e.g., "One strategy a fourth-grade teacher could use to build reading comprehension is:"). Long stems make for complicated questions.

There will be two types of multiple choice questions. Some will be "content questions," which will ask if you know the content of RICA (e.g., "All informal reading inventories will include the following tests:"). The more difficult questions are of the second type. These "contextual questions" will provide a classroom scenario and ask you to analyze a specific problem (e.g., "Teacher A has a second-grade classroom with 20 students. She has assessed her students' knowledge of letter–sound relationships and determined that six of her students do not know the *ph* digraph makes the sound of /f/. She should:"). Be sure you read every answer option carefully. As with all multiple choice questions, first eliminate any answer options that are clearly wrong. Then, carefully consider your remaining choices. Select the best possible answer, realizing that sometimes a correct answer will not "leap out" at you.

To conclude, answer every question. Don't take more than 90 minutes on this section. Expect some difficult questions with long stems.

(4) Develop an Appropriate Strategy for Answering the Essays

There are two short essay questions. Your answers must fit on a single page and should be between 75 and 125 words. Take about 15 minutes for each of these questions. There are two long essay questions. Your answers for the long questions must fit on two pages and should be between 150 and 300 words. Take about 25 minutes for each of the long questions. Please note: the word totals are suggestions; the real limitation on the size of your answer is the space provided in the answer booklet.

All the essay questions present a hypothetical situation. You will get information about an entire class, a group of children, or an individual student. Here are some things to remember when you write your answers:

- Answer what they ask, and come directly to the point. The people grading your essays will have lots of papers to read, so don't try to "snow" them.
- Write legibly. Don't expect the person reading your essays to read your essay over and over again to try to figure out what you wrote.
- Be sure to answer each part of the question. For example, on the Practice Test on the RICA website a sample long essay question has these three parts:

  Identify one comprehension need demonstrated by this student To answer this part of the question, simply write a sentence that clearly states the student's area of need and cite the evidence in the question that you relied on to reach that conclusion.

  Describe an instructional strategy or activity to help address this need In this part of your answer, be sure to tell the reader precisely what the teacher and the student will do. Be specific; don't just write something like "implement a direct, explicit lesson on how to predict a story's outcome." Write three or four sentences describing the activity. Also, if you mention a specific instructional approach, like Reciprocal Teaching, do not assume the reader shares your understanding of that approach. Again, take the time to write three or four sentences describing what the teacher and the student will be doing.

  Explain why the strategy or activity you described would be effective for this purpose A portion of a question that asks you to explain why something works is asking for a rationale. How does the strategy help the student? Do not continue to describe what is going on. You could mention the particular strengths of the approach, or you could cite a theoretical or research foundation.

- Use subtitles to structure your essay. Make it easy for the person grading your essay to figure out what part of the question you are answering. For the example provided above, your answer should have three, clearly labeled subtitles:
  1. One Reading Comprehension Need
  2. An Instructional Strategy or Activity to Address That Need
  3. Why the Strategy or Activity Would be Effective

Under each subtopic you would write an appropriate number of sentences to fully answer the question.

(5) Plan Ahead to Use an Appropriate Strategy for Addressing the Case Study

The case study probably will be worth 20% of the total points for the test. The case study is very important, and I will define a strategy for answering it Chapter 17.

(6) Recognize the Attitude of the Test Developers

When you take the RICA, you should adopt the attitude of the policy makers who created it: You believe in a "balanced" approach to reading instruction. As you might know, the field of reading instruction has zealous proponents of radically different approaches to teaching reading. The people who designed RICA believe that teachers should have a balanced instructional program with:

- The direct, explicit teaching of reading skills and strategies. A reading *skill* is something a reader does automatically. For example, a skillful reader knows that in the word *city*, the *c* makes an */s/* sound. A reading *strategy* is something a reader chooses to do, such as reread a paragraph to clarify meaning. "Direct, explicit" teaching means that the teacher sets the objective for a lesson and teaches it in a pleasant, but no-nonsense manner.
- Opportunities to use the skills and strategies through meaningful reading and writing experiences, such as reading library books and writing stories.

When you write your answers to the RICA, do not appear to be "unbalanced"—that is, an overly zealous supporter of either side of the instructional spectrum. You believe that teachers should directly teach students the skills and strategies they need to be good readers. And, you believe students should spend a great deal of time reading and writing.

(7) Devote More Study Time to the Content Areas Which Are Emphasized

The 70 multiple choice questions are allocated as follows:

Domain 1: 10%

Domain 2: 33%

Domain 3: 13%

Domain 4: 20%

Domain 5: 23%

The totals do not equal 100 because of a rounding error.
The essay questions are allocated as follows:

Domain 1: No essay

Domain 2: Long essay

Domain 3: Short essay

Domain 4: Short essay

Domain 5: Long essay

The case study covers all five domains.

There will be questions on material from each of the 15 competencies, so you must be knowledgeable about each area. *It would be wise, however, to devote more time to the competencies in Domains 2, 4, and 5* (those are competencies 3, 4, 5, 6, 7, 10, 11, 12, 13, 14, and 15).

(8) Read the Content Specifications

Be sure that you have read the *Content Specifications* for the RICA. The *Content Specifications* are on the RICA website at **http://www.rica.nesinc.com**. On the left-side menu, click on "Program Information," then click on "Preparation Materials."

(9) Take the Practice Test on the RICA Website

The Practice Test on the RICA website looks exactly like the exam you will take, with different questions, of course. It is very important that you take the Practice Test. Previous editions of this book have included a sample test, but I have decided not to include one in this edition. Rather, I want you to take the Practice Test on the website. In Chapter 18, I will tell you which parts of this book you need to reread should you miss a question on the Practice Test. On the RICA website, on the left-side menu, click on "Program Information," then click on "Written Examination Practice Test."

COMMON STRATEGIES FOR MEETING THE NEEDS OF ALL LEARNERS

Universal access, providing *differentiated instruction* to meet the needs of all learners, is a major focus of the revised RICA. Instruction is differentiated if the teacher has made adjustments to meet the needs of individual students or a group of students with a common need. Across all competencies, common forms of differentiation are mentioned and it might be a good idea to summarize them here. In the relevant chapters, you will find specific examples of how each form of differentiation can be implemented.

(A) Struggling Readers and Students With Learning Disabilities

(1) FOCUS ON KEY SKILLS.   Although our expectations are the same for all learners, struggling readers will need an instructional plan that identifies the most important reading skills and allocates time to teach them. Less attention will be paid to less important skills.

(2) RETEACH WHAT IS NOT MASTERED.   Although most children might acquire either knowledge or skills in relatively few lessons, struggling readers will need more instruction. Two important points need to be made here. The decision to provide additional instruction to any child should be based on the results of assessment. Second, when reteaching something to a struggling reader, the teacher should use different strategies and materials.

(3) TEACH THINGS IN MANAGEABLE UNITS.   A lesson for most children may contain instruction on more than one aspect of reading development. The content of one lesson planned for other students may need to be broken down into separate lessons for struggling learners. Rather than "manageable units," this form of differentiation is sometimes called breaking assignments into "small steps." One important aspect of this intervention is to help struggling learners monitor their progress during each separate step; the students should have some sense if they are ready to move on to the next step.

(4) PROVIDE CONCRETE EXAMPLES.   This is not always possible, but the more lessons for struggling readers that involve three-dimensional instructional resources, the better.

(5) PROVIDE ADDITIONAL PRACTICE.   Once a skill has been introduced, struggling readers will need more opportunities to practice using it before they master the skill.

(6) USE VISUAL, KINESTHETIC, AND TACTILE ACTIVITIES.   Teachers should plan activities that use the full range of learning modes. Most lessons should feature visual resources (illustrations, charts, diagrams); kinesthetic activity (movement); or tactile experiences (touch).

(B) English Learners and Speakers of Nonstandard English

(1) TAKE ADVANTAGE OF TRANSFER OF RELEVANT SKILLS AND KNOWLEDGE FROM THE FIRST LANGUAGE.   For example, in Chapter 11, you will read about *cognates*, words that look alike and mean the same thing in two languages. There are many cognates between English and German-based languages and between English and the Latin-based languages. Some examples of cognates between English and Spanish: *air/aire, active/activo* or *activa, artist/artista*, and *color/color*.

(2) NOTE DIFFERENCES BETWEEN THE FIRST LANGUAGE AND ENGLISH.   And, when there are differences between the first language and English, these need to be noted. For example, in regards to the directionality of print, English goes left-to-right whereas Arabic and Hebrew go right-to-left.

(3) FOCUS ON KEY VOCABULARY.   English learners face the challenge of learning how to recognize and understand thousands of English words in a relatively short period of time. English learners will need more vocabulary instruction than their English-only peers.

(4) TEACH VOCABULARY WITH CONCRETE ITEMS, PICTURES, CHARTS, AND DIAGRAMS. Lessons using English words to teach the meaning of English words can be frustrating for English learners. When possible, vocabulary lessons should involve concrete items, pictures, charts, or diagrams.

(5) MODELING.   English learners will benefit greatly if their teachers slowly and explicitly model what the English learners are supposed to do during a lesson.

(C) Advanced Learners

(1) INCREASING THE PACE AND COMPLEXITY OF INSTRUCTION.   If it takes five lessons to teach most children something, it may only take two lessons to accomplish the same goals with advanced learners. They catch on fast. Also, lessons planned for advanced learners can involve greater complexity—for example, by asking for more critical thinking and analysis.

(2) EXTENDING THE DEPTH AND BREADTH OF INSTRUCTION.   Advanced learners should study some topics in greater depth than their peers. In this form of differentiation, the advanced learners *learn more about one topic*. For example, all fifth-grade students learn about six common Latin root words; the advanced learners learn 10 additional Latin root words. To differentiate by extending the breadth of instruction, advanced learners *learn about additional topics*. For example, advanced learners would explore English words that have common Germanic root words, while the rest of the class would stick with Latin roots.

(3) BUILDING ON AND EXTENDING CURRENT SKILLS.   Advanced learners should have many opportunities to apply what they have learned in novel and challenging ways. For example, after listening to their teacher read a book aloud, advanced learners could be asked to write a script for a one-act play depicting a key scene from the book.

READY FOR REVISED RICA

A TEST PREPARATION GUIDE FOR CALIFORNIA'S READING INSTRUCTION COMPETENCE ASSESSMENT

CHAPTER 1

Competency 1
Planning, Organizing, and Managing Reading Instruction

INTRODUCTION

This chapter discusses how to plan, organize, and manage an instructional program that helps every child achieve California's *English–Language Arts Content Standards*. It also covers how teachers can promote and assess student independent reading.

There are seven topics in this competency:

(1) Principles of standards-based reading instruction
(2) Key factors in differentiated reading instruction
(3) Organizing instruction to meet the needs of all students
(4) Components of effective instructional delivery in the *California Reading/Language Arts Framework*
(5) Engaging and motivating students
(6) Strategies for promoting and monitoring independent reading
(7) Support systems to promote the skillful teaching of reading

We will now examine each of these eight topics.

(1) PRINCIPLES OF STANDARDS-BASED READING INSTRUCTION

(A) The *English–Language Arts (ELA) Content Standards* and California State Board of Education (SBE)-Adopted Materials

Teachers should plan instruction with the following goal: Every student in the classroom will meet the content standards adopted by the California State Board of Education. The California Department of Education and the State Board of Education have established *English–Language Arts Content Standards for California Public Schools, Kindergarten through Grade Twelve*. These standards state what every child should know and be able to do at each grade level. For example, first graders are supposed to be able to "distinguish long- and short-vowel sounds in orally stated, single-syllable words (e.g., *bit/bite*)."

The *English–Language Arts Content Standards* are important. All textbooks purchased with money from the state of California are aligned with these standards. California's assessment of K–12 students, the Standardized Testing and Reporting (STAR) program, now includes a test that measures student achievement of the standards, the California Standards Test (CST). The *English–Language Arts Content Standards* can be found online at the California Department of Education website, www.cde.ca.gov.

The bottom line is simple: All of your instructional decisions, including the materials you choose, how you group students, the activities you plan, and the pace of your teaching, should enable every student to achieve each of the standards for your grade level.

(B) A Balanced, Comprehensive Reading Program as Described by the *California Reading/Language Arts Framework* of 2007

In addition to the *English–Language Arts Content Standards*, the other state-approved document that is important to you is the *California Reading/Language Arts Framework for California Public Schools: Kindergarten through Grade Twelve* of 2007. The *Framework* "provides a blueprint for organizing instruction so that every child meets or exceeds the language arts content standards" (p. 2). The *Framework* provides guidelines on *what* should be taught at each grade level and *how* to assess and teach that content. It also provides guidelines for the selection of instructional materials. The *Framework* calls for an instructional program in reading and language arts that is (1) balanced and (2) comprehensive.

(1) BALANCED INSTRUCTIONAL PROGRAM.   A balanced instructional program is characterized by the strategic and appropriate selection of what skills should be taught, given a child *not* children's level of reading development. This means that more time is devoted to some categories of skills, and less time to others. For example, in first grade more attention will be given to word recognition skills, whereas in sixth grade more attention would be paid to complex comprehension skills.

(2) COMPREHENSIVE INSTRUCTIONAL PROGRAM.   A program is comprehensive when the teacher works on helping students achieve *all* the grade-level standards. At each grade level there are English–Language Arts standards in each of the following categories: (a) word analysis, fluency, and systematic vocabulary development; (b) reading comprehension; (c) literary response and analysis; (d) writing strategies and writing applications; (e) written and oral English language conventions; (f) listening and speaking strategies; and (g) speaking applications. The key is that teachers should not get bogged down on any one component of the reading/language arts program.

This means that the children in your classroom should receive direct, explicit instruction in reading skills and strategies; *and* they should have opportunities to use those skills and strategies to read a variety of texts and write in several formats.

A *skill* is something that a reader does automatically (or, with *automaticity*). The ability to decode is a skill; for example, knowing that the *c* in *cake* is "hard," and makes the /k/ sound, whereas the *c* in *city* is "soft," and makes the /s/ sound. A *strategy* is something a reader consciously chooses to implement. For example, a reader may want to get an overview of a chapter in a social studies textbook, so she previews the chapter by reading the first paragraph, all the subtitles, and the chapter summary.

In a comprehensive instructional program, in addition to direct, explicit, skills and strategy lessons, the instructional program should include *many opportunities for students to read and write*. These activities challenge the students to do many things, such as reading books the teacher has selected, reading books they have selected themselves, reading social studies and science textbooks, reading plays through readers theater, chanting poems and rhymes aloud, writing in journals, composing and sending emails to students in other countries, authoring original poems and stories, and discussing books and stories in small-group formats.

(C) Instructional Decisions Based on Ongoing Assessment Results

We will discuss this principle in greater detail in the next chapter. You should make instructional decisions on the basis of the results of ongoing assessment that utilizes a variety of assessment tools. For example, you want your first graders to hear the difference in long and short vowel sounds in single syllable words (the difference between *bit/bite, bat/bait, bed/bead*). Ideally, you would test your students to determine who has achieved this standard and who has not. Those students who have met the standard will work on other reading activities while you provide direct instruction to those children who have not yet met the standard.

(D) Systematic and Explicit Instruction—Preventing Reading Difficulties Before They Occur

Recently, there has been an emphasis on the importance of *systematic*, *direct*, and *explicit* skill and strategy instruction. There are two dimensions of *systematic* teaching. First, the teacher knows precisely what skills and strategies each student at each grade level should master, as defined by the relevant set of content standards. Second, the teacher is "systematic" in that the results of assessments focus instructional planning—those students who are not acquiring a skill or strategy are grouped together for additional lessons. *Direct and explicit* skill and strategy lessons are teacher-directed, and though the teacher may use any of a number of resources, the objective of the lesson is to teach a specific reading skill or strategy. These lessons are best taught to small groups of students who share a common need. For example, a first-grade teacher implements three lessons for five children who are having difficulty understanding that in words with the CVCe pattern, the vowel is long (words like *bite* and *cake*).

The goal of systematic and explicit instruction in the early grades is to prevent reading difficulties. Effective reading/language arts programs focus on *prevention rather than remediation* (remediation is the process of helping a child "catch up" and learn what his or her classmates have already mastered). Even the most successful instructional programs will have some children who are struggling readers. Remedial programs that focus on our youngest readers who are having difficulty are called *early intervention* programs. These programs try to address reading difficulties at the first possible opportunity. Many offer individualized instruction, like Reading Recovery, which features highly trained teachers working in one-to-one settings. Other programs provide intervention to children in small groups.

(E) Mastery of Skills—Developmental Issues and Foundational Skills

The *English–Language Arts Content Standards* define what skills and knowledge children should acquire at each grade level. There is a developmental aspect to learning to read in that some skills that are appropriate for children at one grade level would be difficult, if not impossible, to teach at an earlier grade. At the same time, some skills and knowledge cannot be learned unless children have mastered prerequisite skills and knowledge.

For example, one of the standards requires fifth graders to "draw inferences, conclusions, or generalizations about text and support them with textual evidence and prior knowledge" when reading grade-level-appropriate texts (Comprehension and Analysis of Grade-Level-Appropriate Texts, 2.4). Obviously, this would be a difficult standard for a second grader, especially if she or he were reading a fifth-grade textbook! The acquisition of many skills is a prerequisite for a fifth grader to achieve this standard. For example, a fifth grader who had not mastered the second-grade standard of "knowing the meaning of simple prefixes and suffixes" could not make generalizations from a chapter in a fifth-grade social studies textbook, which would be filled with many words with common prefixes and suffixes.

(F) Differentiated Instruction

Teachers must address the full range of learners in the classroom and convey high expectations to all learners. Almost all teachers will have students who are acquiring English as a second language (English learners), children who speak nonstandard dialects of English (speakers of nonstandard English), students who have difficulty learning to read (struggling readers), students with learning disabilities (students with special needs), and students with extraordinary ability (advanced learners). Because each child's needs are unique, teachers must differentiate instruction to meet individual differences. Instruction is differentiated if the teacher has made adjustments to meet the needs of individual students or a group of students sharing the same need.

One way instruction becomes differentiated is when a teacher no longer relies solely on whole-group lessons. Teachers should use a variety of grouping formats. (See Section (3) below.)

In addition to grouping, instruction becomes differentiated when the teacher selects appropriate strategies for different groups of children. For example, for struggling readers, a teacher may narrow the focus to a skill, reteach certain concepts, and increase the number of concrete examples used in a lesson.

Finally, differentiated instruction means that the teacher chooses different resources and materials for different groups of students. Advanced learners, for example, may be asked to read texts that would be far beyond the comprehension of their classmates.

(G) Short- and Long-Term Goals and Learning Objectives

Long-term planning is for the school year, often organized for each month. Short-term planning covers a briefer time span, such as a week or two. Successful short-term and long-term planning requires that the teacher have a thorough understanding of the relevant grade-level standards. For long-term planning, the teacher should allocate enough time so that the full range of standards will be covered. Many school districts provide teachers with *pacing guides*, which describe how long a teacher should take to teach something.

A goal is a broad target to be achieved over the long term (the school year) or the short term (a week or two). To achieve a goal, a teacher will implement several lessons, each with a small number of learning objectives. For example, a second-grade teacher's long-term goal in the area of literary response and analysis would come from the *English–Language Arts Content Standards*, which state that second-grade students should "read and respond to a wide variety of significant children's literature." A short-term goal for 2 weeks would be to have students achieve standard 3.1, which is that students will "compare and contrast plots, settings, and characters presented by different authors." The *Framework* provides "A Curricular and Instructional Profile" for this standard and recommends that the first couple of lessons use two brief stories with some similarities and differences. The *Framework* recommends *Peter Rabbit* and *Curious George*. The first lesson may focus on the prerequisite skill of the identification of plot, setting, and character. Students can't compare plots, settings, and characters unless they first are able to identify those elements. A learning objective for that lesson would be "students will identify the setting in *Peter Rabbit*."

It is important that teachers define *evidence-based* learning objectives for lessons. This means that the teacher has defined some source of evidence that will indicate whether or not each individual child has met the objective. Such evidence is not limited to paper-and-pencil tasks; the evidence can be something the students say or do, but it is more difficult to keep accurate records of oral or nonwritten evidence. For the objective listed in the previous paragraph, identifying the setting in *Peter Rabbit*, the teacher's evidence could be a worksheet the students complete after listening to the story. Given a description of several story settings, the students would put an X next to the one that describes the setting of *Peter Rabbit*.

(2) KEY FACTORS IN DIFFERENTIATED READING INSTRUCTION

When planning reading instruction that will meet the needs of all learners, teachers must consider each of the following factors:

(A) Students' Knowledge and Skills

Throughout this section, we will use the following first-grade standard (Decoding and Word Recognition 1.15): "Students will read common word families (e.g., *-ite, -ate*)." The first-grade teacher should have collected data on an ongoing basis and know which of his students are strong in the area of decoding and word recognition and which students have difficulty in this type of task.

(B) Prerequisite Knowledge and Skills

More specifically, the teacher must have data on each student's mastery of prerequisite skills and knowledge. For this standard, students must have mastered their initial consonant sounds. For example, for students to read words with -*ate*, such as *date*, *fate*, and *mate*, they must be able to associate the correct sound for *d, f,* and *m*.

(C) Pacing of Instruction

Once the teacher has a good sense of where students are in regards to the knowledge and skills in the area of decoding, and once the teacher knows where the students are in regards to prerequisite knowledge and skills, the teacher must make instructional pacing decisions. This includes how many lessons it will take to achieve the objective and how long each lesson should take. To differentiate instruction, some children may need more lessons than their peers and some children may need adapted lessons that go at a slower pace.

(D) Complexity of the Content/Skills to Be Presented

The difficulty of the skill students are asked to learn will affect several instructional decisions. The teacher may conclude that reading words with -*ite* and -*ate* is not a particularly difficult one for first graders. Thus, the teacher would plan less differentiation than with a more complex skill.

(E) Scaffolds

The *Framework* defines a scaffold as the "temporary support, guidance, or assistance provided to a student on a new or complex task" (p. 361). For this standard two levels of scaffolds should be defined: (1) those that will be included in initial lessons for the whole group, and (2) those that will be used for small-group or individualized lessons for students having difficulty.

    For an initial, whole-group lesson, where students are asked to blend *d, f, g, m,* and *r* with -*ate* to make *date, fate, gate, mate,* and *rate,* the teacher would model the blending process, using her left hand to pretend to "hold" the consonant sound and her left hand to hold -*ate*. As the teacher blends the sounds to make words, her two hands would come together. When working with a small group of children struggling with this standard, the teacher might provide a scaffold by starting each of three "booster" lessons by reviewing the initial consonant sounds involved.

(3) ORGANIZING INSTRUCTION TO MEET THE NEEDS OF ALL STUDENTS

(A) Flexible Grouping, Individualized Instruction, and Whole-Class Instruction

Teachers will form *flexible* groups so children who share the need for a reading skill or strategy will be taught efficiently. Groups are flexible because they exist for a single purpose and will be disbanded as soon as the teacher has completed the lessons planned for the group. For example, a kindergarten teacher has assessed her students and determined that 5 of her 19 students do not have the concept about print called "directionality," that English texts go left to right, top to bottom. That group of five students would receive a three-lesson sequence of remedial lessons.

    For other lessons, especially to teach comprehension, children will be organized so that each group is composed of readers with the same instructional reading level. These are *homogeneous* groups—because the children in each group have the same ability. Finally, some groups will be composed of children with different reading abilities (*heterogeneous* groups). For example, a group performing a reader's theater presentation may have students with several instructional reading levels, yet there can be roles that require different levels of reading proficiency.

    Those students who are having particular difficulty will need *individualized instruction*. These one-on-one sessions can be provided by the classroom teacher, a reading coach, or an adult volunteer who has received appropriate training.

    Whole-class instruction usually takes place at the beginning of a multiple-lesson instructional sequence. After all students have received the initial lessons, the teacher should conduct progress-monitoring assessments to determine which children are getting it and which children will need extra, or booster lessons.

(B) The Use of Core California SBE-Adopted Materials

The California State Board of Education (SBE) approves (or "adopts") five different program types of materials for reading/language arts instruction.

First, almost all school districts will purchase SBE-adopted reading/language arts basic programs. These programs are called *basal reading programs* and feature, at each grade level, the following components: a teacher's manual, a student text (called a "basal" or a "reader"), student workbooks and/or reproducible worksheets, supplemental books, CDs with additional resources, and a package of assessment tools. The program must have resources to help English learners, struggling readers, and advanced readers. More specifically, these programs must have support materials for struggling readers that provide 30 additional minutes of instruction, and lesson plans for this additional instruction must be included in the teacher's edition and student materials.

The other four types of SBE-adopted instructional programs that school districts might purchase include programs that provide *additional* instruction for English learners, programs written in languages other than English, intensive intervention programs for struggling readers in grades 4 through 8; and intensive intervention programs for English learners in grades 4 through 8.

(C) Benchmark, Strategic, and Intensive Groups

All students who are having difficulty and need differentiated instruction are not equal. That is to say, they will have different levels of difficulty and effective teachers will implement different levels and types of intervention. One system used to classify students who are struggling uses the following three categories: *benchmark*, *strategic*, and *intensive* groups. In some schools all struggling readers are placed into one of these three groups.

Students in a benchmark group are experiencing a small level of difficulty in achieving standards. Differentiated instruction for benchmark students does not involve separate resources. Usually, a small amount of extra help using the basal reading program will allow the students to acquire the knowledge and skills they need. The classroom teacher can provide the help benchmark students require.

The strategic group, on the other hand, consists of students who are one or two years behind their peers. Simply reteaching from the basal reader will not work for these students. Classroom teachers will need to plan special lessons and use additional resources. Specially trained tutors may help the classroom teacher.

Students in the intervention group need considerable help. They are often more than 2 years behind. Many will be in special education programs. Lessons for children in the intervention group will have the highest level of differentiation, using special resources. Almost all lessons will have a slower pace. Lessons will be designed so that complex skills and complicated knowledge will be broken down into more manageable "chunks."

(4) COMPONENTS OF EFFECTIVE INSTRUCTIONAL DELIVERY IN THE *CALIFORNIA READING/LANGUAGE ARTS FRAMEWORK*

The *Framework* presents a model of instructional delivery for reading lessons that includes the following components:

(A) Orientation

In this first phase of a lesson, the teacher can do a number of things to orient students to the knowledge and skills they will be taught. The teacher, in most cases, will provide an overview of what will take place in the lesson, stressing what students will be expected to do. The teacher might do something to motivate students so they are engaged in the lesson. This could include bringing an artifact to show the students, displaying an illustration, writing an important word on the board, or asking a stimulating question.

(B) Presentation

In this next section of the lesson, the teacher provides students what they need to acquire the knowledge and skills they are expected to learn. In most lessons, this involves direct, explicit instruction by the teacher (e.g., "Homophones are two words that sound alike but have different meanings ..."). If the lesson focuses on a process, then the teacher usually will model what students are expected to do (e.g., "Watch me blend the sound the *m* makes with the sound that *-ate* makes to build a word ..."). In some instances the presentation is not made by the teacher. The teacher might show a video, play an audiotape, invite a guest to talk, or invite an "expert" student to model something.

(C) Structured and Guided Practice

In the next phase, students complete some task under the close supervision of the teacher. This may be a paper-and-pencil task, it may be a small-group discussion, or it may be some overt, physical action by the students (e.g., "I want you to do the first three items on page 16 in your workbooks while I watch you ..."). While the teacher observes the students, he or she would stop and do the following with individual students:

1. The teacher might reinforce what has been learned, either by restating something or re-modeling a process.

2. The teacher might question students to see if they can explain what they are doing.

3. The teacher might provide feedback, noting when students are doing things correctly, while pointing out mistakes and offering suggestions for those who are on the wrong track.

(D) Independent Practice and Application

Finally, the lesson will conclude with opportunities for students to practice what they have learned or to apply what they have learned. Independent practice differs from guided practice in that the teacher will not be available to monitor student performance and provide feedback. Thus, independent practice can be homework or it can occur in the classroom if the teacher is working with a small group or individual.

(5) ENGAGING AND MOTIVATING STUDENTS

(A) A Stimulating Learning Environment That Promotes Success

The classroom environment can help students become more involved in reading instruction and be excited about reading. Teachers should be positive and upbeat during reading instruction. Excitement is contagious. Teachers should praise students when they do well and be sympathetic when they struggle. Students also need to be polite to their peers and understand that everyone will make mistakes. No "put-downs" should be tolerated. The classroom should have a library with many books. Bulletin board displays should feature student work related to reading instruction.

(B) Appropriate Reading Materials

It should go without saying that children should only be asked to read materials that they *can* read. In Chapter 2, you will learn how to determine each child's independent, instructional, and frustration reading levels. For self-paced, silent reading, teachers need to provide children with books they can read easily. For direct instruction, children should be asked to read material that is challenging, but within their grasp. Books at a child's frustration level, too hard for them to read on their own or without considerable help from the teacher, should only be read aloud to children.

Providing students materials they can read will be a real challenge when teaching social studies and science—because all students have to read the same grade-level textbook. For English learners and struggling readers, teachers should bring to class several books from the library, written at a reading levels easier than the grade-level textbook, that cover the same topics presented in the textbook.

(C) Reading Aloud to Students

Almost all elementary school teachers read aloud daily to their students. This is a good way to introduce students to the best of children's literature. Teachers who read aloud effectively, with enthusiasm and dramatic effect, can affect the reading habits of their students. The key is to bring books that are "related" to the read-aloud selection to class. For example, if a teacher is reading aloud *The Runaway Bunny* to a class of first graders, he or she should bring to class other books written by Margaret Wise Brown, such as *Goodnight, Moon* and *The Little Island*. A sixth-grade teacher who reads aloud *The Book of Three*, the first book in Lloyd Alexander's five-book series, "The Chronicles of Prydain," should have copies of the second book in the series, *The Black Cauldron*.

(D) Book Clubs, Literature Circles, and Author Studies

All of these activities provide formats for small groups of students to talk about what they have read. Discussions about literature, if done properly, can motivate students to read and provide a lifelong appreciation of literature.

(1) BOOK CLUBS.   In the book club format, a small group of students are assigned by the teacher to read the same book. They meet occasionally while they read the book and immediately after they have finished. For example, in a fifth-grade classroom, one group is reading *Holes*, another *Ella Enchanted*, and the third, *Bud, Not Buddy*. Over time, the teacher's goal is to give students control over book club discussions and say as little as possible. The key is to present the members of the book club with questions that are open-ended and provocative, in that they have a good chance to spark spirited discussions. Some teachers use a more structured format, assigning roles to students ("moderator," "recorder," etc.) and using a generic set of questions all groups must answer.

(2) LITERATURE CIRCLES.   This is another small-group discussion format, but here the students have selected what each member of the circle will read. This usually is a book, but it could also be a poem, a story, even a newspaper article. The first step is to help the members of the circle agree on what they will read. Usually the teacher has multiple copies of four or five books. The teacher delivers a book talk on each book, and the students select the book they would like to read. The circles are then formed, and in a process similar to a book club, they meet during and after reading the book for discussion.

(3) AUTHOR STUDIES.   Another format for student discussion about literature focuses on authors, rather than one book. The teacher would assign a group of students to read the books of a prominent author of children's literature. There are several formats author studies can take. In each, members of the group read one book written by the author. For example, in a Scott O'Dell group, all members read *Island of the Blue Dolphins*. The group meets and discusses this common book. Individual members of the author study group choose other books by the author to read—in this example two students read *Zia*, one read *Sing Down the Moon*, and one read *The King's Fifth*. Students present book talks on these books. Under the teacher's guidance, the students would then critically analyze the author's work to answer the question, "What makes this author's books special?"

(6) STRATEGIES FOR PROMOTING AND MONITORING INDEPENDENT READING

Independent reading refers to reading at times other than as a part of a teacher-directed lesson. The material children read independently will usually be fiction, but should also include biographies, information books, magazines, and newspapers. Please note that in this book I use the word *text* to refer to any printed material—books, magazines, recipes, newspaper articles, traffic tickets, the RICA, a Coca-Cola can—anything that uses letters and words and can be read.

Teachers should guide students to high-quality children's books and, in some cases, assign books for their students to read. Most independent reading, however, should be *self-selected* and *self-paced*. Reading is self-selected if the child chooses what she will read, and it is self-paced if the child reads the book with no externally imposed deadline.

Independent reading plays a critical role in a child's overall development, not just as in the area of literacy, but also in other academic areas and in their moral and ethical growth. Consider the following potential advantages of independent reading:

1. Provides greater familiarity with language patterns
2. Increases reading fluency
3. Increases vocabulary
4. Broadens knowledge in the content areas
5. Motivates further reading

We will now examine the strategies teachers should use to promote student independent reading.

(A) How to Teach Students to Select Books at Appropriate Reading Levels

Effective teachers connect children with books for independent reading that are just right for them. For the most part, these will be books that are at each student's *independent reading level*, books that can be read easily with little help from the teacher. The definition of independent reading level will be provided in Chapter 2. In that chapter you will also learn how to determine each child's independent reading level.

A far greater challenge for teachers is to teach children themselves to select books at appropriate levels of difficulty. The general rule—sometimes called the "Goldilocks Test"—is to tell students to pick a book that is not too easy, not too hard, but just right. A test for readers in second grade or higher is sometimes called the "Five Fingers Test." The student selects a book and turns to a page in the middle of the book. The page should have at least 50 words on it. The child then reads that page, putting one finger up each time he or she comes to a word he or she cannot read. If the child has five fingers up before coming to the end of the page, it is time to "waive good-bye" to the book and select something easier.

(B) Students' Personal Interests

Students will read more if they are encouraged to read books that fit their personal interests. Teachers need to connect students to such books and that requires the teacher to know what topics each student finds most interesting.

(1) INTEREST INVENTORIES.   Reading interest inventories are surveys of student reading behavior. They should be given orally to younger children; older students can write their answers on the inventory itself. These inventories include two types of questions: (a) those that try to determine to what extent the child values reading as a recreational activity; and (b) those that try to determine the child's reading preferences. Questions on an interest inventory might include:

If your teacher said you can spend one hour doing any school activity you wanted, what would you choose?

How much time each day do you spend reading books at home?

Who is your favorite author?

Which of the following types of books do you like to read? Check as many as you like:

   Animal stories
   Fairy tales
   Mysteries
   Historical fiction (stories that take place in the past)
   Adventures
   High fantasy (such as the Harry Potter books)

As with any form of survey, teachers should interpret the results of an interest inventory cautiously, especially with older students. Many students have learned that reading is important to teachers and thus will claim to read a lot more than they really do. The results of an interest inventory should be used in concert with the data gathered from student reading logs and your records of individual conferences.

(2) PUTTING IT TOGETHER: THE "I + I STRATEGY"—INTERESTING BOOKS AT THE STUDENTS' INDEPENDENT READING LEVEL.   So far, we have stressed the importance of using two factors to connect students to books that are most appropriate for independent reading: (a) the student's independent reading level and (b) the student's personal interests. These two factors can be put together in the I + I Strategy to motivate independent reading. It is not easy to get reluctant readers to read, but your best bet is to remember this formula: Independent reading level + Personal interest = Best chance of success. First, determine the child's independent reading level. Next, either administer an interest survey or ask the student what type of book he or she likes to read. Then, go the school library or public library and find a book that meets both criteria. This will be a book that the student will be interested in, written at a level he or she can read easily. To get things rolling, it will help if you read the first part of the book to the child.

(C) Structured Independent-Reading Opportunities in Class

(1) SUSTAINED SILENT READING (SSR).   SSR is a time when everyone in the classroom reads silently. Held at the same time every day, this may be as little as 5 minutes a day during the first weeks of first grade or as much as 30 minutes a day in a sixth-grade classroom. Children select their own reading material, which may be books, newspapers, encyclopedias, magazines, or their textbooks. It is very important that everybody, the teacher and any visitors to the room included, read silently. No interruptions are acceptable. SSR also is sometimes called DEAR (Drop Everything and Read).

(2) READERS' WORKSHOP.   Some teachers implement an instructional format called Readers' Workshop. This is an hour or more a day when children read silently, small groups work on projects, and the teacher meets with individual students and groups of children. The format was often expanded to include both reading and writing. A balanced, comprehensive approach to reading instruction makes it difficult for teachers to use readers'/writers' workshop every day. It simply isn't a format conducive to the amount of direct, explicit teaching expected of teachers at the current time. Recently, I have seen teachers with balanced reading programs who use readers'/writers' workshop one or two days a week. This provides time for direct instruction and time for independent reading and writing.

(D) At-Home Reading

Virtually all parents want their children to become good readers and are willing to work with teachers to support the at-home reading of their children. Here are some ideas to support parents:

(1) EVERYONE HAS A ROLE: TEACHERS, STUDENTS, PARENTS/GUARDIANS.   The key to promoting at-home reading is to create a system where teachers, students, and parents/guardians all have well-defined roles. The teacher makes sure that the student leaves the classroom with a book to read at home and a form that parents/guardians will sign verifying that the student read at home. The parent/guardian provides a quiet time and place for the student to read and signs the form verifying that the student read. Students are responsible for reading at home and coming back to school with their books and the verification forms.

(2) LET CHILDREN TAKE HOME BOOKS FROM THE CLASSROOM OR SCHOOL LIBRARY.   Both your classroom and school libraries should have checkout systems so that everyone knows which books a child has borrowed. The vast majority of children will return books promptly. Some children will struggle with returning books and, in those cases, teachers and parents must work together to help children be responsible.

(3) PROVIDE LISTS OF BOOKS THAT CAN BE CHECKED OUT OF THE PUBLIC LIBRARY.   Parents of kindergarteners and first graders welcome a list of books that they can read aloud to their children. Teachers can also prepare lists of books for children to read on their own. I know one teacher who provided each parent with a list of "Fifty Great Books for Fourth Graders." Lists of information books on topics in social studies and science also should be sent home. To promote books and independent reading, all children should have public library cards.

(4) SUPPORT FOR PARENTS OF ENGLISH LEARNERS.   One final point. Almost 40% of our K–12 school population is acquiring English as a second language. We can support our English learners (ELs) by acknowledging their bilingual status. All communication with parents should be in the language the parent understands. Parents should be encouraged to read to their children in their native language and, if possible, in English. During SSR at home, some of the books read may be in the EL's first language because our goal is the development of the "reading habit." Lists of good books written in a language other than English at public libraries should be made available to parents.

(E) Methods for Monitoring Student Independent Reading

(1) STUDENT-MAINTAINED READING LOGS.   Each student should keep a record of the books he or she has read independently. A child in the grade 1 or 2 can write the name of each book, the book's author, the date he or she finished the book, and a personal response on an index card. The cards can be held together with yarn or stored in a file box. Older children should enter the same information on a reading log, which is kept in a folder. Yes, it is true that some children may commit fraud and enter books they haven't finished to impress the teacher. The results of individual conferences and common sense, however, will allow you to determine who has been "fudging." These reading logs reveal important information about the independent reading habits of your students. Some teachers now have computer-based reading logs. There is a template that each student fills in when he or she has finished reading a book independently; the templates are stored electronically in a database the teacher maintains.

(2) BOOK REPORTS.   Book reports require the student to do more than record the minimal information provided in a reading log. A caution is in order here—the task of completing a book report should never be so onerous that it serves as a deterrent to reading. Some teachers create a "generic" book report form for fiction and another for information books. For example, the generic fiction book report might ask students to write something about the characters, setting, plot, and theme of a book. Other teachers have a "menu" of options for book reports that include writing activities (e.g., write a sequel to the story or write a review of the book); performing arts options (e.g., act out a scene from the book); and visual arts options (e.g., create a collage or a diorama).

(3) FORMAL AND INFORMAL ORAL PRESENTATIONS.   Teachers can also use both formal and informal student oral presentations to monitor student independent reading. Formal presentations tend to be oral versions of a written book reports. Students talk about the characters, setting, plot, and theme of the book. A more creative option is to ask students to review books orally, like the late Gene Siskel, Roger Ebert, and their successors have done for feature films on the "At the Movies" television program. These formal presentations should be rehearsed. Informal presentations are more difficult. For example, students who have read similar books may constitute a panel and the teacher serves as moderator, asking questions that the students answer.

(4) INDIVIDUAL CONFERENCES.   Although they require a one-on-one setting, teachers should hold regular, individual conferences with their students. During and immediately after these conferences, teachers should take notes. Some teachers record these notes on laptop computers. Each child comes to the conference with his or her literature journal, his or her reading log (a record of the books read), and the book he or she is currently reading. The teacher uses the conference to discuss what the child has read, to help the child find new books to read, and to work on a skill or strategy the child has not mastered. The child may read to the teacher or the teacher may read to the child. Even if the conferences are held as infrequently as every 2 weeks, they yield important data.

Reading logs, book reports, oral presentations, and individual conferences can all be used to monitor student independent reading. Whatever option the teachers decides to use, the key is that it should provide the teacher with useful information. These monitoring options should help the teacher do each of the following: (a) determine whether or not the student did, in fact, read the book with some reasonable level of understanding, (b) learn more about the student's reading interests, and (c) learn more about the student's ability to read, write, and speak.

(7) SUPPORT SYSTEMS TO PROMOTE THE SKILLFUL TEACHING OF READING

Elementary school teachers have support systems that can improve their teaching of reading, including reading coaches, grade-level meetings, and professional development opportunities.

(A) Reading Coaches

Many school districts in California have teachers who serve as reading coaches (also called *literacy coaches*). Though this varies from district to district, most reading coaches have advanced training and hold either the California Reading/Language Arts Specialist Certificate or Credential. Reading coaches can play many roles, but their main focus should be to provide ongoing, consistent support to classroom teachers. Teachers should know that reading coaches are not administrators, coaches do not evaluate the teachers they support.

Reading coaches are most effective when classroom teachers honestly assess their teaching and ask for help in specific aspects of their teaching (e.g., "I need help meeting the needs of my struggling readers—they don't seem to make any progress"). The reading coach can help in a number of ways. The coach can observe the classroom teacher, model effective strategies, co-plan with the teacher, or help interpret assessment data. Effective reading coaches understand that "one-shot" presentations or haphazard interventions don't work—they know that they need to work with teachers throughout the school year.

(B) Grade-Level Meetings

Within a school or the larger school district, teachers at the same grade level share many challenges. Meetings of teachers at the same grade level can be productive if they are well planned. The focus of the meetings should be on the grade-level *English–Language Arts Content Standards*. Some grade-level meetings are sharing sessions, with an open agenda—teachers share assessment tools and instructional strategies. Other meetings focus on specific tasks. For example, a second-grade standard is that all students will "understand and explain common antonyms and synonyms" (Word analysis, fluency, and systematic vocabulary development, 1.7). Let's assume there are four second-grade teachers. In their first meeting, the teachers designed a pretest and posttest for the standard. In their second meeting, the teachers designed an instructional sequence of five lessons for this standard.

(C) Professional Development

Effective teachers of reading are lifelong learners. The largest international organization dedicated to reading instruction is the International Reading Association (IRA). University professors, state and federal policy makers, reading coaches, school administrators, classroom teachers, and other interested members of the public all belong to the IRA. The state affiliate of the IRA is the California Reading Association (CRA). The annual conferences of the IRA and the CRA are multiday events with hundreds of valuable sessions for classroom teachers. Local school districts often make reading instruction the topic of ongoing training sessions for their teachers, with or without special funding from the state or federal governments. Over the last 6 years, however, the federal No Child Left Behind Act has provided large amounts of money for reading-related training for classroom teachers.

CHAPTER 2

Competency 2
Reading Assessment

INTRODUCTION

Assessment is the process of gathering, interpreting, and using data. The assessment of reading development is complicated because there are many aspects of reading that must be measured. Here I am using the broader word *assessment*, rather than *testing*. Although many aspects of reading development can be measured by tests, there are other ways of gathering information. In this chapter, we are concerned with the general principles of assessment, some terminology you should know, and informal reading inventories (IRIs). You will read about specific assessment instruments and procedures for each of the major areas of reading development in Chapters 3, 4, 6, 7, 9, 11, 13, 14, and 15.

There are six topics in this competency:

(1) The three primary purposes of reading assessment
(2) Alternative assessments for students with an Individualized Education Program (IEP) or a Section 504 Plan
(3) Quality indicators that apply to standardized assessments
(4) Interpretation and use of assessment results
(5) Students' independent, instructional, and frustration reading levels
(6) Communicating assessment results

(1) THE THREE PRIMARY PURPOSES OF READING ASSESSMENT

The *California Reading/Language Arts Framework* distinguishes three types of assessment: (a) entry-level assessments, (b) monitoring of progress assessments, and (c) summative assessments.

(A) Entry-Level Assessments

Entry-level assessments are implemented *prior to* instruction to determine (1) which students possess prerequisite skills and knowledge and (2) which students already have mastered the skills that are going to be taught. Let us look at an example. A fifth-grade standard in the area of Literary Response and Analysis is that students will "identify the main problem or conflict in the plot and explain how it is resolved" (3.2).

A prerequisite skill is that students would be able to identify the main events of a plot and explain their causes; this is a fourth-grade standard. A teacher might plan two entry-level assessments prior to teaching a seven-lesson unit on this standard. In the first entry-level assessment the teacher asks students to read a short story and list the three main events of the plot and explain what factors led to them. Students who have difficulty with this task will have little chance of successfully identifying central problems in stories and explaining how they are resolved.

The second entry-level assessment would determine which students have already achieved the standard. Students would be asked to read a short story, identify the main problem in the story, and explain how it is resolved.

The Framework makes it clear that the purpose of entry-level assessment is not to keep some students from attempting to acquire a standard. Rather, entry-level assessments indicate which students will need more help.

(B) Monitoring of Progress Assessments

Monitoring of progress assessments take place *during* an instructional unit. These assessments tell the teacher which students are making adequate progress toward achieving the target standard(s). Let us continue with our fifth-grade example on identifying the problem in a story and explaining how the problem was resolved. The teacher would plan several progress-monitoring assessments.

The first two lessons teach students that in many stories the problem is a conflict between the protagonist and the antagonist. The protagonist is trying to achieve something and the antagonist attempts to thwart her. The first two stories the students read should have clearly defined protagonists and antagonists; a simple conflict; and a single, clear resolution. The teacher plans a formal monitoring of progress assessment after the second lesson. Working in isolation, after reading the story, the students must complete four simple, paper-and-pencil tasks: (1) identify the protagonist, (2) identify the antagonist, (3) state what the conflict is, and (4) explain how the conflict is resolved. Later lessons will deal with stories with complex problems, unsuccessful attempts to resolve them, and more vague resolutions.

On the basis of this monitoring of progress assessment, the teacher will identify which students will receive an extra lesson on protagonists, antagonists, and how their actions create conflict.

Two final points need to be made. First, not all monitoring of progress assessments need to be formal, "test-like" assessments. Teacher observation of student behavior during instruction is also an important source of data. Second, the results of monitoring of progress assessments need to be analyzed at the individual and classroom levels. If large numbers of students are not "getting it," the teacher should replan the unit of instruction. If, on the other hand, almost all of the class finds the skill easy to master, then the teacher may accelerate instruction for the whole class, while teaching small-group lessons to students who are struggling.

(C) Summative Assessments

Summative assessment determines which students have achieved the target standard(s). Some summative assessments measure student achievement of a single standard, whereas others, often given quarterly, midyear, or at the end of the year, measure achievement of many standards.

With our fifth-grade example, the summative assessment would have two parts. In the first, the students read a story they *have not seen before* and answer two questions: (1) what was the problem in the story? and (2) how was the problem resolved? In the second part, each student would *write* two brief endings to a story. The students would be given the first two thirds of a story. The students would write two resolutions, one in which the protagonist is triumphant and one in which the protagonist does achieve his objective.

It is important that summative assessments measure whether knowledge and skills can be "transferred." That is, that the students be confronted with something new to them. If students had learned how to decode CVVC words (e.g., *boat*), then the words they are asked to read should be words that were not used in previous lessons. That is why in our example, for the summative assessment, the students read a story they had not read before.

(2) ALTERNATIVE ASSESSMENTS FOR STUDENTS WITH AN INDIVIDUALIZED EDUCATION PROGRAM (IEP) OR A SECTION 504 PLAN

Children with disabilities should have either an IEP or a Section 504 Plan. IEPs are mandated by the Individuals with Disabilities Education Act (IDEA). An IEP is required for a child who cannot make progress in a regular, general education program. Other children with disabilities who can make progress in a regular classroom may still require accommodations, and they would have a Section 504 Plan, as required by the Americans with Disabilities Act (ADA).

The most important thing for you to remember is that you must provide whatever specific testing adjustments are specified in either an IEP or a Section 504 Plan.

There are a number of ways teachers can differentiate assessment for students with special needs:

(1) GIVE STUDENTS MORE TIME. In our example, where the fifth graders are expected to write two endings to a story, students were given 40 minutes to complete the task. Students with special needs, however, would have 60 minutes.

(2) DIVIDE THE ASSESSMENT INTO SMALLER UNITS. Another option in our example would be to break the task of writing the two endings in half and spread it over 2 days. On the first day, the student with special needs would have 30 minutes to write the "happy" ending. On the second day, the student would have 30 minutes to write the "sad" ending to the story.

(3) CHANGE THE MODE OF DELIVERY. A third option in our example would be for the teacher to change the task from a written exercise to an oral activity. Working one-on-one with a student with special needs, the teacher would ask the student to *tell*, rather than write, the two alternative endings.

(4) PROVIDE PRACTICE ASSESSMENTS. A fourth option would let the students with special needs practice the assessment task in advance of the summative assessment. This is often done in small groups. In our example, the teacher would work with three students with special needs to complete the alternative ending task with a story other than the one that would be used for the summative assessment. The teacher would "walk" the students through the task, providing feedback along the way.

(5) PROVIDE A SIMPLER VERSION OF THE ASSESSMENT. This option would not be ideal for our example, because the standard requires students to read grade-level-appropriate stories (stories written at a fifth-grade reading level). For some students who cannot possibly read fifth-grade-level material, the most appropriate assessment would be one that requires them to read something written at a simpler level. The teacher would note that the standard was not met with grade-level materials.

(3) QUALITY INDICATORS THAT APPLY TO STANDARDIZED ASSESSMENTS

A *standardized* test is one that has an established, nonvarying procedure. Standardized tests have a manual for the person who administers the test, a script for the person to read. The tests have strict instructions and time limits. You have taken many tests like this—the person administering the test reads aloud something like, "Open your test booklet to page 5. Read the instructions silently. Begin working when I say 'start.' Continue until you reach the last item on page 12. Do not go on to page 13. You have 43 minutes. Start."

(A) Reliability

A test is reliable if the results of the test yield consistent scores across administrations. In other words, if you were to take Form A of a test on April 1 and Form B on April 2, your scores would be considered reliable if they were almost identical.

(B) Validity

A test is valid if it measures what it claims to measure. Validity is a significant issue in the assessment of reading development. You might think that all scores on reading tests, developed by professional test makers, are valid. You might think that these scores always give you an accurate picture of what your students can and cannot do. This is not the case. Consider a typical, standardized assessment of reading comprehension. Students are scored on their answers to questions that appear at the end of reading selections. For some students, these scores could be invalid because students possess the background knowledge to answer the questions at the end of a selection *without* reading it. For example, students read a three-paragraph selection on ancient Egypt. The first question asked, "Why did the ancient Egyptians build pyramids?" If these students had studied ancient Egypt during the school year, they might be able to answer the question even if they had not read the selection. Also, many reading comprehension tests developed long ago present reading selections that do not resemble the type of texts young children normally read now. Almost all stories our first graders read, for example, are illustrated. Until a few years ago, however, virtually all reading comprehension tests administered to first graders did *not* include stories with illustrations.

(C) How to Interpret the Results of Standardized Tests

Commercially produced standardized tests that are administered nationally can yield *norm-referenced* scores. Norm-referenced scores allow for comparisons between the students taking the tests and a national average. The makers of commercially published reading tests, such as the Stanford Achievement Tests (SAT) or the California Achievement Tests (CAT), administer versions of the test to a sample of children. The result of this sample is used to create "norms," which are comparison scores. For example, a fourth grader taking a reading comprehension test gets 42 out of 60 questions correct; 42 is his "raw score." Is this good? Without norm-referenced scores you wouldn't know. If the average fourth grader in the sampling group scored 33, then our fourth grader scored above the average. He might well have a percentile score of 78 and a grade-level equivalent score of 6.3. Both tell us that he was reading above the national norm.

(1) PERCENTILE SCORES.   Percentile scores are norm-referenced scores. Staying with our example, a fourth grader who has a percentile score of 78 had a higher raw score than 78% of the sampling group. The higher the percentile score the better. An "average" score would be 50. Someone with a percentile score of 15 has done poorly on the test, achieving a score higher than only 15% of the sampling group.

(2) GRADE EQUIVALENT SCORES.   Grade equivalent scores are norm-referenced. A student's raw score is converted to a school grade level. Again, our fourth grader got 42 of 60 questions correct (his raw score). His percentile score probably would be around 78. It depends, of course, on how well the children in the sampling group did. His raw score is above average, so his grade equivalent score would be something like 6.3. This means his performance corresponds to what a sixth grader in the third month of school would, on the average, achieve.

(3) STANINE SCORES.   Stanine scores are norm-referenced. "Stanine" is short for "standard nine." Raw scores are converted to a nine-point scale. The number 5 is average, 9 is the top, and 1 is the bottom. Our fourth grader would have a stanine score of 8.

(4) INTERPRETATION AND USE OF ASSESSMENT RESULTS

(A) The Results of Assessments—Grade-Level Content Standards and Benchmarks

Assessments must provide data that will allow a teacher to determine whether or not each child has met each standard. This is the *summative* function of assessment—to reach a judgment on the student's level of performance. In many school districts assessments have been developed for most or all of the *English–Language Arts Content Standards.* Along with these assessments, there are scoring rubrics, which establish criteria for judging and classifying each student's performance.

Whether you teach in a school district that has developed standards-based assessments or not, the daily performance of students on lessons and activities will provide data on whether or not they have met grade-level standards. In any case, the teacher must interpret the data and, in regards to any one standard, be able to place students in three different categories:

1. Some students may be performing *below* the expected level of performance—they have not yet met the standard.
2. Other students, on the basis of their performance on assessments, are *at* the expected level of performance—they have met the standard.
3. And some students have performed at a level that is *above* the expected level of performance—they have not only met the standard, but exceeded it.

(B) How to Analyze, Interpret, and Use Results: Individual Profiles

One function of assessment, then, is to reach a conclusion about whether or not individual students have met grade-level standards. The data from assessments should also be used for instructional planning. Teachers should organize the results of assessments at two levels. First, there should be *individual profiles*, a chart or summary of how each child is doing in regards to the standards. The profile would reveal whether or not the child was below, at, or above the expected level of performance for each standard. Second, a teacher should develop some type of *class profile*, a chart or summary of how all the children in the class collectively are performing on the standards.

For example, the individual profiles for Concepts About Print for a kindergarten classroom would include a separate sheet for each of the six relevant grade-level standards. For the first standard, the individual profile might look like this:

Individual Profile: Concepts About Print 1.1

Child's Name ————————————————— Teacher ———————————————

Kindergarten—Concepts About Print

Students will be able to:

1.1 Identify the front cover, back cover, and title page of a book.

Entry-level assessment, Date ——————————————

Student's level of performance is:

————— below expectations for the standard
————— at expectations for the standard
————— above expectations for the standard

Comments:

Monitoring of progress assessment, Dates ——————————————

Student's level of performance is:

————— below expectations for the standard
————— at expectations for the standard
————— above expectations for the standard

Comments:

Summative assessment, Date ——————————————

Student's level of performance is:

————— below expectations for the standard
————— at expectations for the standard
————— above expectations for the standard

Comments:

On the basis of the data recorded on the individual profile, the teacher can plan interventions to help each student. Students who are really struggling will need individualized remediation lessons. Students who are having some success, but are still below expectations on the same standard, can be grouped for small-group lessons.

One other important point about the interpretation of the results of any assessment: Teachers should place the results of any one assessment in the context of other recently administered tests. Is the result consistent with how the student has been doing lately? Or is the result inconsistent with how the student has been performing, in which case the assessment should be readministered.

Finally, in many schools a "team" approach is taken for students who are struggling, but do not have IEPs. The team might include the classroom teacher, the parents, the principal, and any other teachers who work with the student (PE specialist, music teacher, speech therapist, etc.). The individual profile will provide the information the team needs to develop a plan to help the student—a specific description of the student's strengths and weaknesses.

(C) How to Analyze, Interpret, and Use Results: Class Profiles

The teacher should also compile a class profile for each standard. The class profile could like this for the same standard:

Class Profile: Concepts About Print 1.1

Child's Name _____   Teacher _____

Kindergarten—Concepts About Print

Students will be able to:

1.1 Identify the front cover, back cover, and title page of a book.

Entry-level assessment: 10/5—10/8 (formal, one-to-one)
Monitoring of progress assessment: 10/9—10/23 (ongoing, observation)
Summative assessment: 11/1—11/2; 11/18—11/19 (formal, one-to-one)

Results for entry-level and summative assessments:

Name	Below Expectations	At Expectations	Above Expectations
Allen		10/5	11/1
Christina			10/5
DeSean			10/5
Grace	10/5, 11/1		11/18
Hannah		10/5	11/1
Jay	10/5, 11/1		11/18
Latsamy	10/5		11/1
Marya		10/5	11/1
Michelle C			10/6
Michelle D			10/6
Nadia		10/6	11/2
Orlando			10/6
Ralph	10/8, 11/2, 11/19		
Sarah		10/7	11/2
Sydney			10/8
Tiffany		10/8	11/2
Wayne			10/8

The class profile can be used to adjust instruction for the whole class. Is it okay to move on? What types of lessons were successful? In this example, a high number of students were above the standard at the entry-level assessment (Christina, DeSean, Michelle C., Michelle D., Orlando, Sydney, and Wayne). They did not need instruction to help them learn how to identify the front cover, back cover, and title page of a book. The other children did need help, and took part in a three-lesson sequence. Some students were clearly below the standard at the entry-level assessment and made little progress during the three-lesson sequence and in the days after. They still had not met the standard by the time of the first round of summative assessments (Grace, Jay, and Ralph). They took part in small-group remediation lesson. Ralph had a difficult time and had not met the standard after a second round of summative assessment. He would need individual intervention.

(5) STUDENTS' INDEPENDENT, INSTRUCTIONAL, AND FRUSTRATION READING LEVELS

(A) Assessments Used to Determine Students' Reading Levels

(1) INFORMAL READING INVENTORIES.   An informal reading inventory (IRI) is a battery, or collection, of assessments administered individually to students. For an IRI, one adult gives the assessments to one student. No two IRIs have to contain the same collection of assessments. The selection of assessments for the IRI depends on the student's reading level. For example, an IRI for a sixth grader with average ability would *not* include assessments of concepts about print, phonemic awareness, and phonics. An IRI for a first grader with average ability would. Here are the types of assessments generally included in an IRI:

> Word Recognition Lists (described in this chapter)
>
> Graded Reading Passages (described in this chapter)
>
> Reading Interest Survey (described in Chapter 1)
>
> Assessments Measuring Concepts About Print (described in Chapter 4)
>
> Phonemic Awareness Assessments (described in Chapter 3)
>
> Phonics Assessments (described in Chapter 6)
>
> Assessments of Reading Fluency (described in Chapter 9)
>
> Structural Analysis Assessments (described in Chapter 7)
>
> Vocabulary Assessments (described in Chapter 11)
>
> Spelling Tests (described in Chapter 5)

(2) WORD RECOGNITION LISTS.   In this chapter, we will take a closer look at the word recognition lists and graded reading passages. The word recognition lists are sometimes called "graded word lists." These are lists of words, usually 10 in each list. There is a list for every reading level. The first list for kindergarteners is called the *preprimer* level, or "PP." It will have words such as *the, am,* and *or.* The next list for kindergarteners, with slightly more difficult words, is at the *primer* level, "P." Then there is a list of words for every grade level from first grade to eighth grade. Some IRIs include word recognition lists for the high school grades, too. The words on the eighth-grade list will be difficult, such as *psychology* and *endorsement.* The word recognition lists from one IRI, the *Bader Reading and Language Inventory* (3rd edition) are in Appendix A at the end of this book.

Children are asked to read aloud each word. The word recognition lists serve three purposes: (a) to provide a rough guess of the child's reading level so that whoever is administering the tests knows where to start on the graded reading passages; (b) to provide information on the child's "sight" vocabulary, the words the child can correctly identify; and (c) to provide information about the student's ability to use sound–symbol relationships (phonics) to decode words. The child's errors will provide a partial picture of what letters and letter combinations the child knows and which ones he or she needs to learn.

An example of a teacher's scoring sheet for a third grader's performance on the Bader Graded Word Lists is included as Appendix B. Different IRIs will have different instructions for how to administer the word recognition lists. Basically, students read the words and the teacher records the results, placing a check by words read correctly, noting which words are read with hesitation, and writing the word a child says when he or she misidentifies a word.

(3) GRADED READING PASSAGES.   The most important part of the IRI is the graded reading passages. Like the word recognition lists, the graded reading passages are provided for every reading level from preprimer for kindergarteners to eighth grade. Some IRIs include graded reading passages for the high school grades. Since the graded reading passages can be used in a number of ways, an IRI usually includes two or more passages for each grade. An example of one of the first-grade passages from the *Bader Reading and Language Inventory* is included as Appendix C. A sixth-grade passage is Appendix D. Typically, the student is asked to read the passage aloud.

Miscue Analysis.   While the student reads the passage aloud, the teacher keeps a detailed record of the student's performance. Though many teachers can record what the student says while the student is reading, it is easier to tape record the child. The most popular form of this process is called a "Running Record," which was developed in New Zealand. By looking at the student's errors we can gain a better understanding of how he or she reads. Patterns of errors will emerge and reveal how the child goes about decoding print. Examining a record of a student's oral reading to identify and classify errors is called a *miscue analysis*. Each commercially published IRI uses a different system for teachers to record the child's oral reading performance on the graded reading passages. One system is included as Appendix E. A scoring sheet for one child's oral reading is Appendix F. Oral reading errors fall into three categories.

Graphophonemic Errors.   *Graphophonemic* comes from the Greek words for *symbol* and *sound*. These are errors related to the sound–symbol relationships for English, such as reading *feather* for *father*. The words sound alike, but *feather* wouldn't make sense in a sentence where the correct word is *father*. A child who repeatedly makes graphophonemic errors is either (a) reading word by word and depending too much on phonics to decode each word or (b) reading a passage that is too difficult. Children who are reading word by word need to be taught to speed up (see Chapters 8 and 9). Children who don't use the meaning of the sentences and paragraphs to decode words need to be taught to use what are called *contextual clues* (see Chapter 9).

Semantic Errors.   These are meaning-related errors, such as reading *dad* for *father*. The student has relied too much on the semantic cueing system—and hasn't used graphophonemic clues. A child who repeatedly makes semantic errors understands what he or she is reading, but needs to be taught to use phonics skills to be sure that every word read makes sense from a graphophonemic sense (phonics is covered in Chapters 5 and 6).

Syntactic Errors.   To a linguist, syntax is the way words are placed in order in sentences. A syntactic error would be reading *into* for *through*. Both are prepositions. Syntactic errors make sense in that the error is the same part of speech as the correct word. As with semantic errors, a child who repeatedly makes syntactic errors needs to pay more attention to phonics.

(B) How to Define Frustration, Instructional, and Independent Reading Levels

After the child has read the passage aloud, he or she is then asked to answer some comprehension questions for the passage. The questions are included in the IRI examiner's manual. The teacher reads the questions and the child responds orally. An alternative for younger children in kindergarten, first grade, and second grade is for the teacher to ask the child to *retell* the story. The IRI provides a list of characters, places, and events in the passage the child should mention. This form of measuring comprehension, called a retelling, has been shown to work well. The administration of the graded reading passages of an IRI will allow the teacher to determine each child's frustration, instructional, and independent reading levels. This information is essential for teachers to know. Different IRIs use different formulas, but those listed below are fairly standard.

(1) INDEPENDENT READING LEVEL.   Books and stories at this level can be read and understood by the child without assistance by the teacher. A student's independent reading level is the *highest* passage for which the student reads aloud 95% or more of words correctly *and* answers 90% or more of the comprehension questions correctly.

(2) INSTRUCTIONAL READING LEVEL.   Material at this level can be read and understood by the student with help from the teacher. The student's reading textbook (basal reader) should be at this level. The social studies and science textbooks should be at this reading level. A student's instructional reading level is the highest passage for which the student reads aloud 90% or more of the words correctly *and* answer at least 60% of the comprehension questions correctly.

(3) FRUSTRATION READING LEVEL.   Books at this level *cannot* be read and understood by the child, even with help. The child can listen to the teacher or someone else read material at this level and understand it. For a passage at this level, the child correctly read aloud less than 90% of the words *or* did not answer 60% of the comprehension questions correctly.

   Don't forget: To determine instructional and independent reading levels, you must know both (a) the percentage of words the child read aloud correctly *and* (b) the percentage of comprehension questions the child correctly answered.

(6) COMMUNICATING ASSESSMENT RESULTS

(A) How to Communicate Results to Students

It is important that the students have a good idea of how they are progressing. This is a challenge for primary-level teachers. Communication should be based on the *standards*. For example, "Fred, we have been working on words that mean the same thing, called synonyms, and you have shown me that you know what synonyms are." The important thing is to make the communication specific, while avoiding global comments ("you aren't doing well"). Students will receive communication about their progress in a variety of formats.

(1) COMMUNICATION ABOUT DAILY PROGRESS.   Teachers will give feedback to the students informally on a daily basis. Much of this will be oral. Written feedback will be provided on many assignments. Whether oral or in writing, teachers should let students know when they have done well, and when they are struggling, the child needs to know what he or she can do to make more progress.

(2) INDIVIDUAL CONFERENCES.   I describe conferences with parents below, and in some school districts, students accompany their parents/guardians. Teachers, however, should plan regular individual conferences with students. Time is an issue, but if a teacher can meet with each student once every 3 weeks for about 15 minutes, much can be accomplished. Successful individual conferences have a narrow focus—the teacher should focus on a single standard. The teacher should review the child's progress and provide corrective feedback.

(3) WRITTEN SUMMARIES OF PROGRESS.   Students should see summaries of how they are doing on several standards. These summaries, perhaps shared each month or quarterly, would need to be in a form the child can understand. Each student would know which standards have been met and which need further work.

(B) How to Communicate Results to Parents/Guardians

First of all, it is important that parents/guardians get the "big picture." Parents/guardians should receive information about the grade-level standards that their children are expected to achieve. They should know how and when they will be informed of their child's progress. All communication should be focused on the *English–Language Arts Content Standards*.

(1) COMMUNICATION ABOUT DAILY/WEEKLY PROGRESS. Although it is not necessary that parents see every paper-and-pencil task their children complete, they should see something every week in the area of English–Language Arts. And, it is important that the teacher's evaluation of the student's work be clear—parents/guardians should know if their child's effort was satisfactory and they should know what specific areas of need or strength the assignment reveals.

(2) PARENT/GUARDIAN CONFERENCES. Although most California school districts require a conference with each parent/guardian in late October or early November, effective teachers meet much earlier with the parents/guardians of three groups of students: (a) English learners, (b) students who are struggling, (c) advanced learners. These early conferences would focus on the special needs of the child, discuss what classroom interventions the teacher has planned, and provide guidance for how parents/guardians can help at home.

(3) WRITTEN SUMMARIES OF STUDENT ACHIEVEMENT OF THE STANDARDS. In most school districts, a written evaluation form of some sort, listing each standard and an evaluation of the student's progress on meeting each of them, will be part of the Fall and Spring parent/guardian conference. In many schools, however, teachers send these to parents more frequently.

(4) EMAILS AND TELEPHONE CALLS. If something of particular note occurs one day, whether positive or negative, an email or a telephone call to the parent/guardian is in order.

(C) How to Communicate Results to School and District Personnel

Most school districts will have formal methods for transmitting data to school administrators and district personnel. Written summaries of student achievement are kept in a "cumulative record" (a file) in the school office. The record follows the student to middle and high school. Many districts have standardized assessments that all teachers at a grade level complete, and the results are transmitted to an assessment officer at the school district office. California's Standardized Testing and Reporting (STAR) system, involving several tests administered each Spring, generates data that are compiled at the state level and released to the public.

If a teacher is working with a reading coach, it is important that the coach and the teacher develop an assessment plan, work together to implement it, and meet regularly to analyze the results. Principals like to be informed and classroom teachers should meet from time to time to discuss how individual students, particularly those who are struggling or advanced, are progressing. Some principals make this a more formal arrangement and meet with each teacher every quarter.

CHAPTER 3

Competency 3
Phonological and Phonemic Awareness

INTRODUCTION

Phonological awareness is the knowledge that oral English is composed of smaller units. A child who has phonological awareness can identify and manipulate sounds in many different "levels" of language: (1) individual sounds—that is, phonemic awareness, and (2) sounds in larger units of language, such as words and syllables.

Phonemic awareness is a subcategory of phonological awareness involving the ability to distinguish the separate phonemes (or sounds) in a spoken word. When a child can identify *duck* and *luck* as rhyming words or say that *duck* has three sounds and they are /d/, /u/, /k/, he or she is phonemically aware. The development of phonemic awareness is an important teaching goal for kindergarten and first-grade teachers.

Phonics is knowledge of letter–sound correspondences; knowing, for example, that in the word *phonics* the letters *ph* make the /f/ sound (see Chapter 5).

Definitions

For both this chapter and the next you will need to know the following definitions.

THE ALPHABETIC PRINCIPLE.   This principle states that speech sounds are represented by letters. English is an alphabetic language because symbols represent sounds. The sounds are called phonemes.

PHONEME.   Most linguists would define a phoneme as a speech sound in a language that signals a difference in meaning. For example, /v/ and /b/ are English phonemes because there is a difference between *vote* and *boat*. A simpler definition is: Phonemes are the smallest units of speech.

THE PHONETIC ALPHABET AND GRAPHEMES.   There are two ways to represent phonemes. *Phonetic alphabets* are created by linguists so that each phoneme is always represented by the same symbol. There is one-to-one correspondence between the phoneme and the symbol. For example, the phonemic symbol /e/ always represents the "long a" sound. This sound can be represented by several graphemes, such as the *ay* in *say*, the *ei* in *neighborhood*, or the *ey* in *prey*. *Graphemes* are the English letter or letters that represent phonemes. Some graphemes are a single letter. For example, the phoneme /b/ in *bat* is represented by the grapheme *b*. Other graphemes consist of more than one letter. For example, the phoneme /k/ in *duck* is represented by the grapheme *ck*.

VOWELS.   Vowels are sounds made when the air leaving your lungs is vibrated in the voice box and there is a clear passage from the voice box to your mouth. In English, the following letters always represent vowel sounds: *a, e, i, o, u*. Two letters sometimes represent vowel sounds: *y*, in words such as *sky*, and *w* in words such as *cow*. Vowel sounds are said to be long when they "say their own name," as in *bake* and *bite*. Short vowels occur in such words as *cat, pet, bit, cot, but*. R-controlled vowels are neither long nor short, as in the sounds *a* makes in *car, e* as in *her, i* as in *girl, u* as in *hurt,* and *o* as in *for.*

CONSONANTS.   Speech sounds that occur when the airflow is obstructed in some way by your mouth, teeth, or lips are called consonants.

ONSETS AND RIMES.   Think syllable! Onsets and rimes occur in a single syllable. In a syllable, the onset is the initial consonant sound or consonant blend; the rime is the vowel sound and any consonants that follow. In the chart below, the onsets and rimes are represented by graphemes (rather than the phonemic symbols):

Syllable	Onset	Rime
Cats	c	ats
In	-	in
Spring	spr	ing

Remember: Onsets and rimes occur in syllables. All syllables must have a rime. A syllable may or may not have an onset. What would you say if someone asked you what the onset and rime was in the word, *napkin*? You should answer, "think syllable!" The onset in *nap* is *n*, the rime is *ap*. The onset in *kin* is *k*, the rime is *in*.

PHONOGRAMS.   These are rimes that have the same spelling. Words that share the same phonogram are *word families*. Rime or phonogram: *at*. Word family: *cat, bat, sat.*
Now, we can move on to the five topics in this competency:

(1) The role of phonological and phonemic awareness in reading development
(2) How to teach phonological awareness, including phonemic awareness
(3) The relationship between phonemic awareness and development of phonics knowledge and skills
(4) Meeting the needs of all learners
(5) Assessment of phonological awareness, including phonemic awareness

(1) THE ROLE OF PHONOLOGICAL AND PHONEMIC AWARENESS IN READING DEVELOPMENT

Longitudinal studies of reading acquisition have demonstrated that the acquisition of phonemic awareness is highly predictive of success in learning to read. In fact, the level of a child's phonemic awareness in kindergarten correlates strongly with his or her level of reading achievement (word recognition and comprehension) at the end of first grade. Why? Phonemic awareness is the *foundation* for understanding the sound–symbol relationships of English, which will be taught through phonics lessons.

(2) HOW TO TEACH PHONOLOGICAL AWARENESS, INCLUDING PHONEMIC AWARENESS

(A) How to Teach Phonological Awareness of Larger Units of Language

(1) WORD AWARENESS.   The goal here is to help children become aware that sentences are made up of words. Word awareness requires children to detect and identify *word boundaries* (e.g., that the sentence *I like ice cream* has four words). Lessons should use one-word, two-word, and three-word sentences, each word with one syllable. For example, the teacher has several cards, each with one word written on it. The teacher then builds two-word sentences (*Tom runs*). The sentence is read as a whole, and then each word is read separately, with the teacher tapping the word card. Finally, a third word is added to the sentence (*Tom runs fast*). A more challenging task involves the teacher saying a two-word, three-word, or four-word sentence, and then asking the children to state how many words were in the sentence.

(2) SYLLABLE AWARENESS. Syllable awareness will be more difficult for most children than word awareness because syllables, by themselves, are meaningless. Many children in kindergarten will have no idea that they exist. A venerable instructional activity asks children to clap their hands as they say each syllable in a two-syllable or three-syllable word. Syllable awareness activities are easier if the pronunciation of the syllables is distorted and they are uttered slowly and distinctly.

(3) WORD BLENDING. In this task, the child is challenged to take two single-syllable words and combine them to make a compound word. Pictures can be used. The teacher would say, "This is a picture of a cow and this is a picture of a boy. What do you get when you put *cow* and *boy* together? The child should, say *cowboy*. The teacher would then display a third picture, one of a cowboy.

(4) SYLLABLE BLENDING. Here, children are required to blend two syllables into a word. The teacher would say, "What word do we get if we put *sis* and *ter* together. The children, we hope, will say *sister*.

(5) ONSET AND RIME BLENDING. In an onset and rime blending task, the teacher would say the onset, such as */b/* and the rime, *ank*. The children have to put them together and say *bank*.

(B) How to Teach Phonemic Awareness

Some children will come to school with phonemic awareness. Others will acquire it with little effort. For many other children, however, acquiring phonemic awareness is a significant challenge. There are a number of points to remember about the direct teaching of phonemic awareness:

- Instructional activities focusing on the phonological awareness of larger units of language, such as words and syllables, should take place before instruction in phonemic awareness.
- It is better to focus on one or two phonemic awareness tasks at a time, rather than working on several of them simultaneously.
- It is a good idea to plan some phonemic awareness activities that involve the use of the letters of the alphabet—this helps children see the relationship between phonemic awareness and reading.
- Phonemic awareness instruction should be brief and not exceed 30 minutes for any one lesson. A review of the research showed that the most effective programs in phonemic awareness had less than 20 *total* hours of instruction. The amount of time devoted to phonemic awareness, however, will vary from child to child.

Direct teaching of phonemic awareness consists of lessons focusing on one of the tasks defined below: sound isolation, sound identity, sound blending, sound substitution, sound deletion, and sound segmentation.

(1) SOUND ISOLATION. In sound isolation, the children are given a word and asked to tell which sound occurs at the beginning, middle, or end of the word. The teacher could have a list of words that all have long vowels in the medial position: *cake, day, late, leap, feel, vote, coal, bite, like*. To model the desired response, at the beginning of the lesson the teacher would say each word and then say the medial sound ("*leap*, the middle sound is */e/*"). At some point, the teacher just says the word and the children have to provide the medial sound. It is best to start with beginning sounds, then go to ending sounds, and then to medial sounds.

(2) SOUND IDENTITY. The teacher will need sets of words that all share the same beginning, middle, or ending sound, but have no other shared sounds. For example: *lake, light,* and *low*. Those three words share only one sound, the beginning /l/. The teacher says each of the three words, and then asks, "What sound is the same in each of these words?

(3) SOUND BLENDING. In the simplest lessons to teach sound blending, the teacher says the sounds with only brief pauses in between each sound. The children then guess the word. Example: "Which word am I thinking of? Its sounds are /b/, /a/, and /t/." The answer would be *bat*.

(4) SOUND SUBSTITUTION. In this type of activity, the teacher asks children to substitute one sound for another. The hardest part of this for the teacher is finding phrases that work for this type of task. The easiest ones would be one-word substitutions. The teacher says, "*Cat, cat, cat.* Let's substitute the /b/ sound for the /k/ sound. We get *bat, bat, bat.*" Then, the teacher might try simple alliterations (all start with the same consonant sounds). For example, the teacher says, "*be, bo, ba, bu, bi*" (in this example of non-sense words, all the vowels are long). The students would then chant, "*be, bo, ba, bu, bi.*" The teacher then says, "let's substitute /k/ for the /b/. The students would then chant, "*ke, ko, ka, ku, ki.*" Obviously, it becomes more fun to do sound substitution if you use a well-known chant from a song, such as fe-fi-fiddly-i-o from "I've Been Working on the Railroad."

(5) SOUND DELETION. This activity works best with consonant blends. To avoid using nonsense words, identify words beginning with blends that will generate a new word if one sound is deleted. For example, for the word *block*, take away the *b* to get *lock*. That works! For the word *frog*, take away the *f* to get *rog*. That doesn't work as well. In the lesson, the teacher says, "*Snail*, let's take away the *s*, and what do we have?" The students should say, "*nail.*"

(6) SOUND SEGMENTATION. This is the most difficult of the phonemic awareness tasks. Children are challenged to isolate and identify the sounds in a spoken word. To teach this directly, the teacher should start with words with only two sounds. Remember, the teacher should always model the desired student behavior first. The teacher would say, "I am going to say a word and then slowly say the sounds in the word. *Bee.* (pause) /b/ (pause) /e/. Then the teacher would ask the students to say the sounds in two-sound words. After the children have shown they can segment two-sound words, then lessons should focus on words with three sounds. The lesson challenges children to segment words with minimal differences, such as *cap, cat*, and *cab*.

If children are having difficulty with the sound segmentation task, the teacher may want to simplify the challenge by merely asking how many sounds are in a word the teacher pronounces (for *dog*, the answer would be *three*).

(3) THE RELATIONSHIP BETWEEN PHONEMIC AWARENESS AND DEVELOPMENT OF PHONICS KNOWLEDGE AND SKILLS

Children cannot be expected to learn which letters represent which sounds (phonics) until they are aware of the sounds in a word (phonemic awareness). Thus, the development of phonemic awareness is a prerequisite to teaching phonics.

Please note, however, that this does *not* mean that children first participate in phonemic awareness activities and then, at a later time, move on to phonics lessons. Although some phonemic awareness lessons will precede instruction in letter–sound correspondences, other phonemic awareness activities will take place at the same time children are participating in phonics lessons that teach the alphabetic principle (letters represent sounds) and specific letter–sound correspondences (e.g., that the letter *c* in the initial position can make either the /k/ sound as in *can* or the /s/ sound in *city*).

Thus, in the same week, children will participate in some phonemic awareness activities and some phonics lessons. Also, some phonemic awareness activities that could be done without using letters can have a letter–sound component added to them. Previously, I mentioned that a way of teaching sound blending is to ask children to blend an onset and a rime. For example, use the rime of *-ank*. The teacher would say */b/* and *-ank*. The children should say, *bank*. Then, blend *th* with *-ank* and get *thank*, *cr* with *-ank* and get *crank*. Each time a word is successfully blended, the teacher could display a card with the word written on it. The teacher could say, "Good job. We put */b/* and *-ank* together to make *bank*. Let's look at how the word is spelled." The teacher would then display a card with *bank* written on it and say, "The *b* makes the */b/* sound and *a, n, k* says *-ank*."

(4) MEETING THE NEEDS OF ALL LEARNERS

(A) Struggling Readers and Students With Reading Difficulties or Disabilities

Because the type of differentiation is parallel, our discussion of how to help these two categories of learners will be combined. Some children will have difficulty achieving phonemic awareness. These students will need to participate in small-group or individualized lessons. Teachers should differentiate instruction for struggling readers by using four strategies:

(1) FOCUSING ON KEY SKILLS, ESPECIALLY BLENDING AND SEGMENTING. Blending and segmenting are the most difficult of the phonemic awareness tasks and, to some extent, something of the "final exam" in phonemic awareness. The important point here is that teachers should not consider a child phonemically aware because he or she is successful on the simpler tasks, such as sound identity and isolation. Simply put, the focus of the small-group and individualized remediation lessons should be on blending and segmenting sounds.

(2) RETEACHING SKILLS THAT ARE LACKING. Throughout this book, the importance of teaching at a subsequent time a skill that has not been mastered will be mentioned as an essential strategy to meet the needs of struggling readers. It is important to note, however, that simply repeating verbatim a lesson taught previously will have a minimal impact. Teachers should consider the following: (a) changing the pace of the lesson, that is, going slower; (b) changing the mode of delivery, perhaps by providing more modeling or using clues such as clapping or finger snaps; (c) making the task simpler by providing additional scaffolding; or (d) using different materials.

For example, let us say that a child is having difficulty in word blending. In this task, the child is challenged to take two single-syllable words and combine them to make a compound word. In the example mentioned earlier the teacher used pictures and asked, "This is a picture of a cow and this is a picture of a boy. What do you get when you put *cow* and *boy* together?" The child should say, "*cowboy*." In a remedial lesson, the teacher would differentiate by making the task simpler by first providing the first syllable: "This is a picture of a cow and this is a picture of a boy. What do you get when you put *cow* and *boy* together? We get *cow* . . .?" Hopefully, the child would say, "*cowboy*." The teacher shows a picture of a cowboy. Then, the teacher would ask the child to do the whole task by herself: "Now you do it by yourself." The teacher would show the pictures and ask the child to blend them into *cowboy*.

(3) USING A VARIETY OF CONCRETE EXAMPLES TO EXPLAIN A CONCEPT OR TASK. Struggling readers will almost always be helped if the teacher can use things to help students master a task. This could include pictures or real objects. In the previous example, pictures were used to facilitate success.

(4) PROVIDING ADDITIONAL PRACTICE. Finally, struggling readers will often need more opportunities to practice a skill in order to learn it. For example, most students in the room were successful in segmenting a three-sound word after three lessons. Struggling readers may well need an additional two or three segmentation activities—and parents who are willing to work with their children at home can provide some of the additional practice.

(B) English Learners and Speakers of Nonstandard English

Interestingly enough, almost all of the interventions mentioned in the *RICA Content Specifications* for these two categories of learners focus on English learners. Thus, in this book, most of the suggestions are for ELs. The biggest hurdle for English learners is being able to hear and manipulate sounds that are not phonemes in their first languages. Fortunately, there is some "positive" transfer because many phonemes in English are phonemes in other languages. My examples will be between Spanish and English. The phonemes of /b/, /d/, /m/, /p/, and /t/ are the same in both languages. Further, research done on English phonemic awareness in Spanish-speaking English learners shows that phonemic awareness skills developed in Spanish transfer to English. That is, if a child has mastered the task of blending sounds in Spanish, there is a very good chance that he can blend sounds in English.

On the other hand, teachers should explicitly teach the English phonemes that do not exist in an EL's first language (such phonemes are called *nontransferable*). For example, the sound the letter *h* makes at the beginning of words in English does not exist in Spanish. Likewise, teachers will need to teach *sequences* of phonemes in English that do not appear in the first language. For example, the English blends that begin with *s* do *not* appear in Spanish (*sc-, sk-, sm-, sn-, sp-, st-,* and *sw-* as in *score, skin, small, snail, sports, stop,* and *swim*). Teachers should expect to devote extra time to helping Spanish-speaking ELs hear the two sounds in each of these initial consonant blends.

(C) Advanced Learners

Two ways of differentiating instruction for advanced learners that you will read about repeatedly are (1) increasing the pace of instruction and (2) building on and extending current skills. There are two ways to increase the pace of instruction. One is to spend less time on a lesson, usually by providing less modeling and fewer chances to practice a skill. The second is to devote fewer lessons to a phonemic awareness skill, and thus "move through" the phonemic awareness component of the reading/language arts program at a faster pace.

(5) ASSESSMENT OF PHONOLOGICAL AWARENESS, INCLUDING PHONEMIC AWARENESS

(A) How to Assess Phonological Awareness, Including Phonemic Awareness

In tests of phonological awareness, including phonemic awareness, the teacher talks, the student listens, and then the student says something. No print is involved. Older tests referred to these tests as *auditory discrimination*.

One widely used test for phonemic awareness is the *Yopp-Singer Test of Phoneme Segmentation*. In this test, the teacher says 22 words (*dog, keep, fine, no*). The child must provide each sound of the word in order. So, when the teacher says *dog*, the correct response is /d/, /o/, /g/. Remember, sound segmentation is the most difficult phonemic awareness task. So, if a student does well on the *Yopp-Singer*, you probably can assume he or she can do the other phonemic awareness tasks as well.

Teachers should assess the following word and syllable level phonological awareness tasks: word awareness, syllable awareness, word blends, syllable blending, onset–rime blending.

To do a complete job of assessing phoneme awareness, teachers should measure each child's proficiency in each of the tasks: sound identity, sound isolation, sound blending, sound deletion, sound substitution, and sound segmentation.

It is easy for teachers to develop simple assessments of these tasks. For example, to assess sound isolation, the teacher would create three tasks: one for identifying sounds in the beginning position, another for identifying medial sounds, and one for ending sounds. To assess medial vowel sounds, the teacher would create a list of 15 to 20 words with different medial sounds, such as *bet, feet, cat, take,* etc. For each word, the teacher would say, "Listen to me say this word, *feet, feet, feet.* What is the middle sound in *feet?*"

It is important to remember that the assessment of phonological awareness, including phonemic awareness, should include the following.

(1) ENTRY-LEVEL ASSESSMENT.   This assessment is used to determine each child's level of phonological awareness, including phonemic awareness, *before* a sequence of lessons begins. For example, a teacher should assess students on their ability in word awareness before beginning instruction on that phonological awareness task ("How many words are in this sentence: *Fred ran to school*"?).

(2) PROGRESSING-MONITORING ASSESSMENT.   It is important to assess student proficiency both *during* an individual lesson and *in the middle* of a four- or five-lesson unit. Progressing-monitoring assessment will allow teachers to make two important decisions: (a) which individual students need more help, and (b) at the class level, is it time to stop and reteach the entire class something?

(3) SUMMATIVE ASSESSMENT.   Summative assessments occur *at the end* of instruction and tell a teacher whether a student has not met a standard, met a standard, or exceeded a standard.

(B) How to Analyze, Interpret, and Use Results

As noted in the previous chapter, teachers must analyze and interpret the results of assessment for both individual students and the whole class. All analysis should be based on standards. Assessment for individual students will teach the teacher which students' level of performance is below expectations for the standard, which students' level of performance is at expectations for the standard, and which students' level of performance is beyond expectations for the standard.

Let's look at an example. An *English–Language Arts Content Standard* for first grade in phonemic awareness is that students will able to "Blend two to four phonemes into recognizable words" (1.8). The assessment of this standard will be time consuming because it must be done individually. Perhaps a school district has already created an assessment of this standard, complete with a scoring rubric. If not, the teacher would have to create the assessment, which would not be difficult. Children would be asked blend the sounds in nine words, three with two phonemes (*ice*), three with three phonemes (*cat*), and three with four phonemes (*flip*). The teacher would say each sound in isolation and ask the child to blend them ("/k/ ... /a/ ... /t/ ... makes what word?"). The teacher might define criteria as follows: the expected level of performance is to get at least two out of three correct in each category (two-sound, three-sound, and four-sound).

The results of the assessments will provide the teacher with the information needed to create individual profiles for each student. Students who have struggled and have not met a standard will need intervention. The results for all the children can be used to create a class profile, which tells the teacher how effective overall his or her instruction was. For example, a teacher found that 90% of her students were either at or above the expected level of performance for a standard. The teacher could move on to another standard, while providing extra help to children who need it.

CHAPTER 4

Competency 4
Concepts About Print, Letter Recognition, and the Alphabetic Principle

INTRODUCTION

Concepts about print are essential, basic principles about how letters, words, and sentences are represented in written language. These concepts vary from language to language. Here, of course, we are concerned with English concepts about print. To learn how to read, children must acquire these concepts. They should be learned by the time children leave kindergarten. The actual phrase "concepts about print" was coined by the New Zealand educator Marie Clay, who developed a test of concepts about print. The *RICA Content Specifications* identify the following concepts about print: (1) an awareness of the relationship between spoken and written language and an understanding that print carries meaning; (2) letter, word, and sentence representation; (2) the directionality of print and the ability to track print in connected text; and (4) book-handling skills.

  Letter recognition refers to the ability to identify both the uppercase and lowercase letters when a teacher says the name of the letter ("Point to the big A."). The clue is auditory and the child's action is physical. *Letter naming* is the reverse task, the ability to say the name of a letter when the teacher points to it. *Letter formation*, also called *letter production*, is the ability to write the uppercase and lowercase letters legibly. When talking about letter recognition and letter naming, it is important to note that we are teaching the names of the letters, *not* the sounds letters make (covered in the next chapter).

  The *alphabetic principle* is that in English speech sounds are represented by letters. Simply put, letters represent sounds.

  There are six topics in this competency:

(1) Concepts about print: Their role in early reading development and instructional strategies
(2) The importance of letter recognition in reading development and instructional strategies
(3) The alphabetic principle
(4) Writing and students' understanding of the alphabetic principle and letter– sound correspondence
(5) Meeting the needs of all learners
(6) Assessment of concepts about print, letter recognition, and the alphabetic principle

(1) CONCEPTS ABOUT PRINT: THEIR ROLE IN EARLY READING DEVELOPMENT AND INSTRUCTIONAL STRATEGIES

(A) What Are the Concepts About Print?

(1) THE RELATIONSHIP BETWEEN SPOKEN AND WRITTEN ENGLISH AND THAT PRINT CARRIES MEANING.   This is the most important concept. Children should be aware that printed words are "talk written down." More simply, that the spoken word *cat* and the printed word *cat* are the same thing. Children also need to know that printed words are used to transmit messages as in the stories in picture books, product names in advertisements, and menus in restaurants. It is possible to know this concept and *not* be able to read the printed words in the text. Some young children cannot read every word on the page, but they have acquired the concept that the printed words *are* the story. They know that although the illustrations in a picture book *help* tell the story, a reader must read the words that appear on each page.

(2) RECOGNIZING LETTER, WORD, AND SENTENCE REPRESENTATION.   Again, this concept is *not* the ability to read words and sentences or identify letters. Rather, it is the knowledge of the *differences* between letters, words, and sentences. To fully acquire this concept, children must know how many letters are in a word. A child who has acquired this concept knows *word boundaries*, that is, how many words there are in a line of text. Finally, children need to know where sentences end and begin, which requires recognition of end punctuation (., !, ?).

(3) DIRECTIONALITY OF PRINT/TRACKING OF PRINT.   Students have acquired the concept of directionality when they understand that English is read left to right and top to bottom. Tracking is the physical, observable evidence that this concept has been learned, as the child is able to point to the next word that should be read. Children who have mastered this concept understand they must perform a *return sweep* at the end of each line of text, moving from the far right of one line to the far left of the next one.

(4) BOOK-HANDLING SKILLS.   This is knowledge of how to hold a book when reading, where the front cover of a book is, where the title page is, where the story starts, when and how to turn the pages, and the location of the back cover of a book.

(B) How to Teach the Concepts About Print

Some children will acquire all the concepts about print without direct instruction, especially if their parents or someone else has spent a great deal of time reading to them at home. Other children will acquire concepts about print by taking part in classroom activities such as listening to their teacher read aloud, through shared book experiences, and by dictating stories that are transcribed by an adult. It is important to note, however, that some children will not acquire them easily, through informal activities. Then, these concepts must be explicitly taught.

(1) READING ALOUD TO STUDENTS.   Reading aloud will teach many children that print carries meaning. Reading aloud also will help children recognize the covers of books. If the teacher is reading aloud a standard-sized picture book to a class of 20 students, then the children will not be able to see each word of the text. This means reading aloud will not teach directionality or sentence, word, and letter representation. Teachers should read aloud to the students every day, select high-quality books, and read with enthusiasm and panache.

(2) THE SHARED BOOK EXPERIENCE.   With shared book experiences, teachers attempt to achieve with a group of children what has long been accomplished when an adult, typically a parent, sits and reads a picture book to and with a child. The shared book experience was named by New Zealand educator Don Holdaway. The goals of a shared book experience are to discover good books, to see that reading books is fun, and to teach concepts about print. The shared book experience is a particularly powerful activity because it has the potential to teach all of the concepts about print.

Teachers use *big books* for shared book experiences. Big books are just that, oversized picture books measuring at least 15 × 23 inches. The print is large and can be seen from several feet away. Many big books have been written with predictable phrases or words as a part of the text. These *predictable books* are ideal for shared book experiences. Familiar predictable books include *The House That Jack Built* by Jenny Stow, *The Judge* by Harve Zemach, and *The Napping House* by Audrey Wood.

A shared book experience usually has the following components:

1. Introduction (prereading). Look at cover and point out features of the book, such as the author's name, the illustrator's name, and the title page. Then ask, "What do you think this book will be about?" or some other predictive question.
2. The teacher then reads the story with full dramatic punch, maybe overdoing it a little. The children join in on the predictable text. The teacher may pause to encourage predictions or comments. If the teacher wants to stress directionality and tracking of print, he or she will point to every word as he or she reads it.
3. A discussion occurs before, during, or after the text reading. Children ask questions, or talk about favorite parts or characters.
4. The story is then reread on subsequent days with the whole group, in smaller groups, with student pairs or to individual students—acting out and enjoying the language patterns.

(3) LANGUAGE EXPERIENCE APPROACH (LEA).   The LEA is intended to develop and support children's reading and writing abilities. Children share an experience such as a field trip to the zoo and then dictate an account of that experience to an adult, who records it verbatim. An LEA should record a personal experience that is memorable and provides the child with a great deal to dictate. Together, the adult and child read the dictated text. The text is saved and bound in a child's personal reading book. Class experiences can be dictated by several children whose comments are collected on chart paper. The class then reads the dictated "story" together and the LEA is displayed in the classroom.

The LEA will teach most of the concepts about print. Repeated experiences will help children acquire the big idea—that print carries meaning. Teachers can have children follow along with their fingers as they read aloud. This will teach directionality and tracking of print. The LEA also is a good way to teach sentence, word, and letter representation. Portions of the dictated narrative can be reread, with emphasis on identifying sentences, words, and letters. The LEA, however, *cannot* be used to teach book orientation. LEA experiences also can be used to teach many other things such as letter recognition, phonics, and vocabulary. After the teacher reads the dictated text, and the teacher and child read it together, any portion of the text can be used for a directed lesson.

(4) ENVIRONMENTAL PRINT.   *Environmental print* refers to printed messages that people encounter in ordinary, daily living. This includes milk cartons, bumper stickers, candy wrappers, toy boxes, cereal boxes, billboards, menus, and T-shirts. Teachers should display examples of environmental print on bulletin boards and learning centers. Once displayed, children will see that print carries meaning. Lessons can be based on the letters, words, phrases, and sentences that appear on the items. Obviously, environmental print can't be used to teach book orientation, and it may not work for directionality because many product labels, advertisements, and T-shirts display words in atypical formats, with letters running over the surface in strange configurations.

(5) PRINT-RICH ENVIRONMENT.   All classrooms should be "print rich," with plenty of examples of written language on display. For kindergarteners and first graders, this print-rich environment will help them acquire concepts about print. Children can then "read the room." There are many ways to create this environment:

- *Labels/captions.* Classroom items should be labeled, such as desks, chairs, the clock, and the windows. Bulletin board displays should have easy-to-read captions.
- *Morning message.* The morning message is written on chart paper, in large letters, and provides an overview of the day's activities. For example, "Today is Wednesday, October 11. At ten o'clock we will see a movie about farm animals. We will use

finger paints to make pictures with the colors blue, yellow, and red." The teacher reads the morning message to the students and talks about the day and upcoming events. Students share news with the class. Sometimes, the teacher may wait to write the message until the children are seated in front of an easel with blank chart paper. Then the morning message provides an opportunity for children to see how words become print. The morning message can be used to teach directionality; letter, word, and sentence representation; and the concept that print carries meaning. The morning message, of course, cannot be used to teach book orientation.

- *Mailboxes.* Classroom mailboxes or "cubbies" can be made of milk cartons. They can be used to hold messages as students write to their classmates and the teacher writes to students (for many kindergarteners and first graders, the messages may have to be dictated and transcribed by an adult). Children discover the social purposes of language and that print carries meaning.

(6) EXPLICIT (DIRECT) TEACHING OF CONCEPTS ABOUT PRINT.   The previous activities will be enough for many children to acquire all the concepts about print. For others, you will need to plan direct lessons. For lessons on book orientation, you can use any picture book, assuming the children can see all the words. Big books are ideal for teaching book orientation to a larger group of children. For the other concepts about print, use any of the texts mentioned previously: picture books, environmental print, the child's dictated LEA narratives, or the morning message. The key is that in a direct, explicit lesson, you have as an objective one of the concepts about print. The concept won't be something children "just pick up" but need to be taught directly.

For example, for a child having difficulty with the directionality and tracking of English print, the teacher would select a picture book. First, the book would be read and enjoyed. Then, the teacher would return to the first page of the text and reread it with the child, guiding the child's finger underneath each word as it is read. For a lesson on word representation, the teacher could work with the morning message. In a direct lesson, children would listen to the teacher read a line, and then chant and clap the number of words on the line.

(2) THE IMPORTANCE OF LETTER RECOGNITION IN READING DEVELOPMENT AND INSTRUCTIONAL STRATEGIES

(A) The Importance of Letter Recognition in Reading Development

Research shows that accurate and rapid letter recognition is an essential component in learning to read. In fact, the ability of kindergarteners to identify letters is a strong predictor of future achievement in tests of word identification and comprehension. The key is that children need to be accurate and swift in both recognizing a letter (pointing to a letter the teacher names) and naming a letter (saying the name of a letter when the teacher point to it). Letters are the "building blocks" of printed language, and subsequent reading instruction, especially in phonics, requires students to know their letters.

(B) How to Teach Letter Recognition, Letter Naming, and Letter Formation

Teachers should use a variety of multisensory methods to help children recognize, name, and form the uppercase and lowercase letters of English. Some activities are primarily visual, whereas others tap auditory, tactile, and/or kinesthetic modes of learning. All three capacities (letter recognition, letter naming, and letter formation) develop simultaneously through the following types of activities:

(1) ASSOCIATING NAMES AND THINGS WITH LETTERS.   The teacher could display a large letter on the blackboard, such as a *J*, and then ask everybody with names beginning with *J* to stand underneath the *J*. Some teachers have 26 shoeboxes, each labeled with a different letter of the alphabet. Teachers then ask children to place toys or common classroom objects in the appropriate box, depending on the letter of the alphabet the object begins with. In the *B* box, for example, we would have books, balls, and a bandage.

(2) SINGING THE ALPHABET.   Many generations of children have sung the alphabet song. Remember, to teach the names of the letters, the song needs to be sung slowly as someone points to each letter. This is a good auditory experience.

(3) ABC BOOKS.   Teachers should read aloud books that are organized by the letters of the alphabet. There are dozens of these ABC books. Two of my favorites are *26 Letters and 99 Cents* by Tana Hoban and *Animalia* by Graeme Base.

(4) PRACTICE WRITING BOTH UPPERCASE AND LOWERCASE LETTERS AND WRITING WORDS.   Children learn the names of the letters as they practice writing them. These direct, explicit lessons should include instruction on how to make the letters and a reasonable amount of time for practice. Remember, kindergarteners are only 5 years old and most have not developed the fine motor skills to write letters perfectly. Many teachers have children say the name of a letter each time they practice writing it to provide the auditory link to the visual form of the letter. As children learn to form the letters, they will want to use them to write words, and teachers should encourage them to do so, even if the result is inaccurate spelling.

(5) TACTILE AND KINESTHETIC METHODS.   *Tactile* refers to touch. Tactile lessons include the use of concrete materials to practice the configurations of letters. For example, children could make three-dimensional letters out of modeling clay or trace their fingers over letters cut out of sandpaper. *Kinesthetic* refers to motion. Kinesthetic lessons ask children to make exaggerated movements with their hands and arms, as they pretend to write letters that are 2 feet in height in the air.

(C) How to Systematically Introduce Visually and Auditorily Similar Letters

There are some general principles governing the order in which you teach children to recognize, name, and form letters. First, teach either all the lowercase letters first or all the uppercase letters first; don't teach both at the same time. Second, teach one letter at a time, and each time you introduce a new letter, review the ones that have been learned previously.

The greatest challenge for the children will be learning to recognize, name, and form letters that are either visually similar, auditorily similar, or both. Two letters that are visually similar are *m* and *n*. Two letters that are auditorily similar are *p* and *d*. Two letters that are both visually and auditorily similar are *b* and *d*. Some teachers teach letters that are similar one after the other, rather than teaching the words in alphabetically order. The key is that children learn to recognize, name, and form the *b* before they go on to the *d*.

For visually similar letters, such as the *m* and *n* or the *b* and *d*, many teachers help students distinguish the two letters by asking them to trace the letters with their fingers, focusing on the different direction or the different movements the fingers take for each letter.

(3) THE ALPHABETIC PRINCIPLE

(A) The Role of the Alphabetic Principle

There are close interrelationships among understanding the alphabetic principle, learning letter–sound correspondences, phonemic awareness, and the complex decoding skills such as sounding out words and blending sounds. A child who understands the alphabetic principle knows that the purpose of letters is to represent the sounds of words. Phonemic awareness activities teach children to hear and manipulate those sounds. Phonics instruction teaches children letter–sound correspondences and how to apply that knowledge to sound out words and blend sounds. Perhaps it is easier to understand these relationships if we consider a child who has *not* acquired the alphabetic principle. Such a child would not understand that each of the sounds she hears in a word must be represented by a letter. In fact, the child would have little idea what purpose the letters serve!

(B) Implications of the Alphabetic Principle

When children take part in phonics instruction, they will learn which graphemes (letters) go with which phonemes (sounds). Teachers can see children apply their knowledge of the alphabetic principle both when they read and when they write. When children try to "sound out" a word, they show that they know that sounds are represented by letters. When children are writing and they struggle to identify the appropriate letter(s) to represent a sound, they show they know that all sounds in a word must be represented by at least one letter. Thus, instruction in phonemic awareness, phonics, and spelling all teach and reinforce the alphabetic principle.

(4) WRITING AND STUDENTS' UNDERSTANDING OF THE ALPHABETIC PRINCIPLE AND LETTER–SOUND CORRESPONDENCE

Knowledge of the alphabetic principle and letter–sound correspondences will be reinforced when children write. When they write, young children face the challenge of spelling words correctly. They apply their understanding of the alphabetic principle as they attempt to write the appropriate letters for the sounds in a word. Phonics activities alone cannot fully develop a child's knowledge of letter–sound correspondences. They must write.

(A) Phonetic Spelling

When young children write, their spelling will reflect their still-developing knowledge of English letter–sound correspondences. What they produce is called *phonetic spelling*, or *temporary spelling*, or *invented spelling*. This is what occurs when a child writes a word, but doesn't know the accurate spelling. The result? Some sounds may have no letter at all (*lum* for *lump*) and other sounds in words will be represented by the wrong letters (*bote* for *boat*). Teachers should encourage children to do the best they can and keep writing for two reasons. First, an overemphasis on correctness will stop some children dead in their tracks. They will write very little and that is not good—they need the challenge of trying to figure out how words are spelled. Second, phonetic spelling provides important assessment data on a child's knowledge of letter–sound correspondences.

Two important points must be made. Phonetic spelling is what happens when young children write, *but* it should always coexist with formal spelling instruction that leads to correctness. And, the older children are, the less their spelling should be phonetic and the more it should be accurate.

(5) MEETING THE NEEDS OF ALL LEARNERS

(A) Struggling Readers and Students With Reading Difficulties or Disabilities

The *RICA Content Specifications* recommend the following forms of differentiated instruction to help struggling readers and students with reading disabilities: (1) focusing on key concepts and skills; (2) reteaching concepts, letters, and skills that are lacking; (3) using a variety of concrete examples to explain a concept or task; (4) providing extra practice; and (5) using visual, auditory, kinesthetic, and tactile techniques.

In regards to the concepts about print, many struggling readers and children with reading disabilities have difficulty with the concept of directionality/tracking of print and the difference between letters and words. These are two key concepts.

Reteaching the concept of directionality should involve one-on-one intervention and a strong kinesthetic element. The child needs to guide the teacher's finger as he or she reads left-to-right and makes the return sweep. Then the child needs to point to the next word as the teacher reads, the teacher moving the child's finger if necessary.

Understanding the difference between letters and words may require concrete examples. Many children understand the difference between letters and words by simply looking at a page of book and counting the number of words on a line and the number of letters in a word when asked to do so by the teacher. Struggling readers, however, may need to use letter tiles. The teacher would give the students a tile with the letter *c*, another tile with *a*, and a third with *t*. The student would be asked place them apart from each other and then move them close together to form *cat*. This is an analogous activity to blending sounds.

Struggling readers will have difficulty in recognizing, naming, and forming the letters of the alphabet. Here, tactile interventions are usually necessary. Children need to write letters on their desktop with the bare fingers or write the letters in sand. Many will need to form the letters three-dimensionally with modeling clay.

(B) English Learners and Speakers of Nonstandard English

The *RICA Content Specifications* suggest teachers help English learners to (1) capitalize on the transfer of relevant knowledge and skills from their primary language; and (2) recognize that not all languages are alphabetic and that key features of alphabets vary, including letters, directionality, and phonetic regularity.

(1) CONCEPTS ABOUT PRINT.   If a child has previously learned to read in a language other than English, many or all of the concepts of print will transfer, depending on the first language.

(2) BOOK-HANDLING SKILLS.   At one time there were significant differences in the way some cultural groups prepared texts that were to be read. For example, some groups used scrolls instead of a bound-text format. In the present day, however, almost all cultural groups use books that look alike and are handled the same way. If a child has learned to read in any language other than English, he or she will most likely have acquired book-handling skills.

(3) PRINT CARRIES MEANING.   Likewise, a child who has learned to read in any language will understand that print in books transmits the message. What will differ, however, is what the print looks like (see below).

(4) DIRECTIONALITY AND TRACKING OF PRINT.   This may or may not transfer. If a child has learned to read in any of the Latin-based languages (e.g., Spanish) or any of the German-based languages (e.g., Danish), then they will already understand that print moves left to right, and a return sweep must be made at the end of each line. Most Semitic languages, however, including Arabic and Hebrew, move right to left. Though historically both Chinese and Japanese were written vertically, in modern times these Asian languages have adopted left-to-right horizontal forms.

(5) LETTER AND WORD REPRESENTATION.   This will have a positive transfer for alphabetic languages, including those that have orthographies that resemble English (Latin-based and German-based languages) and those that have alphabets that look very different (Cyrillic, Arabic). Things can get complicated; for example, words are formed differently in Arabic than in English—Arabic words are based three-letter roots. Children who have learned to read any Chinese language, such as Mandarin or Cantonese, will not understand the relationship of letters to words. Chinese is not an alphabetic language, it is logographic, using thousands of symbols to represent morphemes (words and affixes).

(6) LETTER RECOGNITION, NAMING, AND FORMATION.   The greatest level of positive transfer, again, will be from Latin-based and German-based languages—all have alphabets that look a great deal like English. Even then, however, there will be differences that will have to be learned. The letters will have different names. For example, in Spanish *x* is *equis*, *y* is *i griega*, and *z* is *zeta*. And some letters in Spanish do not exist in English (*ll* and *ch*). Children who learned to read in a language with a different alphabet than English (e.g., Korean) will have a greater challenge learning to recognize, name, and form the 26 letters of English. Children who learned to first read a logographic language, such as Mandarin, will face the greatest challenge of all—they will not be use to symbols representing sounds.

(C) Advanced Learners

Many advanced learners will need no instruction at all in concepts about print or letter recognition, letter naming, and letter formation. They will come to school already understanding the alphabetic principle. For advanced learners who do not need to learn these concepts, the *RICA Content Specifications* again mention two ways of differentiating instruction: (1) increasing the pace of instruction and (2) building on and extending current knowledge and skills.

Letter recognition and letter naming provide an opportunity to increase the pace of instruction. Advanced learners will need fewer instructional activities to recognize and name the letters. What takes most children 3 days to master might well be learned in a single lesson.

Some advanced learners with special gifts may want to build on their knowledge of the English alphabet by learning about different orthographies—especially logographic Chinese characters. Lessons on a sound-based alphabet that looks different than English, such as Korean, could also be interesting. They would be challenged to learn the differences among these alphabets while understanding their common purpose—to transmit messages.

(6) ASSESSMENT OF CONCEPTS ABOUT PRINT, LETTER RECOGNITION, AND THE ALPHABETIC PRINCIPLE

(A) Formal and Informal Assessments of Concepts About Print

(1) TESTS OF CONCEPTS ABOUT PRINT.   Marie Clay, the influential educator from New Zealand, developed a test called *Concepts About Print* test, which at one time was popular in kindergarten classrooms in the United States. Now it seems that more and more teachers are relying on tests provided by the basal reading system their school district has adopted, such as Open Court or Houghton Mifflin. To administer Clay's *Concepts About Print* test, the teacher uses one of two special books, *Sand* or *Stones*. The books have some pages with the print upside down, some words with the letters reversed, and some lines of print in odd configurations. The teacher asks the student to do things like point to the front of the book, to identify where the teacher should start to read on a page, and to recognize the beginning and ending of a word. The test measures book orientation, directionality, beginning and ending of a story, word sequence, and recognition of punctuation and capital letters.

(2) INFORMAL ASSESSMENT BY THE TEACHER.   It is relatively easy for classroom teachers to assess concepts about print by using (a) any picture book that has at least three or four lines of text displayed in conventional form on most pages and (b) paper and pencil. The teacher asks students to perform tasks and keeps a record of the results.

For example, to assess directionality and tracking of print, the teacher, at the start of a new page, would ask the child to point to where the teacher should start reading. The child should point to the first word on the first line of the text. Then, as the teacher reads slowly, the child would be asked to put his or her finger under each succeeding word to track the flow of the print. To assess word boundaries, the teacher could cover up all but one line of text and ask the child how many words are on that line.

To assess whether or not a child understands that print carries meaning, a teacher can simply ask the child to write something. If the child writes letters, rather than squiggles or illustrations, then the child understands that, in English, letters are used to convey written messages.

Teachers should also use observation of student behavior to measure acquisition of concepts about print. Some school districts have developed checklists for this purpose. The checklist, for example, might include the following: "book in appropriate position when reading," "demonstrates return sweep," "knows where to start reading on the page."

(B) Formal and Informal Assessment of Letter Recognition, Letter Naming, and Letter Formation

All three of these skills are easy to assess. For letter recognition, you name the letter and the child points to it on a list of all 26 letters. For letter naming, do the reverse. On a list of the 26 letters, point to the letter and ask the child to name it. This is similar to going to the optometrist for an eye exam. By the end of kindergarten, all children should be able to perform both tasks with high levels of accuracy and speed.

More needs to be said about assessing letter formation, which requires two sources of data. First, a teacher should assess the child's ability to write the letters in *isolation*—the teacher calls out the name of the letter and the child writes it. The real test of letter production, however, is whether or not the child can form each letter legibly when writing. This is an encoding in *context* task. Teachers would gather samples of student writing to judge the ability of each student to produce each letter.

(C) Formal and Informal Assessment of the Alphabetic Principle

Assessing students to determine whether they have acquired the alphabetic principle is relatively easy. Please note that this is not the same as the assessment described in the previous section to determine whether or not a child understands that print carries meaning. In that test, the teacher asked the child to write something. If the child writes letters, rather than squiggles or illustrations, then the child understands that, in English, letters are used to convey written messages. This does not reveal whether or not the child understand that letters represent sounds and that every sound must be represented by at least one letter.

Evidence that children have acquired the alphabetic principle can be gained while observing children read aloud and write. If children try to sound out words—if they struggle with finding the right sound for a letter—then they have mastered the alphabetic principle. Likewise, when children write and struggle with choosing the correct letter(s) for a sound, they are demonstrating they understand the relationship between letters and sounds in printed English.

(D) Entry-Level, Monitoring of Progress, and Summative Assessment

Most of the assessment strategies mentioned above can be used for any of the three purposes of assessment. Basically, entry-level and summative assessment should be more formal, whereas monitoring of progress assessments can be based more on observation.

(1) ENTRY-LEVEL ASSESSMENT.   For the concepts about print, it is important that kindergarten and first-grade teachers do a formal assessment of each student early in the school year. The assessment should be administered one-on-one and could use either a commercially prepared test of concepts about print, such as those found in the Open Court or the Houghton Mifflin basal readers, or the teacher-developed format I described using a picture book, paper, and a pencil. For the letters, entry-level assessment should include one-on-one assessment of each task: letter recognition, letter naming, and letter formation.

(2) MONITORING OF PROGRESS.   Teachers should rely on the observations to determine which students are learning what they need to know and which students are struggling. Noting the results of observations is essential. For example, if during an oral reading activity, a child is visibly trying to sound out a word—that is evidence that he or she has mastered the alphabetic principle. If a child reads a book with an adult and the child holds the book appropriately and turns the pages when all the words on a page have been read—that is evidence that the child has mastered book-handling skills.

(3) SUMMATIVE ASSESSMENT.   This needs to be fairly formal, covering all the concepts about print and letter recognition, letter naming, and letter formation. The assessments need to be administered in a one-to-one format.

(E) How to Analyze, Interpret, Use Results

In regards to analysis and interpretation, two points made earlier need to be reiterated here:

(1) ANALYSIS AND INTERPRETATION OF ASSESSMENT RESULTS SHOULD BE BASED ON STANDARDS.   Teachers need to know which students' level of performance is (a) below expectations for the standard, (b) at expectations for the standard, or (c) above expectations for the standard. In many school districts, assessments have been developed for each *English–Language Arts Content Standard*, with criteria defined for each level of performance. If not, then teachers will have to develop their own assessments, and the trickiest part will be defining specific criteria for being below, at, or above the standard.

Let's look at an example from the *English–Language Arts Content Standards*. In the area of Concepts About Print, kindergarten standard 1.5 is that students will be able to "Distinguish letters from words." This assessment can be done with any picture book in a one-to-one format. The teacher selected *Where the Wild Things Are* and chose the text that appears on the seventh page: "That very night in Max's room a forest grew." The teacher read the page and asked the student to count how many words were on the page (nine). Then the teacher asked the student to point to the first word (*That*) and count the number of letters in the word. Finally, the teacher pointed to word *night* and asked how many letters were in that word. A child below expectations would not be able to come up with the correct number of words or the correct number of letters in a word, *or* he or she would take a long time to come up with correct answers. Thus, both *accuracy* and *time* would be criteria for success. A child who meets the standard would be correct and would not take a long time to complete the tasks. A child above expectations would provide the correct answers in a very short period of time.

(2) ANALYSIS AND INTERPRETATION MUST GO FURTHER TO DETERMINE WHY CHILDREN ARE PERFORMING BELOW EXPECTATIONS. The results could also tell the teacher why a child was performing below expectations. A child who stares blankly at the page when asked to count the words obviously needs a great deal of help—the concept of *word* is clearly missing. On the other hand, a child who counts the correct number of words but hesitates before providing the correct number of letters in *That* and *night* understands what words are, but doesn't have the concept of *letter*.

(3) TEACHERS SHOULD USE RESULTS TO CREATE STANDARDS-BASED INDIVIDUAL PROFILES FOR EACH STUDENT. As noted in previous chapters, results of assessments will provide both individual data and whole-class data. Teachers should build individual profiles for each student, clearly listing each relevant grade-level standard and indicating which students are below, at, or above expectations. Individual profiles will tell the teacher which students need additional instruction.

(4) TEACHERS SHOULD USE RESULTS TO CREATE STANDARDS-BASED CLASS PROFILES. Class profiles will allow the teachers to decide whether the entire class needs to work more on distinguishing letters and words; if so, an additional sequence of lessons should be planned. On the other hand, if only a few individuals need help, then their needs can be met with individualized or small-group lessons.

An example of an individual profile and a class profile for one standard in the area of Concepts About Print were provided in Chapter 2.

CHAPTER 5

Competency 5
Phonics and Sight Words:
Terminology and Concepts

INTRODUCTION

Word identification is the ability to read aloud, or decode, words correctly. Please note that word identification does not mean knowing the word's meaning. The *RICA Content Specifications* distinguish word identification, knowing how to pronounce a word, and *word recognition*, which is making a connection between the word being pronounced and its meaning. For all readers there are words we can identify but not recognize. My guess is that almost all of you can pronounce *galah*, but few of you know what a *galah* is (answer at the end of the chapter). When children acquire efficient word identification skills, they can read with automaticity. That is, they do not get "bogged down" with decoding words. They can focus their attention on understanding what they have read. Children can use the following word identification strategies to identify words:

Phonics.   Phonics is the ability to make the correct association between the sounds and the symbols of a language. Using the Greek roots for symbol and sound, these are often called graphophonic or graphophonemic relationships. Phonics is a set of many skills, such as the knowledge that the letter *c* makes both the /k/ sound (*cake*) and the /s/ sound (*city*). We will discuss the terminology, concepts, and role of phonics instruction in this chapter. How to teach phonics, including specific instructional strategies, will be the focus of the next chapter.

Sight words.   Children should be taught to identify some words as whole units without breaking the word down by phonics or morphology. Four types of words should be taught as sight words:

1. *High-frequency* words that appear most frequently in the printed texts children read (*as, the, of*). Many available lists identify these high-frequency words, including Edward Fry's "The New Instant Word List."
2. Words with irregular spellings, such as *dove* and *great*.
3. Words that children want to know, usually because they want to use them in their writing (*dinosaur, Burger King*).
4. Words that are introduced in content-area lessons in social studies and science (*insect, butterfly*).

Morphology.   To a linguist, morphology is the study of word formation. Children use morphological clues to identify words when they rely on root words, prefixes, and suffixes. *Structural analysis* is the process of recognizing words by analyzing prefixes, suffixes, and base words. *Syllabic analysis* is the process of recognizing words by analyzing the syllables in a word. We will discuss structural analysis and syllabic analysis in Chapter 7.

Context clues.   In many instances, children can figure out an unknown word if they know the meanings of the words surrounding the unknown word. When children do this, they have used the context of the sentence or paragraph to identify the word. The use of context clues, which enables children to both identify and know the meaning of an unknown word, will be covered in Chapter 10.

There are three topics in this competency:

(1) The role of phonics and sight words in word identification
(2) The sequence of phonics and sight word instruction
(3) The interrelationships between phonics development and stages of spelling development

(1) THE ROLE OF PHONICS AND SIGHT WORDS IN WORD IDENTIFICATION

This first topic explains the importance of phonics and sight words in the reading process. Knowledge of phonics and sight words facilitates swift and accurate word identification, which is a prerequisite for word recognition, reading fluency, and reading comprehension.

(A) How Word Identification Contributes to Word Recognition

All young readers know the meanings of many words that they cannot pronounce in printed form. For example, a 5-year-old may have a very good sense of what chocolate ice cream is, and be able to say "I want some chocolate ice cream," but be unable to decode the words *chocolate*, *ice*, or *cream*. When children learn to identify in print words that exist in their oral vocabulary, they increase the number of words that they "recognize," that is, that they know the meaning of. This is the process of associating the correct printed form to a known word.

(B) How Automaticity in Word Recognition Leads to Fluency and Comprehension

The goal for all students is to achieve *automaticity* in word identification and word recognition. A child achieves automaticity when his or her word identification is swift and accurate. Automaticity is essential for *fluent* reading, that is, reading at an appropriate pace with appropriate expression. Obviously, a student who is stumbling over several words in a paragraph will not achieve fluency. And research shows fluent reading is essential for the reading comprehension. This is because slow, struggling readers often lose track of the meaning of what they are reading.

(2) THE SEQUENCE OF PHONICS AND SIGHT WORD INSTRUCTION

This second topic identifies the sound–letter correspondences that will be taught and stresses the importance of starting with the simplest linguistic units (consonant sounds) and progressing to more complex linguistic units (irregular words).

(A) Types of Consonant Sounds

(1) REVIEW: DEFINITION OF A CONSONANT.   To review, consonants are speech sounds that occur when the airflow is obstructed in some way by your mouth, teeth, or lips. In some consonant sounds the obstruction is total, and the flow of air stops. In other consonants sounds, the obstruction is partial and some air can flow around the obstruction.

(2) CONTINUOUS SOUNDS.   With continuous consonant sounds, it is possible to "hold" the sound and stretch the sound out. When in the initial position in a word, the sounds made by the letters *f, l, m, n, r, s, v,* and *z* are continuous consonant sounds.

(3) STOP SOUNDS.   On the other hand, with stop consonant sounds, the sound must be uttered quickly with a "quick" puff of air. Stop sounds are also called *clipped* consonant sounds and include the following letters in the initial position in a word: *b, c, d, g, j, k, p, qu,* and *t.*

(B) Common, Regular Letter Combinations

(1) CONSONANT DIGRAPHS.   Digraphs are two-letter combinations that make one sound. For example, *ph* in *phone* and *sh* in *share.* Don't forget: The *ph* in *digraph* is a digraph!

(2) CONSONANT BLENDS.   Blends are two- or three-letter combinations, said rapidly, and each letter in a blend makes a sound. Examples of consonant blends are *pl* in play and *spr* in *spring.* Remember: The *bl* in *blend* is a blend!

(3) VOWELS.   To review, vowels are sounds made when the air leaving your lungs is vibrated in the voice box and there is a clear passage from the voice box to your mouth. In English, the following letters always represent vowel sounds: *a, e, i, o, u.* Two letters sometimes represent vowel sounds: *y,* in words such as *sky,* and *w* in words such as *cow.* Vowel sounds are said to be long when they "say their own name" as in *bake* and *bite.* Short vowels occur in such words as *cat, pet, bit, cot, but.* Some vowel sounds are called "R-controlled" (*car*) or "L-controlled" (*milk*).

(4) VOWEL DIGRAPHS.   Vowel digraphs are two-vowel combinations that make a single sound. For example, the *oa* in *boat* makes the long *o* sound; the *ea* in *teach* makes the long *e* sound.

(5) DIPHTHONGS.   Diphthongs are glided sounds made by such vowel combinations as *oi* in *oil* and *oy* in *boy.* When pronouncing a diphthong, the tongue starts in one position and rapidly moves to another.

(6) R-CONTROLLED VOWELS.   R-controlled vowels are neither long nor short, as in the sounds *a* makes in *car, e* makes in *her, i* makes in *girl, u* makes in *hurt,* and *o* makes in *for.*

(7) L-CONTROLLED VOWELS.   Likewise, L-controlled vowels are neither long nor short, as in the sound *a* makes in *chalk, e* makes in *help, i* makes in *milk, o* makes in *cold,* and *u* makes in *bull.*

(C) Common, Inflected Morphological Units Taught as Part of Phonics Instruction

Morphological units include prefixes (*inter-* or *intra-*), suffixes (*-est* or *-ment*), and words without prefixes or suffixes (*pizza* or *elephant*). We will cover morphology in Chapter 7. *Inflected* morphological units are suffixes that do not change the part of speech of the root word. For example, *walk* and *walked* are both verbs, and *big* and *bigger* are both adjectives. Frequently used inflected suffixes include *-ed, -er, -est, -ing* and *-s.* These inflected suffixes should be taught as a part of phonics instruction. For example, children should be taught how to pronounce *-er* and *-est* and understand how they change the meaning of the root words they are attached to.

(D) Common Word Patterns of Increasing Difficulty

(1) VC.   Please note that the abbreviation *V* stands for *vowel,* and the abbreviation *C* stands for *consonant.* In the VC pattern, the vowel is short as in *am, it,* and *up.* There are exceptions to each pattern in this section—words with "irregular" spellings. In this case, the word *to* has an irregular spelling and is an exception to the VC pattern because the *o* does not make the short *o* sound.

(2) CVC.   The medial (in the middle) vowel is short as in *man, pet, lip, tot,* and *bum.*

(3) CVCC. Words in this pattern include *balk*, *cost*, and *film*. The vowel is short. It will confuse children to include words that end with a consonant digraph, where the final two consonants make only one sound, such as *bath* and *fish*.

(4) CCVC. Most of these words start with a consonant blend, such as *brat*, *clap*, or *skip*. The vowel is short.

(5) CVVC. Many, but not all, of the words in this pattern have vowel digraphs (two vowels, one sound): *bait*, *team*, and *goat*.

(6) CVCE. The vowel in this pattern makes a long sound as in *made, like, cone*, and *huge*. Beware of those irregular exceptions, such as *love* and *live*.

(E) Common Syllable Patterns and Syllabication as Applied to Decoding Multisyllabic Words

There are rules for dividing a word into syllables, such as the six that are listed below:

1. Compound words, divide between the words: *in-side, foot-ball*.
2. Single-syllable prefix, divide between the prefix and the root: *un-kind, pre-test*.
3. Never divide a consonant digraph: *bush-el, teach-er*.
4. Two consonants in the middle of a word that are not digraphs, divide between the consonants: *sis-ter, but-ter*.
5. Single consonant in the middle of a word between two vowels, the vowel preceding the consonant is short, divide after the consonant: *cab-in, lev-el*.
6. Single consonant in the middle of a word between two vowels, the vowel preceding the consonant is long, divide before the consonant: *be-long, fe-ver*.

(F) Why Some Words Are Phonetically Irregular and Never Decodable

For a variety of reasons, there are a large number of words in English that are phonetically irregular—that is, they do not follow the decoding generalizations that usually work. For example, the irregular words *of, the, was*. Some words are phonetically irregular because of the etymology (word origins)—they reflect the spelling of another language. Other words are now phonetically irregular because of pronunciation shifts in English over hundreds of years.

(G) How and When Irregular Words Fit Into the Continuum of Phonics Instruction

Because many of the words that appear most frequently in English are phonetically irregular, many of them must be taught as sight words in kindergarten, first, and second grade. Sight words are words that are taught as a whole "unit," so that students do not need to decode them by applying their knowledge of phonics. For example, the three phonetically irregular words listed in the previous section are among the most frequently used in printed English (*of, the, was*). In the Fry New Instant Word List, which displays the 300 most frequently used words in English, *the* is number 1 (the most frequently used word), *of* is number 2, and *was* is number 12.

Many of the irregular, high-frequency words are neither nouns, verbs, nor adjectives, but rather they are *function words* with no clear meaning: prepositions, pronouns, or conjunctions (such as *of, the, was*). These words, taught as sight words, are particularly hard for children to remember.

(H) Why Some Decodable Words Must Be Taught as Sight Words Until Their Phonetic Pattern Has Been Taught

Some words that are decodable should be taught as sight words because (1) they are high-frequency words children need to know early on and (2) some sound–symbol relationship in the word will not be taught until much later. The *RICA Content Specifications* sight *park* as an example; it is a word that many young children will want to use in their writing, but the R-controlled *a* in *park* may not be taught until second grade. Another example would be the high-frequency word *each* (number 43 in the Fry New Instant Word List). The *ea* vowel digraph is usually not among the first sound–symbol relationships taught to children, but as a high-frequency word it must be taught as a sight word late in kindergarten or early in first grade.

(3) THE INTERRELATIONSHIPS BETWEEN PHONICS DEVELOPMENT AND STAGES OF SPELLING DEVELOPMENT

The development of phonics knowledge and learning how to spell are closely related. This final subtopic examines that relationship.

(A) Stages of Spelling Development

In our discussion, we will use five stages of spelling development: precommunicative, semiphonetic, phonetic, transitional, and conventional. It is essential to note, however, as with any developmental stage theory, sometimes children don't fit neatly into these five categories. If a child is on the cusp of one of these stages, he or she might appear to be in two of the stages at the same time. Also, the jump from one stage to another doesn't occur overnight; children gradually move from one stage to another. Knowing the child's level of spelling development is important because it will tell you what type of instruction the child needs.

(1) PRECOMMUNICATIVE.   Precommunicative spelling shows no understanding that letters represent sounds. Rather than letters, the child "writes" by drawing pictures or making squiggles. Or, if letters appear, they are randomly assigned. There is no understanding of the alphabetic principle. For example, a child wrote *aaLLo Sbav* to represent *My Dad's new car.*

(2) SEMIPHONETIC.   Children attempt to use letters to represent sounds. The child's knowledge of sound–symbol relationships, however, is poorly developed. At this level children often do not write at least one letter for each sound in a word; that is, some sounds in words are not represented. For example, *banana* is spelled *baa*.

(3) PHONETIC.   Phonetic spellers know that letters represent sounds and at least one letter represents each sound in a word. The problem is, of course, that many times young spellers do not choose the right letter or combination of letters to represent sounds. To use linguistic terms, all phonemes have a grapheme. Writing at this level is somewhat difficult to read. For example, *I lik two flii a kitt* is *I like to fly a kite.*

One important thing to note about children who are semiphonetic or phonetic spellers, and are making many errors when they write, is that these children should be encouraged to write even though they make mistakes. This is developmentally appropriate practice as long as teachers (a) simultaneously work to improve the child's spelling and (b) expect that correctness will increase as the child gets older.

(4) TRANSITIONAL.   At this level, the child knows most of the orthographic patterns of English. All sounds have letters and for the most part, the child chooses the correct letter or combination of letters to represent sounds. Mistakes frequently occur with sounds that have several spellings such as the long *a*. This is why the child writes *nayborhood*. Transitional spelling is easy to read. For example, *The firefiters have to be able to climb up the sides of bildings.*

(5) CONVENTIONAL.   The child spells almost all words correctly. The only mistakes at this level occur when the child tries to spell new words with irregular spellings. Children at this level generally recognize that a word they have spelled "doesn't look right." (This paragraph was, I hope, an example of conventional spelling!)

(B) The Relationships Among Phonics Knowledge, Spelling Development, and Decoding Skills

We have already discussed how phonics knowledge leads to swift word identification, which is necessary for fluent reading. Phonics knowledge also supports the child's development as a speller. Simply put, research shows that effective phonics instruction makes children better spellers. This topic uses the phrase "orthographic development," which needs to be defined. *Orthography* is somewhat synonymous with *spelling*—the word is usually used as part of the phrase *orthographic patterns*, which are the frequently occurring letter combinations of English spelling (e.g., the rime *-ight*, the suffix *-tion*). Phonics instruction helps children learn these spelling (or orthographic) patterns. Thus, at the same time you teach phonics you teach spelling.

And ... the reverse is true. Spelling instruction that focuses on common orthographic patterns will help children decode words. For example, a child who knows how to pronounce the *-ight* rime will be able to both orally decode words with that rime when reading aloud and encode the word when writing.

(C) The Relationship Between Spelling Instruction and Vocabulary Development

In addition to helping children increase their phonics knowledge, spelling instruction can foster vocabulary development. Usually spelling instruction focuses on both how to spell a word and what the word means. Effective spelling instruction will sometimes select words that share a common prefix (e.g., *inter-*) or a root (*micro*). A fifth-grade spelling list focusing on *micro* might include *microwave, microscope,* and *microphone.* As children learn to spell those words, they will also learn their meanings.

(D) Writing Activities Provide Opportunities for Applying Phonics Knowledge

Teachers will see which sound–symbol relationships students have mastered when they write. Writing activities provide an opportunity for children to apply what they have learned about English sound–symbol relationships. The point here is that phonics knowledge can be revealed both when students decode printed text while they read aloud and when they encode printed text while they write.

Galah is pronounced with four sounds: (1) the *g* as in *go*, (2) the schwa (*uh*), (3) the *l*, and (4) the short *a*. It is a colorful bird that lives in Australia.

CHAPTER 6

Competency 6
Phonics and Sight Words: Instruction and Assessment

INTRODUCTION

The previous competency addressed the background knowledge teachers need to learn to be effective teachers of phonics and sight words. This competency is about instructional methodology and assessment.

We will start with:

(1) The fundamentals of teaching phonics

Then, we will discuss the five topics in this competency:

(2) Systematic, explicit instruction in phonics at the beginning stage
(3) Systematic, explicit instruction in phonics at more advanced stages
(4) Systematic, explicit instruction in sight words
(5) Meeting the needs of all learners
(6) Assessment of phonics and sight words

(1) THE FUNDAMENTALS OF TEACHING PHONICS

Let's start by examining the common elements of teaching phonics to children at any stage of development.

(A) Systematic, Direct, and Explicit Phonics Instruction

(1) INSTRUCTION SHOULD BE SYSTEMATIC. Teachers should have a clear list of the sound–symbol relationships students at their grade level should know. Students should be assessed to determine which sound–symbol relationships they have mastered and which they need to learn. Sound–symbol relationships should be taught in a sequence that moves from simple to complex linguistic units.

(2) INSTRUCTION SHOULD BE DIRECT AND EXPLICIT. Some authorities in the field of reading instruction have been concerned that too many teachers appear to either teach phonics in a haphazard manner or not teach it at all. Although it is true that some children will acquire some sound–symbol relationships with seemingly little effort as they take part in a variety of literacy activities, most children need to be taught phonics directly. In a direct, explicit lesson, the teacher's objective is to teach a sound–symbol relationship. These lessons are best taught to small groups of children who share the need to learn the same sound–symbol relationship.

(B) Direct, Explicit Teaching of Phonics: Instructional Approaches

(1) WHOLE-TO-PART LESSONS.   We will focus on two approaches to the direct, explicit teaching of phonics: *whole-to-part* (also called *analytic phonics*) and *part-to-whole* (also called *synthetic phonics*). Both approaches have supporters. Some basal reading textbook series feature whole-to-part lessons in their workbooks (Houghton Mifflin), whereas others rely heavily on part-to-whole lessons (Open Court).

Whole-to-part lessons start with sentences, then look at words, and "end up" with the sound–symbol relationship that is the focus of the lesson. Here is a lesson that teaches the *sh* digraph at the end of words:

1. The teacher presents a set of sentences on a piece of chart paper or on the blackboard, each sentence having a word with the common element. The teacher then underlines the target word.

   My mom went to the bank and came home with a lot of <u>cash</u>.

   We went to the market and bought some <u>fish</u> and potatoes.

   I helped her <u>mash</u> the potatoes.

   After dinner, my brother Fred broke a <u>dish</u>.

2. Students read each sentence aloud with the teacher. Then, the students read aloud the underlined word (*cash, fish, mash, dish*).
3. Then the teacher says, "There is something about the underlined words that is the same. What is it?" The children should note they all end with *sh*. If they don't, tell them.
4. The focus is now on the sound–symbol relationship. The teacher writes the letters *sh* on the board and, as the teacher points to the letters, the children make the appropriate sound.
5. The children then reread the target words one more time.

(2) PART-TO-WHOLE LESSONS.   Part-to-whole lessons begin with the sound and then children blend the sounds to build words. The teaching sequence would be:

1. The teacher writes the symbol(s) on the board (*sh*) and tells children the sound that it makes.
2. The children say the target sound each time the teacher points to it.
3. The teacher shows letter combinations that can be added to the sound to make words. The teacher would write *ca, fi, ma, di* on cards large enough for students to see them easily. The teacher places these cards in front of the *sh* written on the blackboard. The children would then blend the sounds to make a word (for example, *ca* and *sh* are read as *cash*).

(C) Other Approaches to Teaching Phonics

If you have an essay question on phonics teaching on the RICA, describe instruction that is direct and explicit, either the whole-to-part approach or the part-to-whole approach. I would not use these two approaches described here in an essay question, but you may have a multiple choice question about them.

(1) ANALOGY PHONICS.   In this approach students are taught unfamiliar words by comparing them to known words, usually with onsets and rimes. For example, children learning *brick* are first showed two simpler words with the *-ick* rime, *kick* and *tick*. The teacher then introduces the *br* blend and children combine it with the familiar *-ick*.

(2) EMBEDDED PHONICS.   This is teaching phonics incidentally as something that is not the central focus of a lesson. For example, after a teacher has read aloud the picture book *Make Way for Ducklings,* she or he takes a few minutes to work with students on the *-ake* rime that appears in *Make* by having the students generate words that rhyme with *make*.

(D) Practice, Practice, Practice

There is one final thing to remember about teaching phonics. After students have been taught sound–symbol relationships and have practiced associating sounds to a letter or group of letters (in isolation), they should have opportunities to read the sounds in the context of words, phrases, sentences, and paragraphs. Often teachers will need to create special sentences with several words with sounds that have been learned—and challenge students to read aloud the sentences.

This contextual practice may require the teacher to first model the desired outcome—the correct oral reading of the words, phrases, sentences, and paragraphs. Students then read the texts *subvocally* (i.e., reading aloud, moving the lips and tongue, but making no sound). Finally, students would read the texts aloud normally.

(2) SYSTEMATIC, EXPLICIT INSTRUCTION IN PHONICS AT THE BEGINNING STAGE

The *RICA Content Standards* cite four categories of word identification lessons that should be included for beginning readers: (a) teaching sounding out and blending of regular VC and CVC words, (b) teaching whole-word reading of single-syllable, regular words and some high-frequency, irregular sight words, (c) using decodable text for practice, and (d) teaching students to use phonics knowledge to spell VC and CVC words. Children start by sounding out letter by letter and move to recognizing words.

(A) How to Teach Sounding Out and Blending of Regular VC and CVC Words

To review, in regular VC words, the vowel is short as in *am, it,* and *up.* In regular CVC words, the vowel is short as in *man, pet, lip, tot,* and *bum.* These are among the most regular phonics patterns in English and a good place to begin with our youngest learners. Teachers would start by teaching children to sound out the separate sounds in VC and CVC words. This involves displaying the letter that represents the sound and having the children voice the sound. After each sound in a word has been displayed and voiced, the children then "blend" the two or three sounds together. The teacher models the blending process, lingering a little too long on each sound.

You might have recognized that this type of lesson follows the part-to-whole approach and is an appropriate way to teach beginning readers the VC and CVC patterns. For example, a teacher working on the short *a* CVC pattern wants students to pronounce *mad, man,* and *map.* First the students would work on the sound *m* makes, then the students would work on the short *a* sound. Next, students would do the *d* sound, and blend the three sounds into the word *mad.* The students would then work on the *n* sound and blend the three sounds into the word *man.* Finally, students would do the *p* sound, and blend the three sounds into the word *map.*

(B) Single-Syllable, Regular Words and Some High-Frequency, Irregular Sight Words

Hundreds of words follow the regular VC and CVC pattern. These are all single-syllable, regular words. Knowledge of single-syllable, regular words, however, will not allow children to do much actual reading since it is difficult to construct coherent sentences using just words that fit that criteria. Thus, early on children will need to learn some high-frequency sight words with irregular spellings (*the, to, is, you, was, are, have*). We will discuss how to teach sight words later in this chapter.

(C) How to Use Decodable Text

Single-syllable, regular words and a few high-frequency, irregular sight words can be used to write stories in *decodable text.* Beginning readers should read often from decodable texts. Stories written in decodable text have highly controlled vocabulary. Words are selected because they have the phonics elements and the sight words children have been previously taught. For example, after students have learned the regular initial and ending consonants and the short *i* in the medial (middle) position, a decodable text story might consist of just the words *did, pig, hid, mitt, sit, big,* and *slid* along with the sight words *who, where* and *when* (*Where did the pig sit?*). Most preprimer (early kindergarten), primer (later kindergarten), and first-grade basal readers consist of stories written in de-codable texts. Reading from decodable texts reinforces the sound–symbol relationships children have learned.

(D) Spelling VC and CVC Words

There should be a close relationship between phonics and spelling instruction. Once children have learned to read VC and CVC words, words fitting into this pattern should be part of their spelling lists. As noted previously, phonics challenges students to *decode* words orally. Spelling challenges students to use their phonics knowledge to *encode* words in writing. When writing a CVC word like *man*, children should sound the word out as they spell it, saying each sound to themselves as they write the appropriate letters.

(3) SYSTEMATIC, EXPLICIT INSTRUCTION IN PHONICS AT MORE ADVANCED STAGES

In more advanced stages of decoding development, children are required to read words of increasing linguistic complexity. The *RICA Content Specifications* cite six categories of word identification lessons for more advanced learners: (a) Teaching the regular CVCC, CCVC, and CVVC words, (b) teaching regular CVCe words, (c) teaching words with less common elements, (d) continuing the use of decodable text, (e) teaching words formed by adding a common inflected ending, and (f) teaching students to use phonics knowl-edge to spell more complex orthographic patterns.

(A) CVCC, CCVC, and CVVC Words Containing Common, Regular Letter Combinations

In the CVCC pattern, the vowel is short (*cost, film*). Most CCVC words start with a blend (*clip, brat*). CVVC words have vowel digraphs with the first vowel saying its name (*bait, team*). More advanced lessons can follow either the part-to-whole or the whole-to-part approach. Let's assume a teacher's objective was to teach the *ai* digraph in the CVVC pat-tern. In the part-to-whole approach, the lesson would start with the letters *ai* on the board. The children would then repeatedly make the long *a* sound as the teacher taps the board below the *ai*. Then, beginning and ending consonants would be added. First, a *b* and a *t* to make *bait*. Students would blend the sounds to make *bait*. The lesson would continue with other *ai* words such as *paid* and *rain*, each time starting with the target sound–symbol relationship (*ai*), then building words.

Or, the teacher could follow a whole-to-part approach for the same objectives. In this approach, the lesson starts with three sentences on the board:

Sam and his Mom used worms for <u>bait</u>.

Sarah <u>paid</u> for the ice cream.

Steve ran under the tree when it started to <u>rain</u>.

The teacher would read the first sentence aloud, pointing to each word. Then, children would read the first sentence aloud as the teacher points to each word. Next, the teacher would read aloud the underlined target word, *bait*. Then, the children would read *bait* aloud several times. Finally, the teacher would circle the *ai* and ask the students to make the long *a* sound each time he or she taps underneath the word. The lesson would continue in the same format for the other two sentences. In whole-to-part phonics, lessons start with sentences, then examine words, and ultimately focus on sound–symbol relationships.

(B) Regular CVCe Words

Advanced learners would continue their phonics instruction by learning regular CVCe words. In regular CVCe words, the vowel is long and the final *e* is silent as in *huge* and *cone*. Again, teachers could use either a whole-to-part or a part-to-whole approach.

(C) Words Containing Phonics Elements That Are Less Common

The *RICA Content Specifications* state that students in the more advanced stages of word identification should learn phonics elements that are less common. This would include consonant digraphs, where two letters make one sound. The most common consonant digraphs are *ch* (*chair*), *sh* (*hush*), *wh* (*which*) and *th* (*with*). Less common is *ph* (*phonics*). Some authorities now consider *kn* to be a digraph as in *knight* and *knife*, others do not include *kn* as a digraph since at one time, hundreds of years ago, the *k* made a sound in English. In any case, less common elements such as *ph* and *kn* will take extra practice for students to master.

(D) Continuing the Use of Decodable Text

As noted earlier, decodable text provides opportunities for students to practice using the word identification knowledge they acquired. Decodable texts for advanced learners use words fitting more complex patterns, such as CVCC, CCVC, CVVC, CVCe, along with many more irregular sight words. While still decodable, these texts include a wider variety of words and will be more interesting to read than simpler decodable texts written for less developed readers.

(E) Words Formed by Adding a Common Inflected Ending

Students at more advanced stages of decoding development should be taught to identify words formed by adding common inflected suffixes, such as *-ed* (*talked*), *-er* (*quicker*), *-est* (*biggest*), *-ing* (*playing*), and *-s* (*shoes*) to base words. First, teachers should teach the suffix in isolation, using either the part-to-whole or whole-to-part approaches. Then students should be challenged to read whole words with the suffix.

(F) Phonics Knowledge to Spell More Complex Orthographic Patterns

The close relationship between phonics and spelling instruction mentioned earlier should continue with students at more advanced stages of decoding development. Spelling lists should include words from the CVCC, CVVC, CVCe patterns; along with words with less common phonic elements (*ph, kn*) and words with inflected suffixes.

(4) SYSTEMATIC, EXPLICIT INSTRUCTION IN SIGHT WORDS

(A) Explicit (Direct) Teaching of Sight Words

It is best to follow a whole-to-part approach to teaching sight words, as follows:

1. First, the teacher selects the words to be learned (*who, want, there, your*).
2. Then, the teacher would write each word in a sentence, preferably in somewhat of a story format, with the target words underlined:

   "Who has my ball?" Matt asked. "I want it back."

   "There it is," Janet said. "Your coat is on top of it."

3. Next, the teacher reads aloud the sentences, pointing to each word as it is read.
4. The children then read the story aloud with the teacher.
5. The teacher then writes each target word on the board, points to one word at a time, pronounces it, and asks the children to spell it and then say it.
6. As a follow-up, the children can add the words to their word banks (a student-maintained list of words). The words can also be written on flash cards that can be used to review the words.

(B) High-Frequency Words

For young learners, the most important words to teach as sight words are the high-frequency words. A well-researched list of high-frequency words is Edward Fry's "The New Instant Word List," which includes the 300 most common words in English print (*the* is number one; *it's* is number 300).

Some high-frequency words do conform to regular phonics/spelling patterns, but many do not. Among the first 25 words on the New Instant Word list, *and, in, is, that, it, on, as, with,* and *this* all conform to regular patterns. On the other hand, *the, of, was,* and *have* do not. High-frequency words that do not conform to regular patterns will be more difficult to learn and should have more lessons devoted to them.

(C) Factors That Affect the Sequence of Instruction for Specific Sight Words

In which order should the high-frequency sight words be taught? Two factors come into play. First, the sight words that appear most frequently in the students' basal readers deserve priority. Teachers should look at the stories students will read and teach those high-frequency words before students read the text. This will most likely include words such as *and, is, it, was,* and *are.* If students can identify these words, their reading will be more fluent. Second, high-frequency words that are visually similar should be taught together. For example, several words in the first 100 of the New Instant Word List all have the *th* digraph: *the, that, they, this, there, then, them, these,* and *than.* The other sounds in these words vary, but it would make sense to teach all the high-frequency words beginning with *th* right after each other.

(D) Explicit Strategies for Helping Students Master the Spelling of High-Frequency Sight Words

As children learn to decode high-frequency sight words, they should also learn how to spell them. In Chapter 7, you will read more about teaching spelling. Effective teachers would select from several multisensory techniques to help students learn to spell high-frequency sight words.

(1) VISUAL: USE OF COLOR.   This is especially effective with words with vowel digraphs, such as *said.* The students would write *said* 10 times, each time writing the *a* in red and the *i* in green.

(2) AUDITORY.   This works well for many students. The students would write the target word 10 times, each time pronouncing each letter in the word.

(3) TACTILE.   Tactile approaches can be effective because many of the high-frequency words contain few letters (*of, to, in, is*). The children would write the words on a textured surface, such as their desktops, with their bare fingers.

(5) MEETING THE NEEDS OF ALL LEARNERS

(A) Struggling Readers and Students With Reading Disabilities

The *RICA Content Specifications* provide four examples of how teachers can help struggling readers and children with reading difficulties acquire the phonics skills, sight words, and spelling skills they need.

(1) FOCUS ON KEY PHONICS SKILLS AND HIGH-FREQUENCY SIGHT WORDS.   Teachers should prioritize the phonics skills and sight words struggling readers need to learn. Although all teachers should seek to have all their students meet the grade-level standards, the extra time struggling readers require may make this difficult. Struggling readers may need a slower pace of instruction and more review, and this takes time. Thus, teachers need to decide what is most important and teach it first.

(2) RETEACH PHONICS SKILLS AND SIGHT WORDS THAT ARE LACKING.   Progress-monitoring assessments will reveal which skills and sight words individuals lack. Students who have not acquired the same skill should be placed in small groups for reteaching activities. When reteaching a skill, the teacher should not simply repeat a lesson previously taught. The teacher could select any or all of the following modifications: use different materials, teach at a slower pace, or vary the mode of delivery (more or fewer visual experiences; more or fewer auditory experiences; more or fewer kinesthetic experiences; more or fewer tactile experiences).

(3) USE A VARIETY OF CONCRETE EXAMPLES TO EXPLAIN A CONCEPT OR TASK.   For phonics and sight words, teachers may want to use three-dimensional, plastic or wood letters. Other teachers use "letter tiles." Some children need to physically manipulate letters as they learn the sounds they make.

(4) PROVIDE ADDITIONAL PRACTICE.   Although some students may learn a phonics skills in a single lesson, struggling readers may need to practice what they have learned several times for the skill to "stick." Some teachers use activities that seem like games to help struggling readers practice what they are learning. For example, in *Word Sorts*, children are challenged to place cards with words on them in appropriate categories. For example, a teacher prepares cards with following words: *cat, mad, nap, tan, rain, day, page, nail.* The students put the short *a* words (*cat*, etc.) in one box, and they put the long *a* words (*day*, etc.) in another.

(B) English Learners and Speakers of Nonstandard English

The *RICA Content Specifications* cite three interventions to help English learners and speakers of nonstandard English acquire phonics skills, sight words, and spelling skills:

(1) CAPITALIZE ON TRANSFER OF RELEVANT KNOWLEDGE AND SKILLS FROM THE PRIMARY LANGUAGE.   The alphabets of Latin-based languages (Portuguese, Spanish, French, Italian, Romanian) and the German-based languages (German, Dutch, Swedish, etc.) look very much like the English alphabet. And, in some cases, the same letters make the same or very similar sounds. My examples will be between English and Spanish. Several initial consonants make the same sound in both languages: *b, d, m, p,* and *t.* These sound–symbol relationships should be taught first and should be relatively easy for Spanish-speaking English learners to master.

Two words that look alike and mean the same thing in two languages are called *cognates.* There are many cognates between English and German-based languages and between English and the Latin-based languages. These words will be easy for children to identify and recognize (know the meaning of the word in English). Here are some cognates between English and Spanish (English word first): *air/aire, active/activo* or *activa, artist/artista,* and *color/color.*

(2) EXPLICITLY TEACHING SOUNDS THAT DO NOT TRANSFER.   On the other hand, between any two languages there will be phonemes that exist in one language that don't exist in the other. In Spanish, *j, x,* and *y* make different sounds than those letters make in English; and the English sound that the letter *h* makes at the beginnings of words doesn't exist in Spanish. Letters that look the same but make different sounds and sounds that don't exist in the child's native language will take extra work to teach. They must be taught directly and explicitly.

(3) EXPLICITLY TEACHING THE MEANINGS OF SIGHT WORDS, IF NEEDED.   We will cover how to teach the meanings of words in Chapter 11, but there is a point to be made here. Recall again, how for native speakers of English word identification—knowing how to pronounce the word—often leads easily to word recognition—associating a meaning to the word that was pronounced. For example, almost all kindergarteners use the word *now* when speaking. They know what *now* means (do they ever!). When they learn how to pronounce *now* when it is taught as a sight word, there is no need to teach them the meaning of *now.* On the other hand, an English learner faces the task of not only pronouncing *now* but learning what it means. Thus, with many sight words, English learners will need to be taught both how to pronounce the word and what the word means.

(4) ANALYZE PATTERNS OF ERROR.   Depending on their first language, English learners will make many predictable pronunciation errors when attempting to decode English.

Teachers should regularly assess the oral reading of English learners to look for consistent pronunciation errors. The important patterns to note are those errors that would make it difficult for the child to understand what she is reading. When identified, the teacher can then help the English learner acquire correct pronunciation.

(C) Advanced Learners

The *RICA Content Specifications* state two interventions for advanced learners as they acquire phonics skills, sight words, and spelling skills.

(1) INCREASE THE PACE OR COMPLEXITY OF INSTRUCTION.   There are two ways to increase the pace of instruction. First, a lesson that might take 20 minutes for most students need only take 10 minutes with advanced learners. Second, although it may take three lessons for most students to acquire a skill, advanced learners may need only one lesson. In regards to complexity, lessons for advanced learners can often have more objectives than for most other learners (you teach more content in one lesson).

(2) BUILD ON AND EXTEND CURRENT KNOWLEDGE AND SKILLS.   Another way to increase the complexity of instruction for advanced learners is to "skip" lessons that would be pre-requisite for most learners. When a teacher does this, he or she is "building" on what the advanced learner already knows. Advanced learners are able to "extend" or go well beyond what most students know and are able to do. For example, a challenging activity for advanced learners in the area of spelling is called *Making Words*. The teacher selects a target word (e.g., *teacher*). The children are given two or three cards or tiles with each letter from the word (*t,e,a,c,h,r*). First the students are challenged to make small words (e.g., *hat, he, her*). Then, they are challenged to make larger words (*cheater, heart*). Finally, they try to guess the target word (*teacher*).

(6) ASSESSMENT OF PHONICS AND SIGHT WORDS

(A) How to Assess Phonics: General Principles

To completely assess students in phonics, teachers should administer tests that ask students to decode in isolation and in context. Many phonics tests are available. Most commercially published IRIs include phonics tests. Basal reading textbook series often include a set of phonics tests teachers can use. Teachers can develop their own "decode-in-isolation" phonics tests without much difficulty. Let's look at each type of phonics test.

(1) DECODE IN ISOLATION.   Decoding tasks ask the child to read aloud. In this type of test, the child is presented with a list of words and asked to read them. For example, if a teacher wanted to determine which students know the sound of an *a* in the medial position in a one-syllable word, the test might consist of the following words: *mat, map, dad, pan, bad*. The teacher records what the child says for each word. If, for example, the child misidentified *mat* and substituted a long *e* sound, the teacher would write *meet* next to *mat*. Some IRIs include decode-in-isolation tests with nonsense words (*fap, fep, fup*). This provides a "control" on the test because the child must use his or her phonics skills to figure out the word; he or she cannot rely on prior knowledge of the word as a sight word.

(2) DECODE IN CONTEXT.   This is the most important phonics test because it asks students to read part of a story or an informational article. Students read a passage of two or three paragraphs aloud. The teacher keeps a record of the child's miscues, looking for words that are misidentified. The teacher especially looks for sound–symbol patterns that are missed repeatedly. For example, a child missed *felt* and *belt*, two words that share the *-elt* rime. This type of test, as you remember, is done as part of an Informal Reading Inventory.

(B) How to Assess Sight Words

It is easy to assess children's knowledge of sight words. Teachers should give children tests on sight words both in isolation and in context. In isolation, sight words are displayed to a child, either on flash cards or on a list, and the child reads them. It is important to determine if the child can read the words in context as well. When children read aloud from the graded passages in an IRI or from a story in a basal reader, the teacher can check to see which sight words were read correctly.

(C) Entry-Level Assessment, Progress-Monitoring Assessment, and Summative Assessment for Phonics and Sight Words

Entry-level assessment may reveal that the goal the teacher was trying to achieve was too difficult. For example, a teacher planned to teach the -*ate* rime to a group of first graders (*date, fate*). This is part of first-grade Decoding and Word Recognition Standard 1.15: *Read common word families (e.g., -ite, -ate)*.

The teacher individually administers a decoding in isolation assessment to her 18 students. Each student is asked to read the following words: *date, bat, fate, gate, lap, zate, mate, rate, lip*, and *jate. Bat, lap*, and *lip* are put in the list so that students do not think every word has a long *a* and fits the CVCe pattern. These words are not scored. *Zate* and *jate* are nonsense words. Thus, there are seven correct answers. The results showed that six students read less than two of the -*ate* words correctly and had difficulty not just with the long vowel sounds, but with initial consonants. These students need to learn their initial consonants sounds before they work on this more advanced pattern.

Progress-monitoring assessments tell the teacher whether or not lessons have been effective. Continuing with our example, the teacher found that the remaining 12 students in her class could get at least four of the words on the entry-level assessment correct, but no one got all seven correct. She planned a three-lesson sequence on the -*ate* pattern. After the second lesson, she asked students to spell five words they had learned in the first two lessons (*date, fate, gate, mate*, and *rate*). She was pleased that nine of the children spelled all five correctly. She planned a reteaching experience for the three who were struggling, but knew that she was being successful with most of her students and could continue for her final lesson.

Summative assessments determine whether or not students have achieved a goal related to a standard. For her summative assessment, she used two assessments. First, she administered a decoding in isolation task that was more complete than her progress-monitoring assessment. The students were required to read aloud all of the following: *date, fast, fate, gas, gate, hate, jar, jate, kate, late, lap, mate, nate, rate, race, pate. (Fast, gas, jar, lap*, and *race* are not scored. *Jate* and *pate* are nonsense words). Second, students were given a decoding in context task. Each child read aloud a 50-word story that included the words *date, gate*, and *late*. The results from both assessments showed who has learned the -*ate* rime.

(D) How to Analyze, Interpret, and Use Results

To vary our discussion slightly in this chapter, let us simply state that (1) the analysis and interpretation of results should be standards-based, and (2) analysis and interpretation should reveal why children are performing below expectations. In this chapter let us focus on using the results to create and use individual and class profiles.

An individual profile will be created for each child. For example, a teacher assessed her students on their ability to spell common, irregular sight words (*the, have, said, come, give, of, was*). For each child, the teacher will know which *specific* words he or she knows how to spell and which words remain a challenge. Next, the teacher will look for *patterns* of errors. Fred, for example, couldn't spell *have*, he spelled it *av*, and on previous spelling assessments he missed almost all the words with an initial *h* (*has, home, hill*). Thus, his pattern of error is that he doesn't understand *h* as an initial consonant. Again, assessments of phonics skills, sight words, and spelling skills are analyzed and interpreted at the individual level for specific errors and patterns of error.

Next, the results must be analyzed and interpreted at the group level. Sometimes teachers will find that several students are all having difficulty with the same specific word. Other times, teachers will find that several students are making the same type of error. For example, Fred was not alone is missing the initial *h*, five other students share that need. If a majority of students mastered the skill being taught, then the teacher can move on while reteaching the few who need more help. On the other hand, if a majority did not do well, then the skill must be retaught while the few who learned the skill can participate in activities that extend their knowledge.

Results can determine many instructional decisions. Sometimes they reveal that one type of lesson is not effective for individuals or, in some cases, the whole group. For example, a teacher who had tried part-to-whole lessons that were not successful may want to switch to more whole-to-part phonics lessons. At other times, results show that the type of presentation may need to be changed. A teacher who met little success with primarily visual presentations may want to teach with more auditory presentations.

CHAPTER 7

Competency 7
Syllabic Analysis, Structural Analysis, and Orthographic Knowledge

INTRODUCTION

In the previous two chapters we looked at two categories of word identification skills: phonics and sight words. This chapter looks at a three other categories of word identification skills: structural analysis, syllabic analysis, and orthographic knowledge. Chapters 5 and 6 focused on how to teach children to identify single-syllable words. This chapter is concerned with how to teach children to identify multisyllabic words.

Structural analysis, also called *morphemic analysis*, is the process of decoding a multisyllabic word with an affix (prefix, suffix) added to a base word. Students recognize the word by "putting together" their knowledge of the affix and the base word. In the upper grades, instruction on prefixes, suffixes, and roots usually combines learning what *sounds* these word parts make with instruction on what prefixes, suffixes, and roots mean.

Syllabic analysis is the process of decoding a multisyllabic word by examining the word's syllables. Students recognize the word by "putting together" their knowledge of each of the word's syllables.

Orthographic knowledge is what a person knows about how to spell words. *Orthography* is, for the most part, a synonym for *spelling*.

Let's look at some linguistic words and phrases relating to the structure of words.

A *morpheme* is the most elemental unit of meaning in a language. In English, there are only two types of morphemes: some words and all affixes (prefixes and suffixes). Remember, not all syllables are morphemes, and some words have more than one morpheme. For example, *elephant* has one morpheme, whereas *walked* (*walk + ed*) and *chairs* (*chair + s*) have two.

Affixes are either *prefixes*, morphemes that appear before a root word, or *suffixes*, morphemes that appear at the end of a root word. Examples of prefixes are *non-*, *un-*, and *pre-*. Examples of *suffixes* are *-ment*, *-er*, and *-ly*.

Bound morphemes are prefixes and suffixes that cannot occur alone; they must be attached to a root word (*un-*, *-est*).

A *free morpheme* can be uttered alone with meaning (for example, *test*).

Let's look at some definitions relating to syllables. A *syllable* is pronounced with a single, uninterrupted sounding of the voice. A single vowel can be a syllable, as in the *a* in *a-bout*, but a single consonant cannot compose a syllable. All syllables must have at least one vowel. Some languages use as few as 50 syllables, but English has about 2,800.

An *open syllable* ends with a vowel (the single syllable words *be* and *go*, and the first syllable in *bee-tle* or *re-sign*). A *closed syllable* ends in a consonant (both syllables in *kick-ball* and *nor-mal*).

There are six topics in this competency:

(1) How phonics, sight word knowledge, structural analysis, syllabic analysis, and orthographic knowledge work together
(2) How to teach structural analysis and syllabic analysis of multisyllabic words
(3) How to teach spelling
(4) Opportunities to use structural analysis skills, syllabic analysis skills, and orthographic knowledge in reading and writing
(5) Meeting the needs of all learners
(6) Assessment of structural analysis skills, syllabic analysis skills, and orthographic knowledge

(1) HOW PHONICS, SIGHT WORD KNOWLEDGE, STRUCTURAL ANALYSIS, SYLLABIC ANALYSIS, AND ORTHOGRAPHIC KNOWLEDGE WORK TOGETHER

All children need to develop accurate and swift word identification skills. The goal is *automaticity*, the effortless and rapid identification of words—and it cannot be stressed enough how important this is. Readers who struggle to identify words find reading a chore, often an embarrassing one. Reading is avoided, and the less children read, the more they fall behind their peers. On the other hand, students who develop advanced word identification skills find reading an easy, productive process. They read a great deal, and the more they read, they better they get at it. Thus, as the years go by, the gap between proficient and struggling readers widens. Some reading authorities call this the Matthew Effect, after the phrase in the Gospel in which the "rich get richer and the poor get poorer."

Phonics and sight word skills are needed to decode single-syllable words. Phonics will help a reader decode regular single-syllable words. Sight word knowledge will provide students with the ability to recognize high-frequency words, especially ones that do not conform to regular letter–sound patterns. To obtain automaticity in word identification with the more complex texts read in the upper grades, students need a more extensive repertoire of word identification skills—they need structural analysis, syllabic analysis, and orthographic knowledge—which will provide students the skills they need to decode multisyllabic words.

These categories of skills often are applied together when a child reads, often without the child being aware of what is being accomplished. For example, a student could use her structural analysis skills and phonics skills to decode *precede*. Structural analysis decodes the prefix *pre-*, and knowledge of the CVCe pattern decodes *-cede*.

(2) HOW TO TEACH STRUCTURAL ANALYSIS AND SYLLABIC ANALYSIS OF MULTISYLLABIC WORDS

(A) Structural Analysis Skills: Teaching Prefixes, Suffixes, and Roots

(1) DIRECT INSTRUCTION: WHOLE-TO-PART. As with phonics, you can either follow a whole-to-part or part-to-whole approach to teach students about root words, prefixes, and suffixes. In a whole-to-part lesson you would follow these steps:

1. Display several sentences, each with a word that contains the target prefix, suffix, or root word. For example, for the prefix *un-*:

   Roberto was <u>unafraid</u> when he entered the haunted house.

   The zookeeper <u>uncaged</u> the tiger when it was time to move him to another zoo.

   They checked very carefully, but the letter was <u>undated</u>.

   The movie was so long it seemed to be <u>unending</u>.

   Leticia tried her best, but she could not <u>untangle</u> the extension cords.

2. Read again the underlined target words and identify the key common element. You might want to circle the common prefix, suffix, or root word (in this case, *un-*).

3. Work with the students to arrive at the meaning of the prefix, suffix, or root word. If they can't figure it out, tell them what it means.
4. Provide some other words with the common element, or see if the children can provide the words.

You may want to create a word wall of words that share the common element.

(2) DIRECT INSTRUCTION: PART-TO-WHOLE.   In a part-to-whole approach, you would use this sequence:

1. Display the prefix, suffix, or root word on the blackboard, in this case, *un-*. Tell the children what it means (in this case, *not* or *the opposite of*).
2. Prepare some 4 × 6-inch cards with root words that can be added to the prefix or suffix to make words. For root words, you will need to prepare cards with prefixes and suffixes on them. For example, for teaching *un-*, you would need cards that read *afraid, caged, ending, tangled*. Add the cards to the element on the board and make new words.
3. Finally, help the children put each newly formed word into sentences, which can be written on the blackboard or on a piece of chart paper.

(3) ROOT WORDS.   Lessons for common roots would follow the same instructional pattern. Especially in grades 4 to 8, when children are reading more complex social studies and science texts, teachers should focus on common Greek and Latin prefixes, suffixes, and roots. For example, a whole-to-part lesson on the Greek root *-cycl-* ("circle") would start with three sentences displayed, with target words highlighted:

> Fred rode his new <u>bicycle</u> around the block.
>
> Leticia and Rosie put their used paper in the <u>recycle</u> bin.
>
> The police officer rode up on a <u>motorcycle</u>.

The sentences are read, each target word underlined, the root word identified and defined, and additional words with the root provided.

The bottom line is that once children know how to pronounce a common root word, prefix, or suffix, they can apply that knowledge to unknown words. Staying with our example of the Greek root *-cycl-* (circle), a child who can pronounce *bicycle* and *recycle* can apply that knowledge to pronounce *cyclone*, knowing that with *-cycl-* the first *c* is "soft" and makes the /s/ sound and the second *c* is "hard" and makes the /k/ sound.

(B) Teaching Syllabic Analysis

(1) TEACHING CHILDREN TO IDENTIFY THE NUMBER OF SYLLABLES IN A WORD.   The traditional activity is to have children clap their hands as they say each syllable in a multisyllabic word. This is a listening activity. The focus here, however, is on using knowledge of syllabication rules to pronounce multisyllabic words when they are being *read*, rather than being heard. For that, there will need to be instruction in common syllable patterns.

(2) TEACHING MULTISYLLABIC WORDS THAT FOLLOW COMMON SYLLABLE PATTERNS. Knowledge of syllable patterns will help children correctly identify multisyllabic words (these six rules were also listed in Chapter 5):

1. Compound words, divide between the words: *in-side, foot-ball*. Children will rarely mispronounce these words if they know each word that forms the compound.
2. Single-syllable prefix, divide between the prefix and the root: *un-kind, pre-test*. Knowledge of this rule will prevent students from pronouncing pretest as *pret-est*.
3. Never divide a consonant digraph: *bush-el, teach-er*. Knowledge of this pattern will prevent students from pronouncing the two letters in the digraph as separate consonants (*bus-hel*).
4. Two consonants in the middle of a word that are not digraphs, divide between the consonants: *sis-ter, but-ter*. Words that fit this pattern are relatively easy to decode.

5. Single consonant in the middle of a word between two vowels, the vowel preceding the consonant is short, divide after the consonant: *cab-in, lev-el*. This is important—the rule is that in a closed syllable such as *cab-* or *lev-*, the vowel is almost always short.

6. Single consonant in the middle of a word between two vowels, the vowel preceding the consonant is long, divide before the consonant: *be-long, fe-ver*. Though this rule has exceptions, in open syllables, ending with a vowel, the vowel is almost always long.

Lessons to teach these rules should start by stating the rule, then proceed to having children divide the target words appropriately while at the same time correctly pronouncing the word.

(3) HOW TO TEACH SPELLING

(A) Selecting Spelling Words

Effective teachers know how to select appropriate words for their students to learn to spell. The traditional approach of providing a classroom of children with a list of 10 to 20 words to learn each week can be productive if (a) the words are appropriate and (b) proper methods are used to teach children how to spell them. Also, teachers should differentiate the number of words children are expected to learn. A reasonable expectation for some children might be only four to five words per week.

What type of words should students be expected to learn?

1. Groups of words that have commonly occurring orthographic patterns: rimes, blends, digraphs, diphthongs, prefixes, suffixes, common root words.
2. High-frequency words, especially those that have irregular patterns.
3. Common-need words, words that several children in the class have difficulty spelling correctly.
4. Content-area words, words taken from social studies and science units of study.
5. Words that relate to each other, such as synonyms, antonyms, and homophones.

(B) Self-Study

Children should be taught how to engage in self-study of words they are learning to spell. It is a good idea to have a pretest so children know which words need to be given added attention. A simple method for self-study is the following sequence:

1. Look at the word and say it to yourself.
2. Say each letter in the word to yourself.
3. Close your eyes and spell the word to yourself.
4. Write the word, check your spelling.
5. Write the word again.

(C) Multisensory Techniques

Teachers should use multisensory techniques to help children learn to spell. Some of our students will learn best from visual activities, whereas others will need either an oral or kinesthetic approach. The categories of multisensory techniques that teach spelling follow.

(1) VISUAL.   The simplest visually oriented activity is for children to look at a word and then write it three or four times. This works for many children, but for others, writing their spelling words multiple times does not work.

(2) VISUAL: USE OF COLOR.   For some students, the use of color makes an orthographic pattern clearer. For example, let us assume children are learning the *oa* digraph that appears in *boat* and *load*. If some students are confusing the positions of the *o* and *a*, the teacher may have them write each word three times, using a blue crayon for *o* and a red crayon for *a*.

(3) AUDITORY. Other students will learn to spell words with greater ease if they hear each letter of a word each time they write it. This results in a noisy study session, of course, but it can be beneficial. Instead of just writing each word, the child says each letter aloud as he or she writes it. In another approach with a "buddy," as one student writes, the other whispers each letter in his or her ear.

(4) KINESTHETIC. Kinesthetics is the science of human motion. Kinesthetic approaches to spelling include writing words in the air with large, exaggerated strokes.

(5) TACTILE. Tactile approaches are highly motivational and work best with younger students. They involve touch. I have seen teachers use sandpaper, window screens, and shaving cream for tactile spelling activities. For example, with the window screens, each child writes each letter with his or finger on the screen. Be sure all tactile activities are safe!

(6) MENTAL IMAGERY. In this type of activity, the children close their eyes and pretend they see someone write each letter of a word. For example, a group of children are learning to spell *apricot*. Their teacher asks them to close their eyes and visualize the teacher writing *apricot* in blue ink on a whiteboard. The teacher says each letter in the word slowly as the students, with their eyes closed, create a mental image the word being written.

(D) Small-Group and Individualized Spelling Instruction

Spelling lessons and tests designed for an entire classroom must be used in conjunction with small-group and individualized spelling instruction. The results of assessment—spelling tests and analysis of student writing—will reveal that some children share specific needs. These children should be placed in a small group and the teacher should provide direct, explicit instruction on the orthographic pattern they need to learn. Individual intervention in spelling can be very productive. Sometimes all that is required is a 10-minute lesson in a one-on-one setting to teach a child a bothersome pattern that the child repeatedly fails to spell correctly.

(4) OPPORTUNITIES TO USE STRUCTURAL ANALYSIS SKILLS, SYLLABIC ANALYSIS SKILLS, AND ORTHOGRAPHIC KNOWLEDGE IN READING AND WRITING

It is not enough to teach structural analysis skills, syllabic analysis skills, and orthographic knowledge in isolation. Students must have many opportunities to apply these skills when they read and write. Students should be challenged to read texts that contain words using affixes, syllable patterns, and orthographic patterns and rules already taught. By the time students are in fourth grade, grade-level reading material will include these types of words. It is essential that students read extensively informational texts, including their social studies and science textbooks, information books, and reference materials. Science texts, especially, will include many words with Greek and Latin affixes and roots.

Teachers may have to plan writing activities that require students to apply their knowledge of more complex orthographic patterns and spelling of multisyllabic words. Teachers should assign topics that lend themselves to multisyllabic words ("At the Doctor's Office"). Some written assignments may include a "word bank," of five to ten words that the students must use in a story or a short essay. For example, students would have to use four of the following words in their fictional account of a trip to see a physician: *stethoscope, antibiotic, precaution, bronchitis, tibia, antiseptic,* or *examination*.

(5) MEETING THE NEEDS OF ALL LEARNERS

(A) Struggling Readers and Students With Reading Disabilities

Of the many possible interventions for struggling readers and students with reading disabilities, let us discuss here: (1) focusing on key skills and knowledge, and (2) using tactile and auditory techniques.

(1) FOCUS ON KEY SKILLS.   As for key skills and knowledge, the focus should be on frequently occurring syllable patterns and affixes and related orthographic patterns. Students should receive extra help to spell correctly:

1. The most common prefixes, such as *pre-,* which often can be misspelled *per-* as in *pertest; fore-,* many students forget the *e* as in *forcast*; and *sub-,* which often is spelled *sup-* as in *suptract*.
2. Common suffixes, such as *-less* and *-ness;* students often forget the second consonant as in *helples* and *closenes; -ful,* some students spell the suffix *-full* as in *helpfull;* and *-ion*, students often spell it phonetically, *-shun,* as in *educashun*.
3. Orthographic patterns having to do with adding suffixes, such as dropping a final *e* (*bake* to *baking*) and doubling a final consonant (*bat* to *batting*).

When focusing on these key structural analysis and syllabic analysis skills, struggling readers will need extra practice with considerable repetition.

(2) TACTILE AND AUDITORY APPROACHES.   When it comes to spelling, reteaching concepts and skills should involve tactile techniques. They should write letters with their bare fingers on their desktops, in clay, or in sand. They will also be helped by strong auditory clues, either saying each letter as they repeatedly write a word or having someone else say each letter as they write. This additional oral practice of saying letters as they are written is important.

(B) English Learners and Speakers of Nonstandard English

Depending on what language an English learner first learned to read, there will be some similarities and differences between the first language and English. For example, Spanish uses prefixes and suffixes in much the same way as English. In fact, many Spanish prefixes are cognates with their English counterparts—they have similar pronunciations and mean the same thing (in both languages. *anti-* means *against*, *auto-* means *self*, *bi-* means *two*, and *contra-* means *against*). On the other hand, Spanish speakers are used to using far fewer syllables than the almost 3,000 that appear in English.

It is important to explicitly teach English learners the common English roots and affixes. This will greatly increase their word identification skills.

(C) Advanced Learners

Again, the *RICA Content Specifications* recommend two forms of differentiation for advanced learners: (1) increasing the pace and/or complexity of instruction and (2) building on an extending current knowledge and skills.

In regards to structural analysis and syllabic analysis, advanced learners in the upper grades can advance swiftly through instruction on common prefixes and suffixes. They are ready to learn more complicated roots and their derivatives, such as the Latin roots *-dent-* ("tooth" as in *denture* and *dentist*); *-grac-* ("thankful" as in *grace, gratutity,* and *congratulate*); or *-manus-* ("hand" as in *manual, manicure, manage*).

(6) ASSESSMENT OF STRUCTURAL ANALYSIS SKILLS, SYLLABIC ANALYSIS SKILLS, AND ORTHOGRAPHIC KNOWLEDGE

(A) How to Assess Structural Analysis Skills, Syllabic Analysis Skills, and Orthographic Knowledge

It is important to assess the application of all three categories of skills in both *isolation* and *context*. Tests of structural analysis and syllabic analysis involve oral reading. Spelling tests, of course, require the child to write.

(1) STRUCTURAL ANALYSIS.   Assessment of prefixes, suffixes, and roots in isolation involves presenting the child with a list of words to be read aloud. The teacher carefully records errors. Some of these tests will involve nonsense words. For example, for a test of knowledge of the suffix *-less*, the test might include the following words: *ageless, careless, spotless, jobless, bathless, sadless*.

Assessment of prefixes, suffixes, and roots in context challenges the student to read a selection aloud that has many words with those elements. There are commercially prepared tests that have such reading selections; otherwise the teacher might have to create one. For example, to assess the prefixes *mis-, pre-,* and *re-,* the student would read aloud a selection that starts as follows:

> Fred was a great deal of trouble at school. His teacher could not predict what he would do next. He would misbehave almost every time the teacher wasn't watching him. It seems no matter how many times he was reminded . . .

You get the idea! The selection would have many words that begin with the target prefixes—in this excerpt the words *predict, misbehave,* and *reminded*.

(2) SYLLABIC ANALYSIS.   Tests of syllabic analysis follow the same combination of tests in isolation and tests in context. A test in isolation will require the child to read a list of words that fit the pattern. For example, after being taught that usually the vowel in an initial open syllable is long, the child would be asked to read *robot, ocean, pilot, title, baby, basic, tuna, unit, female,* and *evil*. For tests of the ability to apply syllabic analysis skills in context, most texts contain enough examples that specially designed paragraphs do not need to be created. Several oral readings of grade-level texts will reveal whether the student can apply knowledge of syllable patterns.

(3) SPELLING.   The traditional spelling test, in which the teacher reads words aloud and the children write them, is an example of a test in isolation. Teachers should never rely solely on spelling tests to make judgments about the orthographic knowledge children have acquired. The real test is whether or not children will spell words correctly when they write. Teachers should collect and analyze samples of student work—their journals, their stories, their answers to questions. The teacher should look for patterns in the child's spelling choices. Which letter–sound correspondences are routinely missed? Which common rimes does the child struggle with? Are there affixes and roots that are repeatedly misspelled?

The bottom line is that assessment of structural analysis, syllabic analysis, and spelling requires tests in both isolation and in context. Why both? Tests in isolation allow the teacher to choose what words the child must pronounce or write. Tests in context are the "real thing"—and measure whether skills and knowledge are both remembered and applied correctly.

(B) Entry-Level, Progress-Monitoring, and Summative Assessment

As we move through the remainder of the RICA competencies less time will be spent on this area of assessment and the next one. The basic concepts of the three types of assessment have been explained in previous chapters. Of note here are:

- The importance of doing a thorough entry-level assessment in structural analysis, syllabic analysis, and orthographic knowledge. Many children will already know what you aim to teach and should be involved in other activities. On the other hand, some elementary school students find these types of skills and knowledge to be very difficult. Entry-level assessment will typically only involve the isolation tasks.
- Progress-monitoring assessment is essential in all aspects of reading instruction—but especially here—because some students will need a great deal of help.
- Summative assessment should absolutely involve performance in context, even if the teacher has to create special selections with target words for the children to read.

(C) Analysis, Interpretation, and Use of Assessment Results

The use of individual profiles and class profiles has been explained in previous chapters. Teachers would use the same process here for structural analysis, syllabic analysis, and orthographic knowledge. All assessment should be standards-based.

The purpose of the individual profiles is to determine whose performance is below expectations for the standard, whose performance meets the standard, and whose performance exceeds the standard. Individual profiles will tell the teacher which children need help on any specific standard. Remedial lessons can be planned for groups of children who all are struggling to meet the same standard.

Group profiles tell the teacher how the whole class is performing. The group profile will tell the teacher that, perhaps, so many children are struggling that a new set of lessons on a standard may need to be implemented.

CHAPTER 8

Competency 8
Fluency: Role in Reading Development and Factors That Affect the Development of Fluency

INTRODUCTION

The fluent reader reads accurately, at an appropriate rate, and with appropriate expression. Achieving fluency is important because the nonfluent reader struggles to understand what he or she is reading. Indeed, there is a strong correlation between reading comprehension and reading fluency. During the past decade the importance of developing reading fluency has gained wide acceptance. There are two subdomains on the RICA dealing with fluency. This chapter addresses the background knowledge about reading fluency that all teachers should know. The next chapter focuses on instruction and assessment.

There are seven topics in this competency:

(1) The key indicators of reading fluency
(2) The role of fluency in all stages of reading development
(3) Interrelationships among fluency and word analysis skills, background knowledge, and comprehension
(4) Factors that can disrupt fluency
(5) The role of decodable text in fluent reading
(6) The role of systematic, explicit instruction in promoting fluency development
(7) Independent silent reading and the development of fluency

(1) THE KEY INDICATORS OF READING FLUENCY

There are three indicators of fluent reading: accuracy, rate, and prosody.

(A) Accuracy

Fluent readers pronounce words correctly when reading orally. This involves the application of their phonics skills, sight word knowledge, structural analysis skills, syllabic analysis skills, and orthographic knowledge.

(B) Rate

Fluent readers read a text at an appropriate rate of speed, neither too fast nor too slow. There are really two components here. First is the ability to quickly decode words, and the second is to speedily read phrases and sentences. Please note that all texts should not be read at the same rate. For example, a reader should read the directions for assembling a bicycle slower than a piece of fiction.

(C) Prosody

This may be a word that you have not seen before. It means to read with appropriate "expression," and includes emphasis of certain words, variation in pitch, and pausing. It reflects the reader's understanding of the structure of sentences, punctuation, and, to a large extent, the author's purpose.

Some words in sentences are meant to be emphasized (or *stressed*). For example, in the sentence, *The sheriff took a step toward Johnson and repeated, "I said put the gun down now."* The word *now* should be said louder and longer than the other words in the sentence. Many times writers or editors will indicate words to be emphasized by using boldface or italics. Reading with expression also involves change your pitch (also called *intonation*), which means whether or not you say a word at a low tone or a high tone. Finally, fluent readers pause when they see commas, semicolons, or ellipses (. . .).

(2) THE ROLE OF FLUENCY IN ALL STAGES OF READING DEVELOPMENT

Though ultimately we are concerned with the fluent reading of connected text, fluency is a goal at all levels of reading development. The goal is *automaticity*—swift and accurate reading. Teachers want children to be fluent at many levels. First is the challenge of accurate and swift letter naming. Then, the goal becomes fluency with single-syllable words with regular, letter–sound correspondences and high-frequency sight words. As children grow, they should read multisyllabic words swiftly and accurately, using their structural analysis skills, syllabic analysis skills, and orthographic knowledge. Our oldest elementary school students must meet the challenge of achieving automaticity with the most difficult words to identify, words with irregular spellings and content-area words, especially those from the sciences.

The point is that failure to achieve fluency at any stage will make it more difficult to become fluent at subsequent stages.

(3) INTERRELATIONSHIPS AMONG FLUENCY AND WORD ANALYSIS SKILLS, BACKGROUND KNOWLEDGE, AND COMPREHENSION

Fluent reading is essential for comprehension. *Automaticity theory* explains why. To oversimplify somewhat, automaticity theory states that reading requires the reader to perform two main tasks: to decode words and understand the meaning of the text. If readers are not fluent, then they get bogged down on the decoding task and are then unable to focus on getting the meaning of the text. Or, stating in the positive, fluent readers swiftly and accurately identify words, which frees their minds to deal with the meaning of a text.

Appropriate expression (or prosody) is also essential to comprehend a text. A reader who reads at a steady pace with a monotone voice will have difficulty understanding most complex texts.

(4) FACTORS THAT CAN DISRUPT FLUENCY

What leads to a lack of fluent reading? Both a lack of word identification skills and a lack of comprehension can slow a reader down. One or more of the following can be the problem:

(A) WEAK WORD ANALYSIS SKILLS, WHICH LEADS TO STOPPING FREQUENTLY TO DECODE UNRECOGNIZED OR UNFAMILIAR WORDS.   This is the number one culprit. Weak word analysis skills mean that the child encounters several words that are not recognizable. The child spends too much time trying to figure out how to pronounce these words. Obviously, this slows the child's reading down to a crawl, but it also leads to diminished comprehension. Children who read too slowly often "forget" what they are reading about and fail to understand.

It is important to note that a lack of any category of word analysis skills will lead to many unrecognized words. In the early grades, poorly developed phonics skills and sight word knowledge could be the problem. In the upper grades, children who have well-developed phonics skills and extensive sight words knowledge will still have problems if their structural analysis skills and syllabic analysis skills are weak.

(B) LACK OF FAMILIARITY WITH CONTENT VOCABULARY. As students get older, they will read more and more content texts—social studies and science textbooks, reference sources, information books. Students must be able to both identify and understand the more complex vocabulary of these texts to read fluently. Two types of content words present real challenges: (1) *One-use words* and (2) multisyllabic content words. One-use words are words that are used within the context of one area of study, but are rarely, if ever, used elsewhere. For example, in the field of geology, compare *core* and *lithosphere*, two parts of the Earth. *Lithosphere* is a one-use word, whereas *core* is used in several contexts other than in labeling a part of the Earth. Several content words are multisyllabic and their size alone challenges the young reader (consider *amphibian* and *photosynthesis*).

(C) LACK OF BACKGROUND KNOWLEDGE. Also a factor in achieving fluency is the reader's level of background knowledge of the topics covered in the text. A lack of background knowledge will lead to lack of comprehension, of "not getting it," and can result in the reader slowing down to reread or stop in frustration. Even if you could swiftly and accurately identify the words in a physics textbook, your lack of background knowledge would lead to a slow, confused reading.

(D) LACK OF FAMILIARITY WITH MORE COMPLEX SYNTACTIC STRUCTURES. This is a major contributor to lack of fluency in older readers. As the structure of the sentences they read becomes more complicated, with more dependent and independent clauses, many readers are befuddled and read slowly without appropriate expression. Especially in grades 4 and up, students will read more and more expository texts (e.g., science textbooks, information books). The more complex structures of these texts, full of academic language, will disrupt the fluency of many children.

(5) THE ROLE OF DECODABLE TEXT IN FLUENT READING

You may recall from Chapter 6 that decodable texts use many single-syllable words with regular letter–sound correspondences and only a few, irregular high-frequency words (*The fat cat sits in Ron's lap.*). The frequent use of decodable text is important to build fluency in young readers who are acquiring basic phonics skills and high-frequency sight words. In time, however, decodable texts must give way to more texts with expanded vocabularies. For students to transition to these more difficult texts, they must acquire a complete knowledge of high-frequency words, expand their knowledge of content-related sight words, master advanced letter–sound correspondences, and develop solid structural analysis and syllabic analysis skills.

(6) THE ROLE OF SYSTEMATIC, EXPLICIT INSTRUCTION IN PROMOTING FLUENCY DEVELOPMENT

Despite its obvious importance, instruction in fluency often has been neglected in elementary school classrooms. Almost all children will benefit from systematic, explicit instruction in fluency—this is a key area of reading development that should not be left to chance. Further, research has revealed the components of effective fluency instruction. All this will be covered in the next chapter. You will read that effective fluency instruction involves frequent oral reading experiences and appropriate guidance and feedback from the teacher.

(7) INDEPENDENT SILENT READING AND THE DEVELOPMENT OF FLUENCY

(A) The Limitations of Using Independent Silent Reading to Increase Fluency

Independent, silent reading can play a role in developing fluency, but there are limits on its effectiveness. The problem with relying solely on silent reading to develop fluency is that there is no guarantee that the reader is reading fluently *while reading silently*. In fact, the child might be repeatedly practicing inaccurate, slow, and nonexpressive reading. Students who do not have automaticity will need systematic, explicit instruction in fluency—and this will require oral reading activities.

(B) How to Make Independent Silent Reading More Effective in Supporting Fluency Development

There are two interventions that will allow independent, silent reading to play a positive role in developing reading fluency.

(1) BOOKS AT APPROPRIATE READING LEVELS. First, teachers should ensure that students select books at appropriate reading levels. There are problems if children select books that are too difficult or too easy. Books that are too difficult will have many words that are not recognizable, and the child will have to stop repeatedly to decode them. This results in the child practicing nonfluent reading. On the other hand, books that are too easy can be read fluently, but it does little to help the student improve and become fluent with more complex texts.

(2) HOLD STUDENT ACCOUNTABLE FOR COMPREHENSION. This was covered in Chapter 1 and includes student-maintained reading logs, book reports, oral presentations, partner reading/discussion, and individual conferences.

CHAPTER 9

Competency 9
Fluency: Instruction and Assessment

INTRODUCTION

There are six topics in this competency:

(1) Instructional strategies that will improve all components of fluency: Accuracy, rate, and prosody
(2) Specific strategies for building accuracy
(3) Specific strategies for building reading rate
(4) Specific strategies for building prosody
(5) Meeting the needs of all learners
(6) Assessment of fluency

(1) INSTRUCTIONAL STRATEGIES THAT WILL IMPROVE ALL COMPONENTS OF FLUENCY: ACCURACY, RATE, AND PROSODY

(A) Monitored Oral Reading With the Teacher

Fluency can be improved when the teacher works one-on-one with a student or with a small group of students. First, it is essential that the student reads texts that are reasonably easy for her—the text should be at the student's independent reading level. Remember, that means the student correctly decodes 95% of the words she will read. Also, the text should not be long, from 50 to 200 words, with the length of the text increasing with older children. A variety of types of texts should be selected, including stories and nonfiction. Poetry should be a frequent choice.

There are three components of effective fluency lessons:

(1) TEACHER MODEL.   It is important that children listen to models of fluent, efficient reading. During these lessons, the teacher should read the text aloud, modeling appropriate accuracy, rate, and expression.

(2) STUDENT PRACTICE.   After listening to the teacher read the text, it is the students' turn to read aloud the same text.

(3) TEACHER FEEDBACK.   Being careful to avoid excessive interruptions, the teacher should respond to the each student's effort. Sometimes the appropriate response is to select a phrase or sentence the child found difficult. The teacher would then model an appropriate reading of the phrase or sentence and the child would reread. Other times, the teacher will note when a punctuation mark has been misread ("Be sure to stop when you see a period. Listen to me read the paragraph and listen for the three stops I make at the end of each sentence.").

(B) Repeated Readings

Repeated readings of the same text improve reading fluency. Again, the child should be reading a brief text at her or his independent reading level. The goal should be to have the student read the text four to five times. There are many formats for repeated readings.

(1) STUDENT ALONE. Sometimes students should be told to reread a text on their own after it has been first read aloud by their teacher. This can be done in the classroom or it can be a homework assignment.

(2) TIMED. In this form of repeated reading, the teacher selects a passage for the student and then determines a challenging, but attainable, rate criterion. For example, "Sally, this passage has 150 words, I want you to read it in 2 minutes." The student then reads and rereads the passage until she or he hits the criterion.

(3) TAPE-ASSISTED READING. This is a fluency activity that has been used for many years. It requires a recorded version of a text read aloud by a fluent reader. Note that not all recorded readings of a text are appropriate for tape-assisted reading. Those produced for listening alone are a valuable classroom resource, but they won't work for experiences where the student is expected to read along with taped reader. There should be no sound effects and it helps if the taped reader reads at a moderate rate, not too fast. Teachers should select a passage/tape at the student's independent reading level. The first time, the student follows along and points to each word in the text as it is read. During subsequent readings, the student reads aloud with the taped reader. Eventually, the student should be able to read the text fluently without the assistance of the tape.

(4) PAIRED READING WITH A PARTNER. In this format, student partners take turns reading aloud a text. If the two readers have the same ability, then the two readers simply alternate reading aloud. They might read aloud together. If one partner is more accomplished than the other, then he or she should read aloud first, providing a model for the less fluent reader.

(C) When and How Fluency Instruction Should Be Introduced

As noted in the previous chapter, the development of fluency is an instructional goal at all stages of reading development. First, the goal is swift identification of the letters. Next, fluency instruction focuses on single-syllable words with regular letter–sound correspondences and sight words. Then, the goal is swift, accurate reading of multisyllabic words. At all levels, there is simultaneously fluency instruction with phrases, sentences, and paragraphs.

All children should engage in some fluency instruction, both through monitored oral reading with their teachers and repeated reading activities. The results of assessment, however, will reveal that some children will need considerably more fluency instruction than others.

(2) SPECIFIC STRATEGIES FOR BUILDING ACCURACY

Monitored oral reading with the teacher and repeated reading activities will build all three components of fluency: accuracy, rate, and prosody. There are, however, specific instructional strategies for each of these components.

Poor accuracy requires additional instruction in word identification skills—teachers should focus on building automatic word recognition. For our youngest readers who have difficulty with accuracy, the appropriate intervention is to provide systematic, explicit instruction in phonemic awareness, phonics, and sight words. Phonemic awareness instruction is an essential foundation for fluent reading because some readers will not be able to decode a word because they do not "hear" every sound in the word. Phonics and sight word instruction is essential for swift and accurate reading; these are the basic tools that allow a child to identify words. Similarly, as children get older, slow word identification is often the result of poorly developed structural analysis skills, syllabic analysis skills, and orthographic knowledge.

(3) SPECIFIC STRATEGIES FOR BUILDING READING RATE

In addition to monitored oral reading lessons and repeated reading activities, there are specific interventions if the problem is inappropriate rate, such as the child reading too slowly.

For example, in *whisper reading,* a group of children each read aloud to themselves, using soft voices that resemble whispering. The teacher moves from child to child, monitoring individual performance. The teacher provides feedback, by modeling faster reading, by focusing on specific words that the child is having difficulty with, or by reading aloud with the child. This is a good intervention for children who are embarrassed to read aloud because they make many errors.

For students whose decoding is automatic—children with well-developed word identification skills—a different approach can be used to improve reading rate. And yes, there are some students with good word identification skills who read too slowly. For children who fall into this category, rate can be increased through independent *silent* reading *if* there is accountability for comprehension and *if* the child is reading an appropriate book. For accountability, two students who read at the same rate with good decoding skills could read the same portion of a text together (a page at a time). At the end of each page, the students could quiz each other on what they read. The teacher should help the child select a book that is at her or his independent reading level—a book that can be read with very few word identification errors and with a high degree of comprehension.

(4) SPECIFIC STRATEGIES FOR BUILDING PROSODY

What if the problem is a lack of appropriate expression (or prosody)? One possible intervention is *phrase-cued reading*. Phrase-cued reading lessons use a text that has been specially marked by the teacher. The goal is to get students to move beyond word-by-word reading and to recognize phrases in sentences and read them appropriately. Such a lesson would follow these steps:

1. The teacher, on the basis of assessment, creates a small group of children with a shared need—they read in flat monotone without expression. The children must all have the same independent reading level.
2. The teacher selects and photocopies a text of about 200 words from a book or a basal reader. The text should be at the students' independent reading level. The teacher marks the text using slash marks (/)—one slash (/) between each phrase and two slashes between each sentence (//). Single slash marks should replace commas, be used in front of prepositional phrases and dependent clauses, and be used when a fluent reader might naturally pause. Example, from *Stuart Little,* by E. B. White (p. 18):

   > Stuart glanced / around the room / to see what he could do / to prove
   > to Snowbell / what good stomach muscles he had. // He spied the drawn
   > shade / on the east window / with its shade cord and ring / like a trapeze /
   > and it gave him an idea. // Climbing to the window sill / he took off his
   > hat / and laid down his cane.

3. Each child has a copy of the marked text and the teacher explains the markings.
4. The teacher reads the text aloud, modeling appropriate reading of the phrases.
5. The teacher rereads the text aloud, and this time the students read aloud as well.
6. Students reread the text with a partner, alternating among reading aloud together and taking turns reading aloud.

(5) MEETING THE NEEDS OF ALL LEARNERS

(A) Struggling Readers and Students With Learning Disabilities

The *RICA Content Specifications* suggest the following interventions to help struggling readers become more fluent.

(1) USING TEXTS WRITTEN AT STUDENTS' INDEPENDENT READING LEVELS. All too often, struggling readers are asked to read material that is too difficult for them. This just makes things worse. Monitored oral reading lessons, repeated reading activities, specific strategies such as whisper reading and phrase-cued reading all need to be done with texts written at the students' independent reading level.

(2) FOCUSING ON IMPROVING ACCURACY THROUGH ADDITIONAL WORD IDENTIFICATION INSTRUCTION. Usually, struggling readers will need extra lessons to improve their phonics skills, knowledge of sight words, structural analysis skills, syllabic analysis skills, and orthographic knowledge. Assessment will determine which specific skills each child lacks—and these will need to be retaught.

(3) FOCUSING ON RECOGNITION OF KEY SIGHT WORDS. Another important intervention for struggling readers is to identify important sight words that the reader cannot swiftly identify. For our youngest readers, the most important sight words are high-frequency words, which must be swiftly and accurately decoded by the end of the second grade. For older readers, the key sight words are usually words in the content areas, such as social studies and science.

(4) FOCUSING ON IMPROVING RATE THROUGH ADDITIONAL PRACTICE, USING EITHER ORAL OR SILENT READING DEPENDING ON THE STUDENT'S AUTOMATICITY. Struggling readers will need lots of practice reading to develop fluency. Remember the distinctions drawn earlier: If the child has poorly developed word identification skills, then additional practice should be oral reading. If the child, usually an older child, has fairly well-developed word identification skills, then some of the practice should be silent reading—if the teacher helps the child select appropriate books and holds the child accountable for comprehending what has been read.

(B) English Learners and Speakers of Nonstandard English

English learners need to learn the tonal patterns and rhythms of English. For this purpose, modeling and phrase-cued reading are essential interventions. Another good intervention to accomplish this goal is *echo reading* (or *imitative reading*). The teacher reads a passage aloud, and then the students read it aloud with the teacher. English learners also need to be taught the meaning of English punctuation.

(C) Advanced Learners

Advanced learners are almost always fluent. The *RICA Content Specifications* repeatedly suggest two interventions for advanced learners: (1) increasing the pace or complexity of instruction and (2) building on an extending current knowledge and skills. For fluency, the goal would blend the two interventions by challenging advanced learners to build on their current skills and become fluent with more complex texts.

(6) ASSESSMENT OF FLUENCY

(A) How to Assess Fluency

Fluency can only be assessed through oral reading. Fluency has developmental aspects, especially in regards to rate. That is, what we expect of a first grader will be far different from what is acceptable for a sixth grader. Most veteran teachers know immediately when a child's oral reading has too many errors, or is too slow, or is too "flat" (without expression). More specific assessment in each component of fluency should be performed to verify these initial impressions and to identify the precise areas of need. Available, too, are a number of commercially published tests of oral reading, such as the *Gray Oral Reading Test, 4th edition* (GORT-4), the *National Assessment of Educational Progress Fluency Scale* (NAEP-Fluency), or the Oral Reading Fluency test of the *Dynamic Indicators of Basis Early Literacy Skills* (DIBELS-ORF). Tests developed by teachers of oral reading that measure fluency are generically called oral reading fluency (ORF) tests.

(1) ACCURACY.   To assess accuracy, teachers would follow the same procedures covered in Chapter 2, when I discussed Running Records and miscue analysis. The child reads a passage, and the teacher notes each error. The target is 95% accuracy, the minimum required to place a passage at the student's independent reading level.

(2) RATE.   Assessment of reading rate will require the use of a watch. These are called "timed readings." After a timed reading, the teacher can calculate *words correct per minute (wcpm)*. Again, there are commercially produced tests that can be used to assess reading rate.

An informal test a teacher can easily administer is the *one-minute reading sample*. The teacher selects a passage of 200 to 300 words from the basal reader. The student reads aloud, and the teacher marks a copy of the passage. Words omitted, substituted, and inserted are all errors. Hesitations of less than 3 seconds are okay; longer than 3 seconds are misses. When the minute is up, the student stops reading. The teacher subtracts the total number of errors from the total numbers of words read to find the student's wcpm. There are several sources that offer appropriate reading rates for elementary school children. For example, by the end of first grade, an average score, at the 50th percentile, would be 56 wcpm, whereas by the end of the sixth grade, an average score would 150 wcpm. Remember, of course, this assumes that the first grader is reading a first-grade-level text and the sixth grader is reading a sixth-grade-level text.

(3) PROSODY.   It is far more difficult to assess expression, because there is a high level of subjectivity involved. There is a commercially published, valid test of expression called the *Multidimensional Fluency Scale*. Most teachers, however, can assess prosody informally while listening to the child read aloud. During an oral reading a teacher should listen for:

> *Appropriate pitch.*   The student's voice rises and falls at the appropriate times in a sentence.
>
> *Appropriate response to punctuation.*   The student pauses for commas and semicolons, stops at the end of sentences, uses correct inflection for questions, and displays emotion while reading sentences with exclamation marks.
>
> *Appropriate characterization.*   When reading a story with dialogue, the child reader becomes an actor and sounds like the character should sound.

(B) Entry-Level, Progress-Monitoring, and Summative Purposes

The assessments described above can be used for any of the three purposes of assessment: entry-level, progress monitoring, and summative. As has been noted previously, entry-level and summative assessment should involve formal measures of oral reading. Progress-monitoring assessment can be somewhat less formal. For example, rather than repeatedly administering oral reading tests of accuracy, rate, and prosody, the teacher might keep anecdotal records of student performance during monitored oral reading lessons and repeated reading activities. The teacher would note which children seem to be responding to intervention strategies and which particular words or phrases continue to be problem.

It is important that each purpose be fulfilled. Entry-level assessment will determine which students will need a high level of fluency instruction. The results will provide the teacher with the specific information that he or she needs to be successful. For example, entry-level assessment of accuracy will determine the level of the child's word identification skills. Are they fairly well developed? If so, then accuracy is not the issue—rate or lack of expression is. Such a child can be helped by a combination of oral reading activities.

(C) How to Analyze, Interpret, and Use Results

It never hurts to reiterate two points about the analysis and interpretation of assessment results:

(1) ANALYSIS AND INTERPRETATION OF ASSESSMENT RESULTS SHOULD BE STANDARDS-BASED.   Assessment results should tell the teacher which students' level of performance is (a) below expectation for the standard, (b) at the expectations for the standards, or (c) above expectations for the standard.

(2) ANALYSIS AND INTERPRETATION MUST GO FURTHER TO DETERMINE WHY CHILDREN ARE BELOW EXPECTATIONS.   What specifically do they not know or what specifically can they not do?

In regards to fluency, there is a significant difference between this area of reading and others in regards to how it is treated in the *English–Language Arts Content Standards*. Other areas such as concepts about print, phonemic awareness, decoding and word recognition, vocabulary, comprehension, and literary response and analysis all have several specific standards at each grade level. For fluency, however, at each grade level is a single, broadly stated standard:

> *Kindergarten:* (There is no fluency standard beyond the ability to recognize and name the letters, blend sounds, and read one-syllable and high-frequency words.)
>
> *First grade:* *Read aloud with fluency in a manner that sounds like natural speech.*
>
> *Second grade:* *Read aloud fluently and accurately and with appropriate intonation and expression.*
>
> *Third grade through sixth grade:* *Read aloud narrative and expository text fluently and accurately and with appropriate pacing, intonation, and expression.*

Thus, to meet the standard in fluency in grades 2 through 6, the child must be proficient in each area of fluency: accuracy, rate, and prosody.

(3) INDIVIDUAL PROFILES AND CLASS PROFILES.   As noted in previous chapters, results of assessments will provide both individual data and whole-class data. Teachers should build individual profiles for each student, clearly listing each relevant grade-level standard and indicating which students are below, at, or above expectations. On the basis of the data recorded on the individual profile, the teacher can plan interventions to help each student. The data on the individual profiles will determine which children can be taught in groups, because they share the same need.

The teacher should also compile a class profile for each standard. With fluency, there are few lessons and activities that can be done with large groups of students. Thus, the question is not should the teacher continue to focus on fluency with the whole class, rather it is how effective have the lessons and activities been in helping all children become fluent.

CHAPTER 10

Competency 10
Vocabulary, Academic Language, and Background Knowledge: Role in Reading Development and Factors That Affect Development

INTRODUCTION

A *vocabulary* is a set of words. It is important to note that each person has five different vocabularies:

> *Listening vocabulary.*   Your listening vocabulary consists of the words you understand when listening to other people speak.

> *Speaking vocabulary.*   Your speaking vocabulary consists of the words you use when you talk. It is always smaller than your listening vocabulary.

> *Writing vocabulary.*   Your writing vocabulary consists of the words you use when you write.

> *Sight (reading) vocabulary.*   Your sight vocabulary consists of the words you can recognize and correctly pronounce. We discussed this in Chapter 5, "Phonics and Sight Words: Terminology and Concepts."

> *Meaning (reading) vocabulary.*   Your meaning vocabulary consists of the words you understand when reading silently. The focus of this chapter and the next is on helping children expand their knowledge of word meanings. In this chapter, vocabulary refers to meaning vocabulary.

This chapter also covers the role of academic language and background knowledge in reading development.

> *Academic language.*   Academic language is the language used in textbooks and tests—it is the language of the classroom. Academic language is different than language used in everyday social interaction, which is less formal. Different words are used, many with Greek or Latin roots, and phrases and sentences can be more complex than those used in interpersonal communication.

> Academic language can be further broken down into technical or specific academic language and nontechnical academic language. *Technical (or specific) academic language* are words related to a specific discipline. For example, in history technical language would include *sovereignty, monarchy, tyranny*, and *representation. Nontechnical academic language* runs across disciplines and would include such words as *theory, hypothesis, analysis,* and *synthesis.*

> *Background knowledge.*   Background knowledge refers to what you know about a specific topic. Students will not comprehend what they are reading if they lack essential background knowledge on the topic. Background knowledge is the foundation upon which greater knowledge can be built. For example, a student

reading about the causes of the American Revolution of 1775 will be unable to understand many words if he doesn't understand that the American colonies were then part of the British Empire.

There are three topics in this competency:

(1) The role of vocabulary, academic language, and background knowledge in reading development
(2) Important issues related to the development of vocabulary, academic language, and background knowledge
(3) Factors to consider in developing students' vocabulary, academic language, and background knowledge

(1) THE ROLE OF VOCABULARY, ACADEMIC LANGUAGE, AND BACKGROUND KNOWLEDGE IN READING DEVELOPMENT

The more developed a child's vocabulary knowledge, academic language, and background knowledge, the better he or she will be at all aspects of reading.

(A) Vocabulary and Fluency

Knowing the meaning of words helps in the ultimate achievement of swift, accurate word recognition and in all aspects of fluency—rate, accuracy, and prosody. Understanding the meaning of words makes it easier to recognize words and read fluently. Although there are some readers who are fairly talented at pronouncing words correctly even if they have no idea what the words mean, that is the exception not the rule.

(B) Vocabulary and Reading Comprehension

When it comes to reading comprehension, a child's level of vocabulary is both a key indicator and predictor of whether or not the child understands what he or she is reading. This requires some explanation. A child who comprehends what he or she is reading will be able to define several key words in the text after he or she has read—that is what is meant by vocabulary being a "key indicator" of comprehension. And, if a teacher wanted to make a prediction about whether or not a child would comprehend a text that the child will be asked to read, a test of target vocabulary in the text will be a good predictor. This is all common sense: if you don't understand the meanings of important words in a reading selection, then there is virtually no chance you will understand what you have read.

(C) Academic Language and Comprehension

In addition to an inadequate level of vocabulary, another reason some children don't understand what they have read is a lack of academic language. The failure to comprehend could be a failure to know the meanings of nontechnical academic language, in which case reading about almost any academic topic will be frustrating. Or, the problem could be a lack of technical academic language in a specific area. This explains why some students comprehend better in one subject than in others. For example, the student has a good sense of the specific academic language used in history and comprehends the social studies book, but has poorly developed academic language knowledge in geology and struggles when reading a science textbook.

(D) Background Knowledge and Reading Comprehension

Finally, a third cause of poor comprehension can be a lack of background knowledge of a topic. This, too, is common sense: a reader who knows little about farms will have difficulty understanding a selection about crop rotation. In fact, background knowledge is a key predictor of how well a student will learn new information related to that content.

Thus, in order to comprehend a text, a reader must have adequately developed (1) meaning vocabulary, (2) academic language knowledge, and (3) background knowledge.

(2) IMPORTANT ISSUES RELATED TO THE DEVELOPMENT OF VOCABULARY, ACADEMIC LANGUAGE, AND BACKGROUND KNOWLEDGE

(A) The Role of Early Vocabulary Development in Students' Later Achievement in Reading: The Matthew Effect

You might recall that in reading, "The Matthew Effect" is that over a period of time the gap between high-achieving and low-achieving readers widens. If a child does not gain an understanding of the meanings of thousands of words in the prekindergarten years, kindergarten, first grade, and second grade, then she or he will find reading a frustrating task. Why read if you struggle constantly to understand what the teacher asks you to read? As a result, the child reads less, and as a result of that, the further the child falls behind his or her peers who read a great deal. Effective vocabulary instruction for all children and timely intervention for those who are having difficulty is essential in the primary grades.

(B) Vocabulary Knowledge and Concept Learning

There is a reciprocal relationship between learning the meaning of words and acquiring broader concepts. The more words you know, the more concepts you learn; and, the more concepts you learn, the more words you know. In addition, as a child's level of vocabulary increases, so does his or her level of background knowledge. Again, the relationship is reciprocal. The more words you know, the greater your background knowledge; and, the greater your background knowledge, the more words you know.

(C) Vocabulary Learning as an Incremental Process

Children do not learn the meanings of most words all at once. Rather, there are levels of word meaning knowledge. For each person some words are *unknown*, others are *acquainted*, and others are *established*. Unknown words are just that—these are words that you cannot define, even partially. Acquainted words are words that you have some knowledge of, you know part of their meanings. Finally, established words are words that you know well and immediately understand.

Rarely do words jump from the unknown category to established. Rather, vocabulary learning is incremental. Through a variety of instructional strategies and activities described in the next chapter, words that are unknown become familiar, words that are familiar become established. The most challenging task for a teacher is to teach students the meanings of words that fall in the unknown category.

(D) Vocabulary Instruction, Target Words, and Larger Sets of Words

One other issue to keep in mind is that the goal of vocabulary instruction is not limited to the small groups of words that are the focus of direct instruction (*"target" or "key" words*). For example, for a group of students reading a story about a garage sale, the target words could be *advertising, collectible, bargain*, and *junk*. Teachers must also carefully plan the activities that promote knowledge of larger sets of words. We will see that this includes independent word-learning strategies, word consciousness, and wide reading.

(E) Text Is More Complex Than Speech

The fiction and information books we read tend to use a larger and more sophisticated vocabulary and more complex language structures than speech. This is a challenge for students. It is the additional complexity of written language that requires teachers to teach vocabulary, academic language, and background knowledge.

(3) FACTORS TO CONSIDER IN DEVELOPING STUDENTS' VOCABULARY, ACADEMIC LANGUAGE, AND BACKGROUND KNOWLEDGE

(A) Not All Words Should Be Given Equal Emphasis

It would be impossible to directly teach all the thousands of words children need to learn. And, there are limits to how many word meanings children can be expected to learn in a day, a week, or a month. Thus, teachers must decide which words to teach. Three reasonable criteria are:

(1) FREQUENCY. How often will students encounter the word when they read? The more frequently a word appears, the more important it becomes to teach it.

(2) UTILITY. How often will students want to write the word? The more frequently students will have to write the word, the more important it becomes to teach it.

(3) LEVEL OF KNOWLEDGE. The less students know about a word, words that are in the "unknown" category, the more important it becomes to teach it.

(B) Different Tiers of General Academic Vocabulary

Some authorities in the field identify three tiers of academic words that students should learn. These are words that appear in social studies textbooks, science textbooks, information books, and reference materials.

The *first tier* includes simple words that most children will know without instruction. These are words that are used almost every day and include words such as *flower, water*, and *rain*. Students will encounter many first-tier words when they read.

Words in the *second tier* are more difficult words that appear in several contexts across two or more areas of study. This would include words such as *peninsula, territory, nautical, climate*, and *tropical*. Such words might be used in science and social studies textbooks. Some authorities think these words should be the focus of vocabulary instruction.

Words in the *third tier* are the most difficult of all because they are used only in one specific "domain" or one specific area of study. If a group of students were learning about microorganisms, they would encounter *unicellular, protozoa*, and *amoeba*. These words should be taught as a part of social studies or science instruction. They are often too difficult to be taught with the vocabulary instructional strategies alone; they will also require several well-planned science or social studies lessons that use them.

(C) The Importance of Teaching Nontechnical Academic Language

You should recall that nontechnical academic language consists of words that are used in several subjects—words that children encounter whether they are studying mathematics, social studies, science, or the humanities (literature, music, visual art). These are words that are necessary for performing school tasks, such as *define, identify, illustrate, speculate, summarize*, and *classify*. These words need to be taught to children.

CHAPTER 11

Competency 11
Vocabulary, Academic Language, and Background Knowledge: Instruction and Assessment

INTRODUCTION

This chapter discusses how to teach and assess vocabulary. Remember, in this chapter *vocabulary* refers to *meaning vocabulary*. There are eight topics in this competency:

(1) Research-based principles of vocabulary instruction
(2) Direct teaching of specific words
(3) Independent word-learning strategies
(4) Developing word consciousness in students
(5) How to use wide reading to increase vocabulary, academic language, and background knowledge
(6) Instructional activities to support what students have learned
(7) Meeting the needs of all learners
(8) Assessment of vocabulary, academic language, and background knowledge

(1) RESEARCH-BASED PRINCIPLES OF VOCABULARY INSTRUCTION

Research shows that vocabulary instruction should be based on the following principles.

(A) Instruction Must Fit the Age and Ability of the Students

This is true for all instruction, of course. Research shows that vocabulary instruction that leads to gains in comprehension, the ultimate goal of reading, is developmentally appropriate. A key aspect of appropriate vocabulary instruction is providing children with definitions that are "kid-friendly," that is, easy for them to understand.

(B) Lessons Must Provide Examples of How Target Words Are Used in the Context of Sentences and Paragraphs

Too many vocabulary lessons stop with definitions. After helping students learn the meaning of a word, teachers need to challenge students to read the word in sentences and paragraphs and use the word when they write.

(C) To Learn the Meanings of Words, Children Must Have Repeated Exposure to the Words

Students need to repeatedly listen to, speak, read, and write the words they are learning. Isolated vocabulary lessons don't work. This is especially true when teaching content-area vocabulary—students need multiple exposure to the words they are expected to learn.

(D) Vocabulary Instruction Involves Each of the Following

1. Direct instruction of specific words
2. Teaching students independent word-learning strategies
3. Developing word consciousness
4. Encouraging wide reading

(2) DIRECT TEACHING OF SPECIFIC WORDS

There are dozens of effective techniques for teaching children the meaning of words. First, let's review a few key points. Most teachers try to teach the meaning of too many words each week. Researchers at the University of Pittsburgh have shown that there is a magic number: The "average" elementary school student can learn the meanings of about 350 to 400 words a year—about 9 a week. Thus, teachers should carefully select the words they teach. As noted in the previous chapter, words should be selected for their frequency, utility, and lack of familiarity.

Although many alternatives exist, most teachers rely on two relatively ineffective techniques to teach the meanings of words. The teacher simply displays the word on the blackboard and then tells the children what it means. Or, the teacher asks children to look up the meaning of a word in a dictionary, without some discussion of the results. Both these instructional approaches are an ineffective way to teach meaning vocabulary.

Here, four strategies for teaching the meanings of words will be described:

1. Contextual redefinition
2. Semantic maps
3. Semantic feature analysis
4. Word sorts

(A) Contextual Redefinition

Contextual redefinition makes use of the context surrounding the target word and the power of cooperative learning. It is especially effective when teaching words from a story in a basal reader or from a chapter in a social studies or science textbook. Before the lesson, the teacher finds the paragraph where each target word first appears in the basal reader (or textbook). The teacher copies the sentence in which the target word first appears. These sentences will eventually be displayed to the children with either a computer or an overhead projector.

The teacher also prepares a worksheet in which the set of target words appears four times. There should be a space to write a definition after each word. Contextual redefinition works best with a small group of children. The lesson proceeds as follows:

1. The teacher displays the word and, working independently, students write a definition if they know one. If they don't, they write "I don't know." The teacher should encourage those who venture a guess to explain the rationale for their definition. This is "round one."
2. Working in groups of three, the students come up with "second round" definitions. Moving to the part of the worksheet where the words appear for the second time, the children write a definition for each word. They can stick with the definition they wrote in the first round, borrow a definition from someone in their group, or come up with an improved definition.
3. Then the teacher displays the sentence in which the word first appears. The sentence is read aloud by either a student or the teacher. The teacher encourages anyone who wishes to make a comment about the word to do so. The students now write their "third round" definition of the word.
4. Finally, the teacher asks for volunteers to read their definitions and selects one that is accurate and writes it on the board. The children copy this definition in the space where the word appears for the fourth time.

(B) Semantic Maps

Semantic maps are also called *word maps* or *semantic webs*. Semantic maps are diagrams. They are useful in prereading instruction because they not only teach the meanings of words, but also help children activate their prior knowledge of key concepts associated with the target word. Semantic maps are a very effective tool for a teacher-guided discussion about a word.

The teacher places the target word in the center of a circle. The circle can be written on the blackboard or on chart paper. The teacher supplies the names of the "satellite bubbles" that appear around the target word and are linked with lines to it. The teacher and the students discuss the bubble topics and place words and phrases within the bubbles.

For example, for the target word *dolphin*, one "satellite bubble" was *Characteristics of Mammals*. Words placed in this bubble included *breathes, doesn't lay eggs, has hair*. Another bubble was *Where They Live* and the words inside the bubble included *in the ocean* and *aquatic parks*. A third bubble was *Other Things We Know* and included *looks like a big fish, smiles at you, smart, talk to each other*.

(C) Semantic Feature Analysis

Semantic feature analysis is a good teaching activity for a set of words that share at least one characteristic. It works well with words from social studies and science units. The teacher creates a grid or matrix that identifies traits of the target words. Along the vertical axis, the target words are listed. Along the horizontal axis, the traits are listed. Next to each word, the children place a + under each trait the word shares. Here is a semantic feature analysis for the teaching techniques just presented:

	Teaches meaning	Uses context	Uses a chart
Contextual Redefinition	+	+	−
Semantic Map	+	−	+
Semantic Feature Analysis	+	−	+

(D) Word Sorts

In this vocabulary activity, students sort a collection of words by comparing and contrasting them. A word sort only works if the target words can be placed in two, three, or four groups. The words should be placed on 3 x 5 cards. The teacher and the students discuss each word and then create categories. For struggling readers, the teacher creates the categories in advance. For example, for a fourth-grade social studies unit on pre–Gold Rush immigration to California, the target words were *anchor, blubber, harpoon, hides, tallow*, and *carreta*. The words would be sorted into two categories: *whaling* and *tanning*.

(3) INDEPENDENT WORD-LEARNING STRATEGIES

In addition to teaching directly the meanings of specific words, teachers should teach their students to use three types of word-learning strategies that they can use independently when they are reading:

1. Morphemic analysis
2. Contextual analysis
3. Using the dictionary

(A) Morphemic Analysis

Morphemic analysis requires students to look at the parts of words to determine their meaning. This is also called *structural analysis*. First, you should know some linguistic words and phrases relating to the structure of words.

(1) DEFINITIONS.   A *morpheme* is the most elemental unit of meaning in a language. In English, there are only two types of morphemes: some words and all affixes (prefixes and suffixes). Remember, not all syllables are morphemes, and some words have more than one morpheme. *Shoe, chair*, and *wall* all have one morpheme. Walked has two (*walk* + *ed*) and *unkindly* has three (*un* + *kind* + *ly*).

Affixes are either *prefixes*, morphemes that appear before a root word, or *suffixes*, morphemes that appear at the end of a root word. Examples of prefixes are *non-, un-,* and *pre-*. Examples of suffixes are *-ment, -er,* and *-ly*.

Bound morphemes are prefixes and suffixes that cannot occur alone; they must be attached to a root word (*un-, -est*). A *free morpheme* can be uttered alone with meaning (for example, *test*).

Teachers should teach lessons about each of the following to help them unlock the definitions of unknown words: prefixes, suffixes, common root words, synonyms and antonyms, and Greek and Latin roots and affixes.

(2) TWO FORMATS FOR TEACHING PREFIXES, SUFFIXES, AND ROOT WORDS.   Teaching prefixes, suffixes, and root words should simultaneously teach children to identify these words parts and understand their meaning. You can follow either a whole-to-part or a part-to-whole approach (see Chapter 7). Please note that teaching Latin and Greek affixes and roots is an excellent way for older students to expand their meaning vocabularies.

(B) Contextual Analysis

Morphemic or structural analysis lessons are one way to help children develop the ability to figure out the meanings of words on their own. A second type of activity attempts to teach children to figure out the meaning of an unknown word by using contextual clues.

Many times, readers will be able to correctly guess the meaning of an unknown word by thinking about the words, phrases, and sentences surrounding that word. One technique for helping students use context is to teach them to identify four types of contextual clues:

1. *Definition contextual clues.* The author actually provides a definition for the target word in the text. This is very common in elementary social studies and science textbooks.
2. *Synonym contextual clues.* Another word in the paragraph is a synonym for the target word.
3. *Antonym contextual clues.* Another word in the paragraph is an antonym for the target word.
4. *Example contextual clues.* The author of the text has provided a definition of the target word by listing examples of the word in the text.

Teachers provide examples of each type of clue and model how they can be used. The teacher typically uses "think-alouds" to demonstrate how to use each type of clue. Gradually, the teacher releases responsibility by stating that the children must find a particular type of clue in the paragraph (e.g., "There is a synonym clue is this paragraph that will help you figure out the meaning of the word *clergy*.").

It should be pointed out that there are limits to using contextual clues to figure out the meanings of words. For one thing, it is a difficult strategy to teach. For another, many texts have few clearly stated contextual clues, such as the four categories listed above. More subtle clues, often spread over several sentences, are difficult find and use.

(C) Using the Dictionary

Finally, children can learn the meanings of words by looking for a definition in a dictionary. There are a number of cautions to note here. First, be sure that children use a developmentally appropriate dictionary, one with appropriate words, a large typeface, child-friendly definitions, and plenty of illustrations. Second, there are problems with relying on the dictionary to find the meaning of a word. If you are reading and stop to consult a dictionary, the process is slow and distracts you from the meaning of whatever you are reading. When the children find the target word, they may not be able to understand the definition they read. If the word has more than one definition, the child may not know which definition is appropriate for the word, given the context of the passage. Before children use the dictionary, they need these skills: how to alphabetize words; how to find and use guide words; and how to identify the applicable meaning for a word with multiple meanings. Teachers should prepare lessons that focus on the following:

- Understanding alphabetical order to the third, fourth, or fifth letter. You can't locate words in the dictionary unless you know how to alphabetize words.
- Using the guide words (first and last entry) that appear on each page of a dictionary. Efficient use of guide words will greatly facilitate the use of the dictionary.
- Dealing with multiple meanings. As an exercise, children should be given several words with multiple meanings (e.g., *foul*). Then they should be given sentences with different meanings of the word. For example: *Tucker hit a foul ball. There was a foul smell coming from the refrigerator.* Children should then match the appropriate dictionary meaning to each sentence.

Remember, it is important for teachers to first model the use of the dictionary, then provide students with a reasonable amount of guided practice using the dictionary, and then challenge them to find meanings of words in the dictionary independently.

(4) DEVELOPING WORD CONSCIOUSNESS IN STUDENTS

So far, we have discussed two broad categories of instructional activities that help children learn the meanings of words: (a) the direct teaching of specific words, and (b) independent word-learning strategies. A third broad category is developing word consciousness. *Word consciousness* is an interest in words and their meanings.

(A) Synonyms and Antonyms

A good way to expand the meaning vocabularies of children is to teach lessons and play games with synonyms (two words with similar meanings) and antonyms (two words with different meanings).

One way to teach synonyms is to choose five words, each with a clear synonym, and write a paragraph that contains each of them. Highlight the five words. The paragraph will give children contextual clues to figure out the meanings of the five words if they don't know them. Then provide children with a "bank" of 10 words—five of which are synonyms for the five target words, and the other five will not be synonyms for any of the five target words. Challenge children to come up with synonyms for the highlighted words. You can use the same process to teach antonyms by having the word bank include antonyms for the target words.

Once they have been introduced to word pairs that are either synonyms or antonyms, children can play many games. In one, the teacher divides the class in half. She gives a word, written on a card, to each child. For each word, some child has a word that is a synonym. The children must then find their partners who have the synonym for their words.

(B) Homophones and Homographs

Children enjoy activities centered on homophones and homographs. Homophones are two words with the same sound (*Sunday* and *sundae*, *mail* and *male*). Homographs are rarer in English, two words with the same spelling but two different pronunciations (cool *wind*, *wind* the clock).

(C) Word of the Day

Some teachers develop word consciousness by having a "word of the day." Sometimes the teacher selects the word, and sometimes the word comes from a child's question or comment. The word is displayed in large letters. The teacher should also present the word in context, in a paragraph, by using an overhead projector or a computer-based projection system. The teacher and the class should talk about the meaning of the word. If the word has a common prefix, suffix, or root, then other related words can be recorded. The teacher should stress the importance of the word and provide a rationale for the word's selection.

(D) Playing With Words: Idioms and Puns

Idioms are phrases with the following characteristic: it is impossible to determine the phrase's meaning even if the meaning of each individual word is known. Examples are *It's raining cats and dogs* or *Don't look a gift horse in the mouth*. Puns involve the humorous use of a word, typically by playing with a word that has more than one meaning or substituting one word that sounds like another (e.g., one of Shakespeare's characters remarks about a person who has died, *"Yes, he is a grave man"*). Children like to build collections of idioms and puns and enjoy illustrating them.

(E) Playing With Words: Poetry

In addition to writing their idioms and puns, children will benefit from being challenged to write different forms of poetry (e.g., haiku, limerick). This will expand their vocabularies because they will have to be creative and consider several words before picking the one that "fits." Another worthwhile activity is to expose students to a poem written in a certain form and challenge them to write their own poem using that form.

(F) Etymology

Etymology is the history and development of words. Most college-level dictionaries will provide the etymology of words. Students usually are fascinated to learn how words became words. For example, did you know that the word *limousine* comes a region of France, *Limousin*, where shepherds wore a hooded cape? The first limousines were built in the early 1900s and had the driver sit underneath a covering that looked the hood worn in Limousin.

(5) HOW TO USE WIDE READING TO INCREASE VOCABULARY, ACADEMIC LANGUAGE, AND BACKGROUND KNOWLEDGE

Finally, the fourth way to build meaning vocabulary is to encourage students to read widely on their own. Research shows that children learn the meanings of thousands of words simply through independent reading. The more a child reads, the more words she or he will encounter in print. Although researchers cannot explain it, the more often a reader comes across a word, the better the chance the reader will acquire an understanding of the word's meaning.

Increasing time spent reading will increase a child's general vocabulary. However, to have the most impact, children should expand their reading horizons. Many students will only read the same time type of book—sometimes books from just one series (e.g., *The Babysitters Club*). For such students, teachers should find books with similar characters, settings, and plots, but written at a more difficult level. To increase knowledge of academic knowledge and background knowledge, students' independent reading will need to focus on new and different topics.

Strategies for promoting independent reading were covered in Chapter 1.

(6) INSTRUCTIONAL ACTIVITIES TO SUPPORT WHAT STUDENTS HAVE LEARNED

(A) Listening/Speaking

Students can improve their vocabularies, knowledge of academic language, and background knowledge through two important activities. First, teachers should read aloud both literary (fictional) and informational texts. Please note: far too many teachers only read aloud fiction; it is important that teachers include biographies and information books as well. Second, students should take part in discussions that challenge them to use the words they have learned through direction instruction.

One oral language activity that helps students see the link between oral and written language is called *oral rehearsal*. Before students write something, they say it to themselves, listening to how their words "came out," and, perhaps, modifying their message before they write if it doesn't "sound right." For example, a group of students could take a set of target words that have to be placed in sentences. They could discuss possible sentence options before deciding what the final version of their sentence would look like. This allows students to transfer oral skills to written language.

(B) Reading/Writing

After learning the meanings of words, students should have reading assignments that include the target words they have learned. Likewise, students should be asked to use words they have learned in sentences and paragraphs that they compose. This is important! Teachers must go beyond just teaching the definitions of words—the words have to be used.

(C) Structure of the English language

Knowledge of each of the following will increase a student's vocabulary and knowledge of academic language.

(1) SENTENCE STRUCTURE. Students should learn about subjects and predicates, independent clauses, dependent clauses, and how to avoid writing sentence fragments and run-on sentences. An *independent clause* can stand alone. For example, *Darlene kicked the ball*. A *dependent clause* cannot stand alone. For example, in the sentence *Darlene kicked the ball to Fred, who kicked it to Allen,* the dependent clause is *who kicked it to Allen*. Students should be taught to recognize common patterns in sentences, such as *either/or, neither/nor* sentences.

One activity that is frequently used in the upper grades is *sentence combining*. Students are presented with two, three, or four *simple sentences* (one subject and one verb). They are then challenged to combine the simple sentences into *complex sentences*, with one independent clause and one more dependent clauses. For example:

> *Fred kicked the football to Sam.*
>
> *Sam kicked the football over the fence.*

These sentences could be combined into *Fred kicked the football to Sam, who kicked it over the fence.*

Lessons on sentence structure and activities like sentence combining help students understand the structure of sentences, and consequently, help them better understand what they are reading.

(2) SYNTAX. Students should also learn the rules of *syntax,* the order of words in sentences. For example, they should know that in English a common pattern is article, adjective, noun. (*The yellow house.*)

(3) PUNCTUATION AND CAPITALIZATION. The meaning of any text becomes clearer if students understand the purpose of punctuation and capitalization. Punctuation and capitalization should be taught by providing a kid-friendly rule, then displaying models of correctness, and ultimately challenging students to find errors in specially designed sentences. This is called an *error-analysis task*.

(7) MEETING THE NEEDS OF ALL LEARNERS

(A) Struggling Readers and Students With Learning Disabilities

The following interventions to help struggling readers acquire vocabulary, knowledge of academic language, and background knowledge.

(1) FOCUS ON KEY VOCABULARY AND FOCUS ON NONTECHNICAL ACADEMIC LANGUAGE.   Struggling readers will often find it difficult to learn the meanings of words. Teachers should narrow the focus. Two types of words should become the focus of vocabulary instruction for struggling readers. First are those "key" words that are absolutely necessary for understanding the text. Although most children might be expected to learn the meanings of six to eight words in a lesson, lessons for struggling readers might focus only on three or four absolutely essential words.

Second, struggling readers will benefit from lessons on words that will be used in several contexts: what we earlier defined as nontechnical academic language. Such words include *analyze, synthesize, identify, compare,* and *contrast.*

(2) RETEACH WHAT IS NOT MASTERED.   Although many children will have a good sense of the meaning of the words taught in a single lesson, struggling readers may need additional lessons on the same words. It is important the second and third lessons be different from the first, often by using concrete examples and visual, kinesthetic, and tactile interventions (see below).

(3) PROVIDE CONCRETE EXAMPLES.   For nouns, the best way to help struggling readers understand the meaning of a word is to provide the thing itself. If the target word is *asparagus,* nothing beats having fresh asparagus they can see and touch. If it is impossible to bring in the real thing, then photographs and illustrations work well (for example, with *elephant* and *tractor*).

(4) USE VISUAL, KINESTHETIC, AND TACTILE ACTIVITIES.   As with almost all types of lessons, struggling readers usually respond well to activities that use a variety of learning modes. This is not always easy to do when teaching vocabulary, but opportunities do arise. For example, when teaching the meaning of action verbs, a way of differentiating instruction would be kinesthetic—have the students pantomime the target words, such as *measure, hammer, saw,* and *drill.*

(B) English Learners and Speakers of Nonstandard English

The *RICA Content Specifications* recommend the following interventions for English learners and speakers of nonstandard English.

(1) COGNATES.   One very effective way to teach the meaning of English words to English learners is to focus on *cognates.* This was mentioned previously in Chapter 6. You will recall that cognates are words that look alike and mean the same thing in two languages. There are many cognates between English and German-based languages and between English and the Latin-based languages. Some examples of cognates between English and Spanish are *air/aire, active/activo* or *activa, artist/artista,* and *color/color.*

(2) PROVIDE CONCRETE EXAMPLES.   Again, this is the same form of differentiation as mentioned previously. The rationale for using real things, illustrations, and charts to teach the meanings of words to English learners is that many of the strategies teachers use to teach directly the meanings of specific words use words to teach the meanings of words. English learners will benefit from vocabulary teaching activities that feature real things or have strong visual support.

(3) BUILD KNOWLEDGE OF ENGLISH MORPHEMES.   English learners should be taught the meanings of common English roots, prefixes, and suffixes. This morphemic knowledge will allow them to independently figure out the meanings of words. There is some good news here, especially for Spanish speakers, because many English and Spanish affixes have similar pronunciations and mean the same thing. In both languages, *anti-* means *against, auto* means *self, bi-* means *two,* and *contra-* means *against.*

(4) TEACH ENGLISH SYNTAX.   *Syntax* is the order in which words appear in sentences. When compared to many other languages, there will be differences between English syntax and the syntax of the other language. English learners will need to be taught the differences. For example, in English the preferred order is article, adjective, noun (*the white house*). In Spanish, it is article, noun, and then the adjective (*la casa blanca*).

(C) Advanced Learners

The *RICA Content Specifications* routinely recommend the same two forms of differentiations for advanced learners.

(1) INCREASING THE PACE AND COMPLEXITY OF INSTRUCTION.   One characteristic of most advanced learners is that learning the meanings of words comes easily. Advanced learners will learn the meanings of the same words as their peers in far less time.

(2) EXTENDING THE DEPTH AND BREADTH OF INSTRUCTION.   Vocabulary instruction is an excellent opportunity to challenge advanced learners by asking them to learn the meanings of more words than their peers. As noted in earlier chapters, teachers can accomplish this by either extending the depth or breadth of instruction. Extending the depth of instruction would involve asking advanced learners to learn the meanings of more words on the same topic. For example, when studying the causes of the American Revolution of 1775, all fifth graders would be expected to learn the meanings of *taxation, representation, empire,* and *colony*. Advanced learners might also learn *mercantile system, coercive tax,* and *embargo*.

To differentiate by extending the breadth of vocabulary instruction, teachers would challenge advanced learners to learn the meanings of words on topics that other students would not cover. Using our example of the American Revolution, advanced learners might be asked to study the French Revolution of 1777 and learn the meanings of *absolute monarchy, aristocracy, radical,* and *guillotine*.

(8) ASSESSMENT OF VOCABULARY, ACADEMIC LANGUAGE, AND BACKGROUND KNOWLEDGE

(A) How to Assess Vocabulary and Academic Language—Tests

For meaning vocabulary, teachers can select standardized, commercially published tests, such as the *California Achievement Tests* (CAT) and the *Stanford Achievement Tests* (SAT); vocabulary tests that come with a basal reader series; or tests they have designed themselves to assess a student's level of word meaning. Following are some formats for assessing meaning vocabulary.

(1) USE A WORD IN SENTENCE/MULTIPLE ANSWER OPTIONS FORMAT.   This is the most valid format for assessment of knowledge of word meaning. Standardized tests and the tests that come with a basal reader series usually adopt this format for testing meaning vocabulary. The key is that the target word, underlined or italicized, appears in a phrase or a sentence. It does not appear in isolation. Likewise, the possible definitions should all be phrases, not single words.

(2) CHOOSE A SYNONYM.   Another way to test knowledge of word meanings is to ask students to identify a synonym to a target word.

(3) ANALOGIES.   A third format that can be used to assess meaning vocabulary is analogies. Two words that have a relationship are listed together, and then the target word appears. The student must select a word that has that same relationship to the target word. For example, *head* is to *body* as _____ is to *mountain* (the correct answer is *peak*).

(B) How to Assess Vocabulary and Academic Language—Use in Context

Tests have their limits—they measure student knowledge of word meanings in isolation. The real question, of course, is whether students can show they know the meanings of words when they read, write, speak, and listen. Teachers should plan activities that require students to use the words they have learned. Oral and writing activities can be a very effective way to determine whether children have really learned the meanings of words.

To continue with our fifth-grade example of the American Revolution, the teacher could plan the following assignment. In the first, pretend it is 1775 and write letters to the editors of Colonial newspapers advocating that the Colonies should break from England. In their letters, the students must use the words *taxation, representation, petition,* and *independence.*

(C) How to Assess Morphemic Analysis

Tests of morphemic analysis assess student knowledge of prefixes, suffixes, root words, and compound words. These are sometimes called tests of "structural analysis." Some tests ask students to identify nonsense words with common prefixes or suffixes (e.g., *monotell, semidid*), but these are really tests of prefix and suffix identification, rather than meaning. Other, more meaning-oriented tests ask students to define common prefixes and suffixes (e.g., "What is the difference between a *test* and a *pretest?*").

(D) How to Assess Knowledge of Language Structures

Teachers have several choices for assessing student knowledge of language structures. One technique that is frequently used is a variation on the CLOZE assessment technique. CLOZE was developed to assess comprehension. The teacher would select a passage of about 300 words and delete every tenth word. Students would try to figure out the missing words. To assess knowledge of language structures, the teacher would be more selective in deleting words, choosing some nouns, some verbs, some adjectives, and some adverbs. To fill in the appropriate words, students would have to understand what part of speech is missing.

(E) Entry-Level, Progress-Monitoring, and Summative Purposes

(1) ENTRY-LEVEL ASSESSMENT.   Although it is important in all aspects of reading development, effective entry-level assessment of vocabulary is essential. Entry-level assessment will determine whether too many words have been selected for an instructional sequence, or whether additional words can be added.

(2) PROGRESS-MONITORING ASSESSMENT.   As with most areas of reading development, this will be less formal and depend largely on teacher observation and analysis of student work products. The teacher will decide which words need to be retaught.

(3) SUMMATIVE ASSESSMENT.   Summative assessment should challenge students to use words in context when they talk and write. The focus should not be on repeating definitions, rather it should be on determining whether or not students know words well enough to use them appropriately.

(F) How to Analyze, Interpret, and Use Results

Once again, let's repeat four key points about the analysis, interpretation, and use of assessment results, this time for vocabulary.

(1) ANALYSIS AND INTERPRETATION SHOULD BE STANDARDS-BASED.   Again, teachers need to know, for each standard, which students' level of performance is (a) below expectations, (b) at expectations, or (c) above expectations.

For example, for second grade, one of the *English–Language Arts Content Standards* is that children "identify simple multiple-meaning words" (Vocabulary and Concept Development, 1.10). Such words would include *park, rose, rock,* and *play.* An entry-level assessment could ask children to write sentences that show different meanings of each word and to think of other words that have more than one meaning. A correct response for *park: My Mom will park the car close to the curb. I went to the park to play soccer.* One child continued and noted that another word with multiple meanings is *step. The porch had four steps. He steps around the puddle.*

A child who can provide two appropriate sentences for all four words and identify additional multiple-meaning words is above expectations for the standard. A student who can write the sentences for three of the four words, but cannot come up with additional multiple-meaning words, could be considered to have met expectations. A student who cannot provide sentences for two of the words is below expectations.

(2) ANALYSIS AND INTERPRETATION SHOULD REVEAL WHY CHILDREN ARE PERFORMING BELOW EXPECTATIONS.   In many cases, this involves talking individually with a child to determine why he or she is "not getting it." With multiple-meaning words, the problem could be that the child does not understand that the same word, such as *park,* can be both a noun and a verb.

(3) TEACHERS SHOULD USE RESULTS TO CREATE STANDARDS-BASED INDIVIDUAL PROFILES FOR EACH STUDENT.   For this standard, the individual profiles will be specific. For example, Fred's individual profile shows that he is below expectations when it comes to identifying simple, multiple-meaning words. So far he has learned the multiple meanings of *park* and *rose*, but can't seem to use the verb form of *rock (the cradle rocks)* or the noun form of *play (watched a play at the theater).*

(4) TEACHERS SHOULD USE RESULTS TO CREATE STANDARDS-BASED CLASS PROFILES.   The class profile will tell the teacher how the class has performed as a group. If many children have failed to meet the standard, then a new set of lessons teaching the standard should be planned. If almost all of the children have met or exceeded the standard, then the teacher should move on and plan remedial lessons for those who continue to need help, either individually or in small groups.

Competency 12
Comprehension: Concepts and Factors Affecting Reading Comprehension

INTRODUCTION

Comprehension refers to the reader's understanding of what is being read. The final four chapters of this book address the revised RICA's four competencies on comprehension. This chapter looks at basic concepts and factors affecting reading comprehension. Chapter 13 focuses on instruction and assessment of comprehension with any type of text. Chapter 14 narrows the focus to instruction and assessment of comprehension of literary texts. Chapter 15 looks at instruction and assessment of comprehension of informational texts, study skills, and research skills.

There are six topics in this competency:

(1) How word analysis, fluency, vocabulary, academic language, and background knowledge affect comprehension
(2) Literal comprehension
(3) Inferential comprehension
(4) Evaluative comprehension
(5) The role of sentence structure and text structures in facilitating comprehension
(6) The role of oral language, listening comprehension, text-based discussion, writing activities, and independent reading in facilitating comprehension

(1) HOW WORD ANALYSIS, FLUENCY, VOCABULARY, ACADEMIC LANGUAGE, AND BACKGROUND KNOWLEDGE AFFECT COMPREHENSION

(A) Word Analysis and Fluency

This relationship was explained earlier Chapter 8. You might recall that there we discussed *automaticity theory*. This theory states that reading requires the reader to perform two main tasks: (1) decode words and (2) understand the meaning of the text. If readers have poor word analysis skills and do not read fluently, they get bogged down on the decoding task, and then are unable to focus on getting the meaning of the text. Or, stated in the positive, fluent readers with advanced word analysis skills swiftly and accurately identify words, which frees their minds to deal with the meaning of the text.

As explained in Chapter 10, a student's level of vocabulary, academic language, and background all play roles in determining whether or not a child will understand what he or she is reading.

(B) Vocabulary

Obviously, if a student does not know the meanings of several words in a text, there is little chance that the student will comprehend what she or he is reading.

(C) Academic Language

As students progress through the grades, the better the chance that a lack of academic language knowledge will be a serious impediment to comprehension. As noted in Chapter 10, a lack of knowledge of "nontechnical" academic language, words that appear in many social studies and science textbook chapters, will be a huge problem (words such as *compare, contrast, analyze*). Lack of knowledge of the technical academic language, words related to a single topic, could also block comprehension (in the study of the mathematical operations with fractions, words and phrases such as *denominator, least common multiple,* and *numerator*).

(D) Background Knowledge

Finally, another cause of poor comprehension could be a lack of background knowledge of a topic. Background knowledge is a key predictor of students' comprehension of a selection.

(2) LITERAL COMPREHENSION

(A) Levels of Comprehension Skills

There are many different taxonomies, or systems, that can be used to classify reading comprehension skills. The RICA uses three: *literal, inferential,* and *evaluative*. This is important: Do not think of reading comprehension as one "thing." It is possible to be proficient in literal comprehension tasks and be lacking in inferential and/or evaluative comprehension.

(B) Literal Comprehension: Definition

Literal comprehension is the ability of a reader to understand the surface meaning of a text. Literal comprehension questions have clearly verifiable answers in the text. One way of classifying questions used with primary students places questions in two categories: (1) those with answers that are "in the book," and (2) those with answers that are "in your head." Literal comprehension questions have answers that are "in the book."

(C) Literal Comprehension Skills

Literal comprehension skills include:

- Identifying explicitly stated main ideas
- Identifying details and sequences of events
- Identifying clearly stated cause-and-effect relationship
- Identifying the components of story grammar: plot events, characters, the setting, the story's conflict (if clearly stated), and how the story's conflict is resolved (again, if the resolution in clearly stated)

(3) INFERENTIAL COMPREHENSION

(A) Inferential Comprehension: Definition

Inferential comprehension is the ability of a reader to interpret what she or he has read. The answers to inferential reading questions are not in the text—the reader must speculate based on the surface meaning of the text. Using our primary-level classification system, answers to inferential questions are "in your head."

(B) Inferential Comprehension Skills

Inferential comprehension skills include:

- Inferring main ideas
- Making comparisons
- Identifying cause-and-effect relationships not explicitly stated in the text
- Drawing conclusions
- Making generalizations
- Making predictions using evidence from the text
- Inferring themes, if the theme is not clearly stated

(4) EVALUATIVE COMPREHENSION

(A) Evaluative Comprehension: Definition

Evaluative comprehension is the ability of the reader to make judgments about what he or she has read. Answers to evaluative comprehension questions are not in the text. Using our primary-level classification system, answers to evaluative questions are "in your head."

(B) Evaluative Comprehension Skills

Evaluative comprehension skills include:

- Recognizing instances of bias
- Recognizing unsupported assumptions, propaganda, and faulty reasoning in texts
- Distinguishing facts and opinions in texts
- Judging a text's content, characters, and use of language—did the character do the right thing?
- Analyzing themes—does the author's theme make sense?

(5) THE ROLE OF SENTENCE STRUCTURE AND TEXT STRUCTURES IN FACILITATING COMPREHENSION

(A) Sentence Structure

As students enter the upper elementary grades, the more complex grammatical structures they will encounter when they read. They will read fewer simple sentences and more compound and complex sentences. Perhaps a review of the definitions of simple, compound, complex sentences would help:

A *simple sentence* has one subject and one verb. Simple sentences are also called *independent clauses*:

Fred kicked the football.

A *compound sentence* has two independent clauses, that is, two sets of subjects and verbs. The independent clauses are joined by words called *coordinators*, which include *for, and, nor, but, yet*, and *so*:

Fred kicked the football, and Sally played on the swings.

A *complex sentence* has one independent clause and one or more dependent clauses. A *dependent clause* is not a complete thought—it lacks a subject. In a complex sentence the independent clause and the dependent clause are linked by words called *subordinators*, which include *because, since, after, although, when*; or they are linked by *relative pronouns* such as *that, who, which*:

Fred kicked the football to Sam, who kicked it over the fence. (In this sentence, *who kicked it over the fence* is a dependent clause).

Students need to be taught the different types of sentences and the differences between dependent and independent clauses. Older readers will need to understand unusual and complicated grammatical patterns to understand what they are reading. The *California English–Language Arts Content Standards* require fourth graders to use compound sentences. Fifth graders are expected to able to identify and use dependent clauses. Failure to understand compound and complex sentences will be a barrier to comprehension in the upper grades.

(B) Paragraph Structure

Beyond the sentence level, students will become better readers if they understand the structure of paragraphs. Students should be taught how to write topic sentences expressing main ideas and how to provide supporting details for each topic sentence. This will help students understand the role of topic sentences and, consequently, give them a better chance of understanding the meaning of paragraphs.

(C) Text Structures

Most social studies textbooks, science textbooks, and encyclopedia entries are written in standard patterns or structures. These are called *expository text structures. Expository text* is information based and includes social studies textbooks, information books, encyclopedias, recipes, and "how-to" books. The following are common expository text structures:

(1) CAUSE AND EFFECT.   This structure is common in science textbooks, in which the author shows that some phenomena results from some other phenomena. It also occurs in social studies textbooks when the author explains why a historical event occurred.

(2) PROBLEM AND SOLUTION.   In this type of expository text structure, the author presents a problem and then provides an explanation for the reader.

(3) COMPARE/CONTRAST.   In this structure, the writer examines the similarities and differences among two or more items. Venn diagrams are used to represent this structure.

(4) SEQUENCE.   The author lists items or events in numerical or chronological order.

(5) DESCRIPTION.   The author describes a topic by listing characteristics or features.

As you will see in Chapter 15, teachers can use these structures for several instructional purposes. Students with experiences working with expository text structures can use that knowledge to better comprehend the information-based texts they are asked to read.

Appendix G shows diagrams of these expository text structures.

(6) THE ROLE OF ORAL LANGUAGE, LISTENING COMPREHENSION, TEXT-BASED DISCUSSIONS, WRITING ACTIVITIES, AND INDEPENDENT READING IN FACILITATING COMPREHENSION

The focus of the next three chapters will be on instructional strategies to enhance reading comprehension. The last topic in this chapter, however, is how related language activities can help children better understand what they are reading. Oral language development, listening comprehension activities, structured text-based discussions, writing activities, and independent reading all play important roles in facilitating the development of reading comprehension.

(A) ORAL LANGUAGE AND COMPREHENSION

For many years, theorists and researchers have considered the relationship between oral language development and reading comprehension. Though there are exceptions with some children, the two are related. Children with advanced oral language skills usually have an easier time comprehending words, sentences, and paragraphs than their peers with less-developed oral language skills. It is not clear why this relationship exists—perhaps oral language development and reading comprehension are both reflections of a common, underlying level of language sophistication.

As noted previously, children will acquire an understanding of the meanings of some words by repeatedly hearing and speaking them. Oral language activities, especially those in social studies and science, will enhance a child's vocabulary, which in turn, will aid comprehension.

(B) Listening Comprehension and Reading Comprehension

Listening comprehension activities can help children have better comprehension when they read. Almost all students will be able to understand texts that are read to them that they could not understand if they read them on their own. Thus, a well-designed listening comprehension activity, with the teacher reading aloud to students, can allow children to develop the more challenging comprehension tasks—inferential and evaluative comprehension.

(1) STRATEGIC READ-ALOUDS. One structured format for listening comprehension lessons is called *strategic read-alouds*. Although different authorities propose different models of strategic read-alouds, a common instructional sequence would be as follows:

1. The teacher chooses a text to read aloud. It should be something that the children will find interesting.
2. The text is divided into sections, of about 250 words, depending on how old the students are. The text should be broken at a point that makes sense. For each section, the teacher identifies three or four target vocabulary words and writes both literal and inferential comprehension questions.
3. Before reading aloud, the teacher provides a preview of the section and teaches the meanings of the target words.
4. The teacher reads the section aloud.
5. After reading, the teacher asks the comprehension questions.
6. The text is then reread, and the children listen for the target words.
7. The next day, before starting a new section, the target words are reviewed.

(C) Text-Based Discussions

Well-planned discussions during and after students read a text can facilitate reading comprehension. Three discussion models are worth describing:

(1) INSTRUCTIONAL CONVERSATIONS. Developed for English learners, the instructional conversation format works well with all students. During and after students read a selection, the teacher leads a discussion. The goal of the teacher is to promote more complex language by asking students such questions as, "Tell me more about _____," or "What do you mean by _____?" The teacher asks students to explain their answers by providing supporting details. The teacher avoids asking "known-answer" questions, with one correct answer. As the conversation continues, the teacher should say less and less as the students take more control.

(2) QUESTIONING THE AUTHOR. In this format, students read one or more paragraphs and then attempt to analyze the author's intent, craft, and clarity. Questioning the author works best with information-based texts. Each time they stop, students answer the following five questions:

1. What is the author trying to tell you?
2. Why is the author telling you that?
3. Does the author say it clearly?
4. How could the author have said things more clearly?
5. What would you say instead?

(D) Writing Activities

Several writing activities can be used help support students' understanding of text. Especially important are those that ask students to write a summary of what they have read. This challenges students to isolate and identify the most important parts of the text. Any of a number of formats for creating written outlines of a selection can help students better understand what they have read.

(E) Independent Reading

Frequent and extended periods of independent reading can help students reinforce their reading comprehension skills. The more they read, the better they get at it.

CHAPTER 13

Competency 13
Comprehension: Instruction and Assessment—Before Children Read, While Children Read, After Children Read

INTRODUCTION

This chapter focuses on instructional strategies that can be used with any type of text—a basal reading textbook, a social studies or science textbook, or a novel.

Here, instruction strategies are categorized as those that should be implemented before children read, those that should be used while children read, and those that are appropriate after children have read. There are six topics in this competency:

(1) Instruction before children read
(2) While children read: Question classification/Answer verification
(3) While children read: Strategic reading
(4) Instruction after children read
(5) Meeting the needs of all learners
(6) Assessment of comprehension

(1) INSTRUCTION BEFORE CHILDREN READ

(A) The Context of Comprehension Lessons

There are many instructional models for teaching comprehension skills and strategies. The major basal reading series, Open Court and Houghton Mifflin, both have specific formats for directed reading lessons. Whatever they are called, lessons focusing on reading comprehension should be taught according to the following principles:

- Comprehension lessons should be planned and implemented for a small group of children. Effective lessons require discussions, and for all children to be engaged, you need a small group.
- The children in the group should have the same instructional reading level. It is impossible to design comprehension lessons for students with widely different reading levels. Both the material being read and the tasks the teacher poses must be aligned to the students' reading level.
- The material the students read should be at their instructional reading level to ensure that they do not struggle with word identification.
- As the year progresses, children in a class will be grouped and regrouped depending on their path of development. Children who are having an especially difficult time need individual attention.

(B) Direct Instruction to Activate Background Knowledge: KWL and PreP

Before they begin reading, children will have a better chance of understanding what they are about to read if their teacher helps them call to mind what they know about the topic of the selection. In simple words, we don't know all that we know. This is called "activating background knowledge."

(1) KWL. KWL charts are a popular way to help children activate their background knowledge. These charts help students activate, think about, and organize their prior knowledge. The teacher prepares a chart with three columns: *K, W,* and *L.* Let's assume a small group of children are about to read a story about penguins. The teacher asks the children, "What do you know about penguins?" and records their responses under the *K.* Then the teacher asks, "What would you like to learn about penguins?" and records the students' responses under the *W.* After the story has been read, the final column, under the *L,* is completed as the teacher asks, "What have we learned about penguins?"

(2) PreP. The Prereading Plan (PreP) is another way teachers can help their students call to mind what they know about a topic. PreP is a structured discussion with three steps:

1. *Associations.* The teacher says, "Tell me anything you think of when you hear the word *penguins.*" The teacher records these initial associations.
2. *Reflections on the associations.* The teacher asks some of the students who responded, "What made you think of (whatever the child said about penguins)?" Often, many new associations come forth during this part of the discussion.
3. *Organizing associations.* The teacher then asks, "Do any of you have new or different ideas or thoughts about penguins?" Many children will, at this point, recall additional information about the topic.

(C) Vocabulary Instruction

The prereading phase of a directed reading lesson will usually include teaching the meanings of a few key words in the text that the children will read. We covered this in Chapter 11.

(D) Previewing the Text

Another prereading activity that a teacher may choose to implement would be to preview the text.

(1) PICTURE WALK. For younger readers, the teacher could lead the children on a picture walk. The teacher and the students look at the illustrations that appear in the story before they read. The picture walk can be used to teach vocabulary if one of the target words is illustrated (e.g., target word is *bridge,* and there is a picture of a bridge). In many picture walks, the teacher will stop midway through the story and ask students to make predictions.

(2) USING GRAPHIC FEATURES. For older readers, a preview of the text will focus on graphic features—the title, subtitles, and illustrations.

(E) Setting a Purpose for Reading

Finally, the teacher often will set a clear purpose for reading the text. If the selection being read is informational, then the purpose is easy to state. For example, "Today we are going to read about penguins. We learn three things: where they live, what they eat, and why they take such long walks."

If the children are going to read a story, the teacher might focus on the theme of the story ("Today we are going to read a story that will teach us about friendship"); or an element in the plot ("Today we are going to read about a girl who makes a surprising discovery—let's see what she finds.").

The purpose for reading can have an instructional focus ("Today we are going to read about penguins and we are going to classify questions using the QAR system.")

(2) WHILE CHILDREN READ: QUESTION CLASSIFICATION/ ANSWER VERIFICATION

A good way to help children acquire literal, inferential, and evaluative comprehension skills is to ask them to first classify the question and then verify their answer. Struggling readers typically have poorly developed inferential and evaluative comprehension skills. Usually they cannot answer inferential and evaluative comprehension questions because they treat every question as if it were literal, with an answer clearly stated in the text. Some children waste a great deal of time trying to find the answers to inferential and evaluative questions when, in fact, the answers are not stated clearly in the text.

In the process of question classification and answer verification, children are challenged to first determine which type of question is being asked. Once an answer is offered, students should then be challenged to verify their answer and explain how they "came up" with their answer.

For our youngest readers, in kindergarten and first grade, the classification system should be as follows: Is the answer (a) in the book, or (b) in your head? Middle school and high school teachers could use the grown-up classification system of literal, inferential, and evaluative. The question-answer relationship (QAR) system is good for grades 2 through 6 because it avoids the words *literal, inferential*, and *evaluative* and replaces them with a kid-friendly system. The four types of QARs are:

1. *Right there*. The answer to the question is in the text in a single identifiable sentence. These are literal questions.
2. *Think and search*. The answer is in the text, but it is in two different parts of the text. The complete answer is not in a single sentence. This is a different type of literal question.
3. *Author and you*. The answer is not in the text. You need to think about what you already know and what the author said and put it together. These may be inferential or evaluative questions.
4. *On my own*. The answer is not in the story. You can answer the question without reading the story. These may be inferential or evaluative questions.

Lessons focus on helping children identify and classify questions. A group of children reads a story in the basal reader. The teacher and the students look at a set of questions, such as those provided in the teachers' edition, and classify each question before trying to answer it.

At first, teachers may want to work on just distinguishing "right there" from "think and search" questions because both do have answer sources in the text. Next, the teacher could help children distinguish the two types of questions that do not have answers in the text: "author and you" and "on my own" questions.

Finally, after students have classified the question and provided an answer, they need to explain the basis of their answer. This is "answer verification." For "right there" and "think and search" questions, students will be able to cite a specific paragraph on a specific page. For "author and you" and "on my own" questions, the explanations will be more challenging because there will be several correct answers. Students must be able to provide some textual basis for their speculations or judgments (e.g., an incident in the story, a character's comment).

(3) WHILE CHILDREN READ: STRATEGIC READING

Comprehension strategies are things readers choose to do to help them understand what they are reading. Many are mental and are done in the reader's head (often called *metacognitive*) whereas others involve the use of pencil and paper. Teachers need to help their students become proficient in using these strategies:

1. *Visualizing*—"seeing" the action of the story in your head.
2. *Paraphrasing*—stating in your own words something that happened in the story.

3. *Clarifying*—stopping when you are confused and doing something to bring clarity to the reading act.
4. *Predicting*—making an educated guess as to what will happen next.
5. *Generating questions*—stating questions that will be answered in subsequent sections of the text.
6. *Summarizing*—reducing what has been read, either orally or in writing, to a few sentences containing the main events of the story and its theme.
7. *Adjusting reading rate*—changing the pace of reading according to the difficulty of the text.

(A) Strategy Instruction: Gradual Release of Responsibility Model

There are many instructional models for teaching students how to use these strategies. Almost all follow a model of teaching called the *gradual release of responsibility*. This model is implemented over a sequence of lessons. The teacher starts by doing most of the work, and then gradually releases responsibility to the students. In the first few lessons, the teacher models the target strategy. The students watch and listen. The teacher will usually use think-alouds. For example, the teacher would stop midway through a story and say, "I am going to make what is called a prediction. A prediction is a guess. So far in the story we have learned that Fred has a new skateboard, but he isn't following the rules his parents have set for him when he rides it. I predict that Fred will fall off his skateboard and get hurt."

In the next set of lessons, the teacher performs part of the strategy and the students do the rest. For predicting, the teacher reviews what a prediction is and summarizes the main events of the story up to the point where the group has stopped reading. To provide even more scaffolding, the teacher might give the students three choices of possible predictions and each student picks the one she thinks makes the most sense.

In the final set of lessons, the teacher has completely released responsibility for implementing the strategy to the student. Let's say that the students are reading a story about a garage sale. The teacher would say, "We are going to stop here at the end of page 37. I want you to write down a prediction of what you think is going to happen to Sally at the garage sale." The teacher monitors student performance and provides feedback.

(B) Reciprocal Teaching

Reciprocal teaching, which follows the gradual release of responsibility model, is an instructional process for teaching strategies of:

- Predicting
- Generating questions
- Clarifying
- Summarizing

Research has shown that teachers who consistently use reciprocal teaching will help their students develop better reading comprehension. The teacher decides which strategy will be the focus of the lesson. Everyone has a copy of the same text, and these lessons usually focus on a short selection. In the initial lessons, the selection usually is read paragraph by paragraph; subsequent lessons ask the children to work with longer blocks of text.

The teacher initially models the strategy and then, over time, does less and less as the students do more and more. Over the course of a few weeks, the process would evolve as follows:

1. The teacher describes the strategy and explains how to use it.
2. The teacher models the strategy using oral think-alouds to reveal the cognitive processes. For example, pretending to be confused, the teacher may say, "I am not sure why Sally wants to sell her computer. I am going to reread the last two paragraphs" or "I don't know what a *wardrobe* is. I'd better look it up in the dictionary."
3. After lessons in which the teacher has described and modeled the strategy, the teacher and the small group of students collaboratively practice the strategy. If the

group is working on generating questions, for example, the teacher and students would read a selection together. The teacher would stop at one point and say, "Let's see if we can write some questions that will be answered in the rest of this chapter." The teacher would come up with the first two questions; the students in the group would generate three more.

4. After collaborative lessons, the students are challenged to perform the strategy on their own in a "guided practice" format. The teacher "coaches" the students with corrective feedback as they use the strategy.

5. Finally, the students will be asked to use the strategy independently, with the teacher providing feedback only on the finished product.

(4) INSTRUCTION AFTER CHILDREN READ

After children are done reading the text, teachers can choose from many postreading activities that will help children become better at comprehension.

(A) Format: Discussions, Writing, Visual/Graphic

Teachers should use a variety of formats for postreading activities. Some should involve discussions, others should challenge students to write, and some should challenge students to make graphs or draw illustrations.

(B) Postreading Tasks

(1) SUMMARIZING AND RETELLING.   After some reading experiences, teachers should challenge students to summarize what they have read. Teachers should follow the gradual release of responsibility model to teach this strategy.

(2) SHARING PERSONAL PERSPECTIVES.   Sometimes after reading a story, the teacher will ask students to share their personal perspectives about what they have read. Teachers should ask open-ended questions such as "Did you have a favorite part of the story?" or "Do you think you would like to have (name of character) as a friend?" or "If you were the author, would you have written the same ending?"

(3) TEXT-TO-SELF, TEXT-TO-TEXT, AND TEXT-TO-WORLD CONNECTIONS.   Another possibility for a postreading activity is to ask students to find relationships between what they read and themselves, other stories, and real life. Text-to-self prompts challenge students to discover if they have had similar experiences to something in the story. For example, "Have you ever been to a garage sale like the one in the story?" Text-to-text questions ask students if they have ever read another story with similarities to the one they just read. For example, "Have we read another story that had a detective in it?" Finally, text-to-world prompts ask children to find the connections between the story and the real world. For example, "We just read about a nurse who was a hero. Can you think of any heroes who have been in the news lately?"

(4) VISUAL/GRAPHIC REPRESENTATIONS OF WHAT WAS READ.   Finally, some postreading activities do not involve discussion or writing. Children can be asked to create an illustration—perhaps of an event that was not illustrated in the text. Children can also be asked to create their own semantic maps (discussed in Chapter 11). Remember, that a semantic map has a key concept, theme, or word in the middle (e.g., "Friendship") and "satellites" or "bubbles" of words around it. When making comparisons, even young learners can create Venn diagrams.

(5) MEETING THE NEEDS OF ALL LEARNERS

(A) Struggling Readers and Students With Reading Disabilities

The *RICA Content Specifications* suggest several forms of differentiated comprehension instruction for struggling readers, many that we have covered with previous topics.

(1) BUILDING WORD ANALYSIS SKILLS, FLUENCY, VOCABULARY, ACADEMIC LANGUAGE, AND BACKGROUND KNOWLEDGE. For many struggling readers, improved comprehension will not be the result of more comprehension instruction. Rather, students will become better readers when their "foundation" skills and knowledge have increased. Lessons on each of the areas listed in the subtitle will pay comprehension-related benefits in the long run.

(2) PROVIDING ACCESS TO GRADE-LEVEL TEXTS THROUGH ORAL PRESENTATION. One obvious challenge for teachers with struggling readers is that the children who are having difficulty can't read texts at their grade level. For example, consider a fifth grader whose independent reading level is grade 2. While the fifth grader can have some reading experiences with simple texts, he or she will need to encounter more challenging texts to engage in the crucial critical thinking tasks of inferential and evaluative comprehension. Thus, teacher will have to read grade-level texts aloud to struggling readers so that they can participate in discussions appropriate for their grade level.

(3) RETEACHING, ADDITIONAL PRACTICE, CONCRETE EXAMPLES. As with so many areas of reading instruction, these three tried-and-true methods of differentiated instruction for struggling readers should be used. Struggling readers will need to have more lessons, especially on reading strategies, than their peers. Also, struggling readers will need more opportunities to practice what they have learned. Although some students will understand the process of making a prediction after only one or two opportunities, struggling readers may have to practice the strategy many more time. Concrete examples are always helpful with struggling readers, but are difficult to come up with in the area of comprehension.

(B) English Learners and Speakers of Nonstandard English

Here are some ways to differentiate instruction for English learners and speakers of nonstandard English.

(1) CAPITALIZE ON TRANSFER OF COMPREHENSION STRATEGIES FROM THE PRIMARY LANGUAGE. If an older English learner has learned to read in his or her native language, then there is a very good chance that she or he has learned how to implement several of the strategies mentioned in this chapter (summarize, predict, clarify, take notes, etc.) The focus then should not be on teaching the English learner the English vocabulary necessary to implement those strategies.

(2) EXPLICITLY TEACHING COMPREHENSION STRATEGIES THAT ARE MISSING. With English learners, it is important that teachers complete a thorough assessment of their ability to implement essential reading strategies. Those that are lacking should be taught and retaught.

(C) Advanced Learners

Let's take a look at how the means of differentiation the *RICA Content Specifications* mention apply to comprehension.

(1) INCREASING THE PACE OR COMPLEXITY OF INSTRUCTION. Some of the instructional activities mentioned in this chapter are difficult to learn, such things as question classification/answer verification and learning how to implement reading strategies. Advanced learners, however, may need relatively few lessons to master these processes, and those lessons that are planned can involve less teacher modeling. Advanced learners will be able to assume responsibility for comprehension tasks faster than their classmates.

(2) USING MORE ADVANCED TEXTS. Advanced learners should be asked to read and work with texts well beyond their grade level.

(3) EXTENDING DEPTH AND BREADTH OF ASSIGNMENTS. Advanced learners love a challenge, and in the area of reading comprehension there are many opportunities to do just that. Extending the depth of a comprehension lesson could involve asking advanced learners to move away from the QAR system and, instead, classify questions using the "grown-up" categories of literal, inferential, and evaluative. Extending the breadth of comprehension lessons, both of question classification/answer verification and strategic reading, involves pushing advanced learners to perform those tasks with a wide variety of texts, including information books, biographies, poetry.

(6) ASSESSMENT OF COMPREHENSION

The assessment of reading comprehension is multifaceted, as teachers need to (a) determine each child's independent, instructional, and frustration reading levels; (b) gather data on each child's mastery of comprehension skills at each level (literal, inferential, and evaluative); and (c) gather data on each child's mastery of reading comprehension strategies.

(A) Determine Reading Levels

It is important that teachers know the independent, instructional, and frustration reading levels of every student in the classroom. This information reveals, in a general sense, which level of reading material each student can comprehend. Teachers should use the graded reading passages of an informal reading inventory (IRI) to gather this information. The use of graded reading passages on an IRI and the process of determining reading levels were described in Chapter 2. Remember, these reading levels are a function of (1) the percentage of words the child read aloud correctly and (2) the percentage of comprehension questions the child answered correctly.

After you have properly administered the graded reading passages of an IRI, you will know each student's instructional level. This is important, because most comprehension lessons should require the child to read texts at this level. There are two things that the results of this type of "placement" assessment do not reveal: (1) whether a student will be able to read a specific story or article, because the instructional level generated by an IRI is a rough estimate; and (2) which specific comprehension skills and strategies a child has mastered and which ones need to be developed.

(B) Assess Comprehension Skills at Each Level: Literal, Inferential, Evaluative

(1) USING QUESTION-ANSWER RELATIONSHIPS (QARS).   All too often, teachers only assess literal comprehension. We have discussed the QAR system as an instructional tool in the process of challenging students to classify questions and verify their answers. It can also be used to assess students' mastery of all levels of comprehension skills—literal, inferential, evaluative. Let's look at some examples of questions teachers would ask, using the QAR to determine a student's ability to answer literal, inferential, and evaluative questions.

(2) RIGHT THERE.   This type of question measures literal comprehension. The answer is easy to find in the text. The answer is in a single, identifiable sentence, such as this one from the first chapter of *Charlotte's Web*: "Why did Mr. Arable think he should kill Wilbur?" (Because he was the runt of the litter.)

(3) THINK AND SEARCH.   This is another type of literal comprehension question. The answer is in the text, but it is in two different parts of the text. The complete answer is not in a single sentence. Example: "How do we know that Fern loves Wilbur?" (On page 4, she says, "Oh, look at him! He's absolutely perfect." On page 7, she can't stop thinking about Wilbur and answers that Wilbur is the capital city of Pennsylvania.)

(4) AUTHOR AND YOU.   The answer is not in the text. This type of QAR asks for inferential or evaluative skills. The reader needs to think about what he or she already knows, think about what the author wrote, and put it together to answer the question. Example: "Fern will have to feed and care for Wilbur, feeding him with a baby bottle. She is 8 years old. If you have taken care of a pet, you know what a large responsibility that is. What will Fern have to do to keep Wilbur safe and well? Do you think she can do it?" (Answers to this type of question will vary.)

(5) **ON MY OWN.** The answer to this type of question is not in the story. You can answer the question without reading the story. These can be either inferential or evaluative questions. Evaluative questions ask for students to detect bias or to distinguish fact from opinion. Example: "Fern says that it is 'unfair' to kill Wilbur just because he is small and weak and is the runt of the litter. Is she right? Would it have been unfair? Suppose Fern slept late, and Wilbur was killed. Would you think Mr. Arable had done a terrible thing?" (Again, answers will vary.)

Teachers can assess levels of comprehension by developing a simple comprehension test using QARs. Select a story from a basal reader and write three questions of each type. Have the students read the selection silently and answer the questions. You should have a much clearer idea of each student's ability to answer literal, inferential, and evaluative questions.

(C) Using Retellings to Assess the Literal Comprehension of Young Readers

The use of retellings has become a popular way of assessing the literal comprehension of young readers. Since many kindergarteners and first graders have limited ability to write, comprehension skills must be assessed orally. A retelling is less threatening than having the teacher fire questions at a 5-year-old, a procedure that all too often resembles an interrogation rather than an appropriate primary-grade assessment.

After a student has read a story, the teacher asks the child to retell it.

There are two types of retellings. In an *unaided retelling*, the child simply is asked to retell the story. Unaided retelling is also called *free retelling* or *recall*. The teacher provides no guidance. After the unaided retelling, the teacher usually proceeds with *aided recall* by asking the student if he or she remembers anything about a major component of the story he or she failed to mention. Aided recall is also called *probed recall*. For example, in a retelling of "Jack and the Beanstalk," if the child talked only about the ending of the story, the teacher might ask, "What happened before Jack climbed up the beanstalk?"

The teacher needs a checklist of items that a student should mention. The checklist can be organized by the literary elements (setting, characters, plot events). The teacher checks off each item if the child mentions it. Another way to organize the checklist is by the main events of the story, with supporting details listed under each main event. Again, it is important to note that retellings test literal comprehension. Unless they have been prompted by a question, children rarely make inferences or evaluate what they have read.

(D) How to Assess Reading Comprehension Strategies

Unfortunately, it is somewhat difficult to assess strategies such as prediction, summarization, generating questions, visualizing, and adjusting reading rate. These metacognitive comprehension strategies are internal, mental operations.

(1) **ORAL THINK-ALOUDS.** Think-alouds can be used as a tool to assess which students monitor their reading, reread what they don't understand, and are able to implement the other reading strategies. Any selection from a basal reader or a social studies or science textbook can be used as long as it will be challenging for the child who is reading it.

(2) **WRITTEN ASSESSMENTS OF READING COMPREHENSION STRATEGIES.** It is possible to gather data on students' ability to implement reading strategies through writing assignments ("Write a summary using no more than 25 words of what we just read.") Written assignments, however, do not provide information on the child's thought process.

(E) Entry-Level, Progress-Monitoring, and Summative Purposes

The ability to perform tasks mentioned in this chapter develop slowly over time. It may take months, for example, for a third grader to make any type of reasonable summary of what has been read.

(1) ENTRY-LEVEL ASSESSMENT.   As children get older, the more chance they will already know how to classify questions, verify answers, and read strategically. Entry-level assessment will reveal who already knows how to do these things. Then, the teacher will know that these processes do not need to be retaught. Rather, the emphasis is on applying what the student knows to grade-level texts.

(2) PROGRESS-MONITORING ASSESSMENT.   As with most areas of reading development, progress-monitoring assessment of comprehension skills and strategies will be less formal and depend on teacher observation and analysis of daily written work.

(3) SUMMATIVE ASSESSMENT.   With reading comprehension, it is worth repeating one more time—it is essential to test the students on all three forms of comprehension: literal, inferential, and evaluative.

(F) How to Analyze, Interpret, and Use Results

Let's look at the four key points about the analysis, interpretation, and use of assessment results in relation to comprehension.

(1) ANALYSIS AND INTERPRETATION SHOULD BE STANDARDS-BASED.   Teachers need to know for each standard, which students' level of performance is (a) below expectations, (b) at expectations, or (c) above expectations.

For example, for fifth grade, one of the *English–Language Arts Content Standards* is that children "draw inferences, conclusions, or generalizations about text and support them with textual evidence and prior knowledge" (Reading Comprehension, 2.4). There are two required behaviors for a student to perform at or above expectations. First, the student must consistently make reasonable inferences. Second, the student must consistently support these inferences with evidence from the text.

(2) ANALYSIS AND INTERPRETATION SHOULD REVEAL WHY CHILDREN ARE PERFORMING BELOW EXPECTATIONS.   For this standard, there are two reasons why a student would be unable to make inferences. The student could be unable to infer because he or she didn't understand the literal meaning of the text. This could be caused by a lack of word analysis skills, fluency, meaning vocabulary, academic knowledge, or background knowledge; most likely some combination of these factors. Or, if the student can answer literal questions about the text, but still can not make inferences, then the student needs to be taught (a) how to identify inferential questions and (b) the process of answering questions with answers that are not "in the book."

(3) TEACHERS SHOULD USE RESULTS TO CREATE STANDARDS-BASED INDIVIDUAL PROFILES FOR EACH STUDENT.   For this standard, the teacher should not mark that any student has met or is beyond expectations unless the students consistently can make inferences and support them with textual evidence.

(4) TEACHERS SHOULD USE RESULTS TO CREATE STANDARDS-BASED CLASS PROFILES.   As with the class profiles for all standards, the class profile for this standard will allow the teacher to decide whether the entire class needs to work more on making inferences and an additional sequence of lessons should be planned or, if only a few individuals need help, their needs can be met with individualized or small group lessons.

CHAPTER 14

Competency 14
Comprehension: Instruction and Assessment—Understanding and Analyzing Narrative/Literary Texts

INTRODUCTION

The focus of this chapter is on instructional strategies and assessments that are appropriate to use with narrative or literary texts. In the field of literacy education, authorities distinguish between narrative and expository texts. *Narrative texts* are stories—written accounts of actual or fictional events. Short stories and novels are narrative texts. *Expository texts* are those that provide information about a topic. A social studies textbook, an information book on lions, and a set of instructions for assembling a barbeque are all expository texts. *Literary* means having to do with literature. This opens a can of worms because whether something written is "literature" or not depends on how literature is defined and who applies the definition.

To keep things simple, in this chapter we are talking about fictional stories, which can be called either narrative text or literary text. Stories may be presented as novels, short stories, poems, or dramatic plays.

There are seven topics in this competency:

(1) Strategies to help students recognize the structure and characteristics of major genres
(2) Instruction in the elements of story grammar
(3) Instruction in narrative analysis and literary criticism
(4) Oral language activities with literature
(5) Writing activities with literature
(6) Meeting the needs of all learners
(7) Assessment of comprehension of literary texts and literary response skills

(1) STRATEGIES TO HELP STUDENTS RECOGNIZE THE STRUCTURE AND CHARACTERISTICS OF MAJOR GENRES

Genres are categories, or types, of literature. Teachers can teach children how to recognize the features of different literary genres. This can be done first by exposing children to several examples of a particular genre and then, through direct instruction, listing their common elements. The following genres cover most children's books.

(A) Traditional Literature or Folktales

Folktales have their origins in oral storytelling and have survived through generations. Folktales are also called *traditional literature*. Examples of folktales are *cumulative tales*, such as *The House That Jack Built*; *pourquoi tales*, which explain a natural phenomena, such as *Why Mosquitoes Buzz in People's Ears*; *trickster tales*, such as the B'rer Rabbit stories from Uncle Remus; and *fairy tales*, stories full of enchantment and magic. Traditional literature also includes *tall tales*, with much exaggeration; *fables*, which teach a lesson; and *myths*, which people created to explain the world around them.

(B) Modern Fantasy

Modern fantasy includes those stories that play with the laws of nature and have known authors. This includes animal fantasy, with beasts that can talk, such as *Charlotte's Web*; stories with toys and dolls that act like people; and stories with tiny humans.

(C) High Fantasy

This is a popular type of modern fantasy for older children. High fantasy has a struggle between good and evil set in a fantastic world. The hero or heroine of the story usually goes on a quest of some sort. Examples include *The Lion, the Witch, and the Wardrobe*, by C. S. Lewis, and the Harry Potter books by J. K. Rowling.

(D) Science Fiction

This is a type of modern fantasy similar to high fantasy with one important difference: The story features some "improved" or "futuristic" technology. Science fiction is the genre of time machines, spaceships that travel at the speed of light, and holographic worlds.

(E) Contemporary Realistic Fiction

These stories take place in the present day in the real world. They can be humorous or quite serious. Examples include the Ramona Quimby books by Beverly Cleary and Newbery Medal winners such as *Walk Two Moons* by Sharon Creech and *Missing May* by Cynthia Rylant.

(F) Historical Fiction

Historical fiction includes realistic stories that are set in the past. Good historical fiction makes the past come alive to young readers, in books such as *Roll of Thunder, Hear My Cry*, by Mildred Taylor, and *Island of the Blue Dolphins* by Scott O'Dell.

(G) Biography

Biographies are information books that tell the story of a real person's life. There are excellent picture book biographies written for young readers. In *autobiography*, the author describes his or her own life.

(H) Poetry

The *RICA Content Specifications* list the following poetic genres.

(1) BALLAD.   A ballad is a form of poetry that tells a story and is usually set to music. In many ballads, the stanzas have four lines. Some stanzas are usually repeated to serve as a chorus in a song.

(2) LYRIC.   There are two definitions of *lyric*. Lyrics are the words of a song. In poetry, however, a lyric poem is one that expresses personal feelings. A sonnet is a type of lyric poetry.

(3) COUPLET.   A couplet is a pair of lines in a poem that usually rhyme and have the same meter (internal structure, e.g., same number of syllables). The shortest poems are couplets—just two lines.

(4) EPIC.   An epic is a long poem telling a story, usually about heroic deeds.

(5) SONNET.   A sonnet is form of lyric poetry with 14 lines. Sonnets have a strict rhyming scheme and a strict internal structure (meter).

(I) Teaching Literary Genres

Teachers who want to teach their students the organizational structure and characteristics of a genre will need to develop an instructional unit on that genre. The children will listen to their teacher read aloud examples of the genre and read some on their own.

Lessons then show the unique characteristics of genre for each literary element. For example, let us consider high fantasy (e.g., *The Lion, the Witch, and the Wardrobe*; the Harry Potter books).

(1) CHARACTER.   Almost all books in the genre of high fantasy have two types of characters: (a) An experienced wizard or magician; and (b) an "undiscovered hero," a character who at the start of the story seems quite ordinary but goes on to fulfill a destiny of greatness.

(2) PLOT.   In high fantasy, the plot involves a struggle between good and evil. Typically, there are setbacks for the "good guys" before they triumph over the forces of evil. These are fantastic stories and there will always be characters with magic powers.

(3) SETTING.   In high fantasy, at least part of the story always transpires in a fake place. For example, we must get to Hogwarts or into Narnia.

(4) MOOD.   For at least part of the story, the mood is dark and ominous, sometimes quite scary. Ultimately, though, the mood changes as good triumphs.

(5) THEME.   The themes of high fantasy stories revolve around the nature of good and evil. What makes evil characters? It is often a twisted quest for power. What allows the good characters to triumph? Often, it is the power of working together.

(2) INSTRUCTION IN THE ELEMENTS OF STORY GRAMMAR

The *literary elements* are character, plot, setting, mood, theme, and style. Together, these elements form a *story grammar*, which is unique for every story. The literary elements are at the center of instruction related to the analysis of the literature. Teachers should directly teach each element by defining the element and providing examples. The literary elements also should be the basis for discussions and written assignments.

Below is a brief summary of the literary elements that make up a story grammar.

(A) Character

In children's literature, characters usually are people. Some children's books have animals, plants, or inanimate things as characters such as a stuffed animal, for example. Older students should be able to identify the protagonist(s) and antagonist(s) in a novel. The protagonist is the main character of the story, or in more literary terms, the character who "pushes toward" something. In colloquial terms the antagonist is the "bad guy," the character who pushes against the protagonist and tries to block him or her from achieving his/her goal.

(B) Plot

The sequence of events in a story is its plot. Many novels and plays written in English follow a plot structure that includes an introduction; rising action, during which the reader is introduced to conflict or complication; a climax when the conflict is resolved; and then falling action to wrap things up, called the *denouement*. Some stories break the normal flow of events with flashbacks and flash-forwards, which present events out of chronological order.

(C) Setting

Teachers should help students understand that the setting of a book is both the time and the place of the story. Settings in a story can be described as either *backdrop* or *integral* or somewhere in between. A story with a backdrop setting has a vaguely defined setting and could take place in a number of places or times, like most fairy tales. Integral settings are fully described and the story can only take place in that time and in that place, as with historical fiction.

(D) Mood

Mood is the feeling you have when you are reading the story. In picture books, illustrations convey the mood (spooky, comforting, majestic, etc.). Scary moods usually are represented with dark colors and with things that are "cloaked," or are only partially revealed. Joy and happiness typically are established with lots of light and bright colors. In novels, authors create mood by using descriptive words. A mood of suspense and impending danger can be created by foreshadowing (giving the reader a hint of the trouble ahead).

(E) Theme

A story's theme, its important message, is usually a comment about the human condition. Theme can be clearly stated (explicit), or the reader must infer it (implicit). For example, the Newbery-winning book *Out of the Dust* has an explicit theme. Author Karen Hesse states, "You can stay in one place and still grow." On the other hand, readers must infer the theme of "the grass isn't always greener on the other side of the fence" in *The Little House* by Virginia Lee Burton. Some teachers refer to a theme as being the "moral" of a story. If students are having difficulty identifying the theme of a story, then teachers should first work with simple fables and fairy tales, where the themes are obvious, before moving on to stories with implicit themes.

(F) Style

The style of a story is how it is written, how the author uses words, phrases, sentences, and paragraphs. We will discuss this more in a subsequent section of the chapter.

(G) Instruction in the Elements: Story Maps

When students understand the elements of a story, they will recall details with greater accuracy. Students can be taught to attend to story elements through story maps and story grammar outlines. For story maps and story grammar outlines, teachers first provide complete models to use as a framework to discuss the story. Then, the teacher provides "skeletal" maps and grammar outlines. Students complete these during and after they read, with help from the teacher. Next, students are challenged to complete maps and grammar outlines on their own.

Story maps provide a visual representation of certain elements of the story. Making a story map helps students think about the structure of a story and how the elements relate to each other. In some story maps, the story's title is placed in a circle in the center of the diagram. Characters, events, and locations are placed in satellite positions around it. Lines show relationships. Other story maps actually look like things (fish, spider webs, etc.).

Finally, a popular type of story map is a *star diagram*, a chart shaped like a six-pointed star, with the points labeled *What?*, *When?*, *Where?*, *Why?*, *How?*, and *Who?*. Working in groups, students answer the six questions, writing their answers on the star diagram.

(H) Instruction in the Elements: Story Grammar Outlines

A story grammar outline challenges students to identify the specifics of each literary element. Some story grammar outlines contain all the elements, other focus on character, setting, and plot. A common template for a story grammar would look like this:

Setting:

Characters:

Problem:

     Event 1:

     Event 2:

     Event 3:

Resolution:

Theme:

(3) INSTRUCTION IN NARRATIVE ANALYSIS AND LITERARY CRITICISM

Literary analysis is the process of studying or examining a story. *Literary criticism* is one possible outcome of that analysis, in which a person makes judgments or evaluations about the story. Literary analysis focuses on the literary elements. The *RICA Content Specifications* list the following instructional activities that will engage children in literary analysis.

(A) Identifying the Structural Elements of a Plot

This typically involves using a story map. The teacher and students list the important events of a story and try to understand how they relate to each other. The analysis can be critical and ask whether or not the events are logical and credible. Did it make sense for an event to take place? Should something have occurred sooner or later?

(B) Comparing and Contrasting Motivations and Reactions of Characters

Even our youngest students can begin to question why certain characters do the things they do in a story. Why are some characters behaving in the way they do? What motivates them to be good, evil, heroic, cowardly? When characters react to events, are their reactions consistent with what we know about them?

(C) Evaluating the Relevance of the Setting

Once children clearly understand the where and the when of the story, they need to consider how the setting of the story relates to the other elements. Older students should know the five functions of setting in a story:

1. To provide a basis for conflict between characters. For example, oil is discovered on a property, two brothers both want to control it.
2. To serve as the antagonist. The protagonists are stuck on an island and battle hunger, thirst, beasts, and storms.
3. To amplify character. We never knew a character was a hero until he risks his life to save others during a hurricane.
4. To establish mood. This is a central function of setting. Scary places create scary moods. Warm and fuzzy settings generate warm and fuzzy feelings in readers.
5. To serve as a symbol. As all of us learned in our high school and college English classes, so often a river is not a river—it is a symbol for the flow of time. Or, a deep, dark forest is not just a forest—it is symbolic for the great unknown.

(D) Identifying Recurring Themes

As noted earlier, a story's theme, its important message, is usually a comment about the human condition. The same themes are repeatedly expressed in children's stories. For example, many children's books focus on themes relating to personal growth and development in young characters. A frequent theme in this area is coming to know and accept yourself for who you are. Other recurrent themes focus on friendship and cooperation— that we can accomplish things collectively that would be impossible accomplish individually.

Teachers introduce students to books with common themes. This can be done informally through the teacher's read-aloud program. Or, the teacher can be more formal and plan a unit of instruction based on a literary theme. For example, "Taking Responsibility," a unit that would feature books that all have young characters who are thrust into adult-like roles.

(E) Identifying Elements of the Writer's Style: Analyzing Figurative Language

Style is the way authors use words. It is not the *what* of the story, it is *how* the story is told. Words have both a literal meaning and a figurative meaning. *Figurative language* is the use of words in a nonliteral way that gives them meaning beyond their everyday definition and provides an extra dimension to the word's meaning. Some examples of figurative language are:

Hyperbole.   An exaggerated comparison (example: "scared to death")

Metaphor.   An implied comparison ("The road was a river of moonlight.")

Personification.   Giving human traits to nonhuman beings or inanimate objects. ("The crickets sang in the grasses. They sang the song of summer's ending.")

Simile.   One of the simplest figurative devices, a stated comparison between unlike things using the words *like* or *as* ("He was as big as a house")

In addition to figurative language, there are other stylistic devices authors can use when they write stories:

Symbol.   A person, object, situation, or action that operates on two levels of meaning— the literal and the symbolic (in *The Polar Express*, the small bell is a symbol for the true meaning of Christmas).

Imagery.   Imagery is when the author appeals to the reader's senses—sounds, smells, sights, touch. For example, in *The Lion, The Witch, and The Wardrobe*, C. S. Lewis appeals to the reader's sense of touch when he brings the character Lucy into Narnia for the first time. In one paragraph he uses words such as *soft, crunching, hard, smooth, soft,* and *powdery*.

Irony.   In literature, irony occurs when there is incongruity between what a character says or does and reality. *Verbal irony* is when someone says something that is not consistent with reality. For example, when a character says, "Beautiful weather we are having!"—and it is raining. *Dramatic irony* occurs when the reader or audience knows something and the character does not. Shakespeare was a master of dramatic irony. In *Romeo and Juliet*, at the end of the play, the audience knows Juliet is not dead, she is in a drugged sleep. However, Romeo doesn't know this and when he finds Juliet he thinks she is dead, and so he kills himself.

Foreshadowing.   Finally, foreshadowing is a literary device in which the author drops hints about what might happen later.

(4) ORAL LANGUAGE ACTIVITIES WITH LITERATURE

(A) Plan Discussions About Literature on a Regular Basis

Experiences with literature provide perfect opportunities for children to develop as listeners and speakers. Children's books should serve as the basis for many stimulating discussions. The role of the teacher varies during these discussions. Usually the goal of the teacher is to facilitate, not dominate, any discussion. The more the teacher prompts individual children to respond to the literature, the better. When the teacher wants to focus oral response on a specific part of a book, such as a character, then he must ask more specific questions.

(B) Book Clubs, Literature Circles, and Author Studies

All of these formats, discussed in Chapter 1, will stimulate literary discussions.

(C) Questioning the Author

This format works well with literature-based discussions. We covered it Chapter 12.

(D) Think-Pair-Share

Think-Pair-Share is a cooperative learning format that can be used for any thought-provoking topic. It works well for discussions based on a book that the teacher is reading aloud to the entire class. In the first step ("Think"), the teacher asks a question, in this case one requiring literary analysis—a question about character, plot, setting, theme, mood, or style. In the second step ("Pair"), partners, usually two students sitting close to each other, discuss the question and come up with an answer. In the final step ("Share"), the pairs report their answers, usually in a round-robin fashion.

(5) WRITING ACTIVITIES WITH LITERATURE

(A) Format: Literature Journals

Students should keep records of the books they have read. Many teachers require students to keep a journal dedicated to their reading experiences with literature. These can be called *literature logs, literature journals*, or *reading logs*. Teachers should use a variety of prompts to stimulate written response. Two frequently used formats are *quotes and notes* and *double-entry journals*. In quotes and notes, each child selects a sentence from a book he or she has read, copies it verbatim in his or her journal, and then writes a comment about the quote underneath it. In double-entry journals, each child writes a comment about a book and then leaves space for the teacher or another student to write a reply.

(B) Format: Essays

Some written assignments will not be in journals. Rather, they will be completed on separate sheets of paper. Literary analysis prompts will require children to write some of their first essays. Older students can be challenged to have topic sentences and supporting details.

(C) Topics: The Literary Elements

For the most part, the prompts students write to are focused on the literary elements of character, plot, setting, theme, mood, and style. This literary analysis is important and should be planned frequently.

(D) Topics: Features of the Genres

Other written prompts can focus on the features or characteristics of a book's genre. Recalling our example of high fantasy, a written prompt could look at setting. After students have read *Harry Potter and the Sorcerer's Stone* and *The Lion, the Witch, and the Wardrobe*, they could be asked to compare Hogwarts and Narnia. What similarities do the two settings share? What is different?

(6) MEETING THE NEEDS OF ALL LEARNERS

(A) Struggling Readers and Students With Learning Disabilities

(1) PROVIDING ACCESS TO GRADE-LEVEL TEXTS THROUGH ORAL PRESENTATION. Most struggling readers, especially those in the upper grades, will be unable to read challenging novels and plays written for older children. It is important that they experience these books so that they can, through discussion, participate in the same types of literary analysis as their peers who can read the books independently. A good alternative is to let struggling readers listen to audio recordings of the literature that the class is reading and studying.

(2) FOCUSING ON KEY ELEMENTS OF STORY GRAMMAR. When struggling readers are reading literature, the teacher should plan lessons that explicitly highlight key literary elements. For example, it is important that struggling readers understand the roles that certain characters play. It helps, too, if the teacher talks about devices of style, such as symbols, that struggling readers won't understand on their own.

(3) USING STORY MAPS. Struggling readers need graphic representations of things, including the plots of the stories they are reading or listening to. Story maps will highlight the important events of a story and help struggling readers understand the relationship of events in a story.

(4) RETEACHING SKILLS AND STRATEGIES/USING CONCRETE EXAMPLES.   As with all areas of reading development, some skills and strategies will need to be retaught to struggling readers. It is best if the retaught lessons feature concrete examples. For example, in a primary-level class, if the teacher is using a story map, it would help struggling readers to place photocopied illustrations of events in the proper order rather than written description of those events.

(B) English Learners and Speakers of Nonstandard English

(1) CLARIFYING CULTURAL CONTEXT OF TEXT.   This is important. English learners may be confused by the actions of characters in stories set in the United States because of a lack of cross-cultural understanding. This is especially true for interpersonal relationships in books and the response of characters to other characters' actions. Some explanation of cultural norms in the United States will be in order. For example, at the beginning of *Charlotte's Web*, young Fern challenges her father's decision to get rid of the runt piglet. In some cultural groups, a child would never challenge a parent as Fern did.

(2) PRETEACHING KEY VOCABULARY.   Whether they are listening to their teacher read aloud or reading a book themselves, English learners will benefit greatly from well-designed vocabulary instruction on key words that will appear in the text.

(C) Advanced Learners

(1) USING MORE ADVANCED TEXTS.   Advanced learners should be challenged to engage in the literary analysis of books that are too difficult for their classmates. This is one area where it is relatively easy to differentiate instruction for advanced learners because there are so many excellent, yet challenging books to choose from. Just be sure that the content of the books is developmentally appropriate for the young, advanced reader.

(2) BUILDING ON CURRENT KNOWLEDGE AND SKILLS.   In all areas of reading development, teachers should build on what advanced learners have learned to create special challenges from them. For example, after advanced learners have worked on story maps and story grammar outlines that the teacher has created, for subsequent stories they should be challenged to create their own.

(3) EXTENDING THE DEPTH AND BREADTH OF ASSIGNMENTS.   In many literary analysis activities, both written and oral, only one of the literary elements, such as character, will be focus of the activity. Advanced learners can be asked to do more: in addition to character, they can be challenged to respond to prompts about setting and theme, for example.

(7) ASSESSMENT OF COMPREHENSION OF LITERARY TEXTS AND LITERARY RESPONSE SKILLS

(A) Formats for Assessment of Comprehension of Literary Texts and Literary Response Skills

(1) STUDENT READ AND TEACHER READ ALOUD.   Teachers should assess literary understanding by asking students to analyze both books that children have read themselves and books that the teacher reads aloud.

(2) ORAL AND WRITTEN.   Teachers evaluate students' analysis through oral and written assessments. For younger students especially, it is important that assessment be done orally. Many children cannot express in writing all their thoughts and feelings about books.

(3) FREE AND FOCUSED.   It is important that the assessment of literary understanding be both free and focused. Free response requires the use of open-ended prompts, such as "Who has something they would like to say about *The Polar Express* by Chris Van Allsburg?" or "Write anything you want about *The Polar Express*."

Focused prompts tend to use the literary elements as a basis for questions. For example, "How are Alyce in *The Midwife's Apprentice* and Billie Jo in *Out of the Dust* alike? How are they different?" (question based on character). "We have read two books by Margaret Wise Brown and two books by Dr. Seuss. Do these authors tell their stories the same way?" (question based on style).

(B) Analysis of Results

As teachers analyze oral and written responses, they should see their students do each of the following.

(1) INCORPORATE LITERARY ELEMENTS. Some examples: Do students focus on the characters in a story? Do they mention specific incidents that help the reader understand a character? Do children ever talk or write about the setting of the story? Do they notice how the story's time and place influence what is happening? Do students understand the plot device of conflict? Can they identify the point in a story when the plot's central conflict is resolved?

(2) MAKE CONNECTIONS. We want our students to see the relationship between the literature they read and each of the following:

Text-to-text. Teachers should know if their students are able to see the relationship between a book they are reading and other books.

Test-to-self. Do children, in their oral and written responses, make connections between the books they are reading and their own lives?

Text-to-world. Teachers should determine whether their students are able to see the relationship between a book they are reading and events and people in the real world.

(3) PROVIDE EVIDENCE FROM A TEXT. Finally, are children able to cite specific events or descriptions in a story to support the perspectives they have stated or written? For example, after a child reads *Holes* by Louis Sachar, she writes, "Stanley grew up during the story." Can this student cite an example of how Stanley changed during his experience at Camp Green Lake?

(C) Entry-Level, Progress-Monitoring, and Summative Purposes

Again, entry-level assessment will determine who already has mastered the content and skills of literary analysis, and thus, will need little, if any direct instruction. Progress-monitoring assessment will be based on the results of daily activities. One point here, since many literary analysis activities will be oral discussions, teachers should keep anecdotal records. I know some teachers who do this on their laptop computer; they have a file for each child, and if something noteworthy transpires the teacher makes a note a recess, lunch, or after school (e.g., *5/9/09: Fred make a text-to-text connection today during a discussion without being prompted.*)

Summative assessment will typically be written products. As students respond to prompts posed by the teacher, the results should reveal whether the student has met or exceeded expectations in each of the following areas:

1. Recognizing the structure and characteristics of different literary genres
2. Understanding the literary elements that make a story grammar
3. Engaging in literary analysis and literary criticism

(D) How to Analyze, Interpret, and Use Results

Let's look at the four key points about the analysis, interpretation, and use of assessment results, in relation to comprehension.

(1) ANALYSIS AND INTERPRETATION SHOULD BE STANDARDS-BASED. Teachers need to know, for each standard, which students' level of performance is (a) below expectations, (b) at expectations, or (c) above expectations.

For example, for third grade, one of the *English–Language Arts Content Standards* is that children "determine what characters are like by what they say or do and by how the author or illustrator portrays them" (Literary Response and Analysis, 3.3). The teacher might assess this standard by providing students with the name of a character and a trait. For example, from *Make Way for Ducklings,* "Mrs. Mallard is devoted to her ducklings." The students would then be asked, "How do we know this?" What did Mrs. Mallard do that would lead to this conclusion?"

(2) ANALYSIS AND INTERPRETATION SHOULD REVEAL WHY CHILDREN ARE PERFORMING BELOW EXPECTATIONS.   For this standard, there could be any of a number of reasons students would be unable to discern the relationship between character traits and the reasons we can define those traits. The standard says there are three sources of evidence that help us understand characters in stories: (a) by what they say, (b) by what they do, or (c) by how the author or illustrator has portrayed them. Progress-monitoring assessment should reveal which of the three sources the student understands and which are unclear.

(3) TEACHERS SHOULD USE RESULTS TO CREATE STANDARDS-BASED INDIVIDUAL PROFILES FOR EACH STUDENT.   For this standard, the teacher should not conclude that a student has met or is above expectations unless the students can use all three sources of evidence to define character traits.

(4) TEACHERS SHOULD USE RESULTS TO CREATE STANDARDS-BASED CLASS PROFILES.   As with the class profiles for all standards, the class profile for this standard will allow the teacher to decide whether the entire class needs to work more on understanding the sources of evidence that define character or only a few individuals need help, and whether their needs can be met with individualized or small-group lessons.

CHAPTER 15

Competency 15
Comprehension: Instruction and Assessment—Expository/Informational Texts and Study Skills

INTRODUCTION

The focus of this chapter is on instructional strategies and assessments that are appropriate for expository or informational text. I defined these terms in the previous chapter. In this chapter, I will simplify things by referring to these information-based texts as *expository texts*. Here we are looking at what is sometimes called *content-area literacy*—reading and writing tasks that students complete while learning content. The content areas of the K–12 curricula include social studies, science, mathematics, health, and the study of the visual and performing arts (the history of painting, rather than how to paint).

This chapter also looks at research and study skills children use with encyclopedias, almanacs, and Internet websites.

There are eight topics in this competency:

(1) Characteristics of expository texts
(2) Using text structures
(3) Using text features
(4) Other instructional strategies for content-area textbooks
(5) Oral and written activities for expository texts
(6) Promoting study and research skills
(7) Meeting the needs of all learners
(8) Assessment of comprehension of expository texts and research/study skills

(1) CHARACTERISTICS OF EXPOSITORY TEXTS

Expository texts transmit information and typically are written in formats that differ significantly from narrative texts, which are stories. Here, we are concerned with a variety of expository texts.

(A) Grade-Level Textbooks in Social Studies and Science

When compared to basal readers, social studies and science textbooks have different internal structures, called *text structures* (covered in the next section). And social studies and science textbooks have a far greater array of organizational, typographic, and graphic features, when compared to the stories in basal readers. These *text features* are covered in the third section of this chapter.

(B) Reference Texts

These include encyclopedias, almanacs, thesauruses, atlases, and dictionaries—and they appear in both hard copy and computer-based versions. Reference texts present a great deal of information in a relatively small amount of space.

(C) Other Expository Texts

The list is almost endless—other expository texts include articles in newspapers and magazines, menus, "how-to" manuals, student-generated research reports, and travel brochures.

To repeat, the key thing to remember is that expository texts are different from the stories children are used to reading. The unique content and format of expository texts challenges most young readers. One important difference is that frequently the reader is selective in what he or she reads in an expository text. If the reader's goal is find out what the largest crop is in the state of Iowa, it is not necessary to read the entire entry for Iowa in an encyclopedia. Rather, the reader might look for a subtitle such as "Agriculture" and only read that section. This is far different than reading a story, where readers start at the beginning of a story and continuing reading until the end.

(2) USING TEXT STRUCTURES

In the previous chapter, you read that many stories follow a predictable pattern, and that teachers can use story maps and story grammar outlines to help children understand these patterns. Likewise, most social studies and science textbooks are written in standard patterns or structures. These expository text structures include the following.

(A) Cause and Effect

This structure is common in science textbooks, in which the author is showing that some phenomena result from some other phenomena. It also occurs in social studies textbooks when the author explains why a historical event occurred.

(B) Problem and Solution

In this type of expository text structure, the author presents a problem and then provides an explanation for the reader.

(C) Comparison/Contrast

In this structure, the writer examines the similarities and differences among two or more historical figures, events, or phenomena. The venerable Venn diagram is used represent this text structure and can be used to help students find the similarities and differences between two people, places, or things.

(D) Sequence

The author lists items or events in numerical or chronological order.

(E) Description

The author describes a topic by listing characteristics or features.

Teachers can use these text structures for three purposes: (1) to create a graphic organizer for students to examine before they read; (2) to create a study guide to help students understand the important points of a selection during and after they read; and (3) to assess the content-area reading comprehension.

Students can use expository text structures to become more efficient readers of content--area texts. Readers can use the author's organizational structure to make predictions about which information will be presented, to clarify information that seems contradictory, and to summarize the key points of a chapter.

Appendix G shows diagrams of these expository text structures.

(3) USING TEXT FEATURES

In addition to using text structures to improve comprehension of expository texts, teachers should also teach lessons to help students make effective use of the wealth of text features that are a part of many expository texts.

(A) Organizational/Explanatory Features

Several organizational/explanatory features in expository texts can assist the reader. These include the following.

(1) THE TABLE OF CONTENTS.   I think I can safely assume that you know what a table of contents is.

(2) INDEX.   Few elementary children develop the ability to skillfully use an index, and this should be the focus of lessons at each grade level from grade 2 and higher.

(3) GLOSSARY.   A glossary is a focused dictionary—providing definitions of words within a specific subject. Most elementary school social studies and science textbooks include glossaries.

(4) GUIDE WORDS.   Guide words appear at the top of each page of a dictionary or encyclopedia. They are the first entry word and the last entry word on each page.

(B) Typographical Features

Typographical features are more prevalent in expository text and than in narrative text and include *italics, boldfacing, underlining*, and *color coding*.

(C) Graphic Features

These include *charts, maps, diagrams*, and *illustrations*.

(D) Instruction on Text Features

Teachers should use the gradual release of responsibility model when teaching students to use text features to improve their comprehension of expository texts. You might recall that in this model of teaching, in the first phase the teacher models the process and the student watches and listens. In the second phase, the teacher completes some of the task and the children complete the rest. In the final phase, the students complete the task and the teacher provides feedback. Please note for some complicated processes, there might be several lessons in each phase.

For example, if a teacher were to teach students to use an index, the first two or three lessons would involve the teacher demonstrating how to use the index to find the page number of a specific topic. The teacher would make use of *think-alouds*—explaining his or her thought process while using the index. In the second phase of lessons, the teacher would assist students by picking a topic and providing the page number in the index where the topic appears. Once the children find the topic, the teacher would explain what multiple page numbers after the topic means (e.g., Trade laws, 138–139, 142, 148). The students would then be responsible for going to the relevant page and answering a question the teacher has posed. In the final phase, the students would complete the entire process while the teacher observes and provides feedback—both positive and corrective.

(4) OTHER INSTRUCTIONAL STRATEGIES FOR CONTENT-AREA TEXTBOOKS

Many of the instructional strategies to enhance comprehension presented in Chapter 13, such as question classification/answer verification and strategic reading, can be used with social studies and science textbooks. Perhaps the best way to frame our discussion here is to answer the question, "What comprehension-building instructional activities are unique to content-area textbooks?" We will examine (a) linking what has been learned previously to the present reading assignment, (b) previewing the reading assignment with a graphic organizer, (c) focusing student attention on essential information, and (d) teaching students how to use text structures.

(A) Before Students Read: Linking to What Has Been Learned Previously

One prereading strategy unique to social studies and science textbooks is connecting the content learned previously with the content of the day's reading assignment. Obviously, this is not important with lessons based on stories in a basal reader, because each story usually is unrelated to the stories before and after it. Chapters in a social studies or science textbooks, however, usually are related to each other. In fact, in many instances students will be able to better understand the information presented in one chapter if they review what they have learned previously. For example, a chapter on the habitats of amphibians may be preceded by a chapter on the anatomy of amphibians. Unless students recall the unique aspects of amphibians' bodies, they won't understand why they live where they do. There are many ways to link information students will be expected to learn to what they have learned previously.

(1) REVIEW OF A KWL CHART OR A DATA RETRIEVAL CHART.   If the class completed a KWL chart on the material they learned previously, the chart could be reexamined. Data retrieval charts and summary charts will be described later in this chapter. They could be used to review the material students read the day before a content-area reading lesson.

(2) SELECTIVE REREADING.   Another easy way to review information presented in a previous chapter of a social studies or science text is to take a second look at that chapter. In other words, before reading Chapter 4, the teacher will have the students open their textbooks to Chapter 3. Together, the class again will look at illustrations and discuss major chapter headings. Students might also be asked to reread a summary of the chapter. This is called *skimming* the text.

(B) Before Students Read: Previewing With a Graphic Organizer

Another useful prereading tool is a graphic organizer. Graphic organizers also are called *structured overviews*. A graphic organizer provides students with an overview of what they will read, usually for an entire chapter in a social studies or science textbook. A well-designed graphic organizer presents the key points of a chapter in an easy-to-read format. It is, in fact, a simple outline of the chapter. Graphic organizers are based on the following text structures (included in Appendix G): cause and effect, problem and solution, comparison and contrast, sequence, and description. Remember, a graphic organizer:

1. Is prepared by the teacher,
2. Has relatively few words and summarizes the main points of a chapter, and
3. Is examined before students read.

Appendix H is an example of a graphic organizer.

(C) During and After Students Read: Focusing Student Attention With Study Guides

When students are asked to read their social studies or science textbooks, teachers should emphasize essential information in the selection. This should be done while students read and immediately thereafter. Middle school and high school teachers have used study guides for years (also called *reading guides*). They can also be used effectively with elementary school children. The purpose of all study guides is to focus student attention on key information in the text. Children complete the guides while working in small groups, or the guides may be completed by the whole class with the teacher's assistance, or children may be asked to complete them individually. Study guides can be constructed in a number of formats.

(1) STUDY GUIDES BASED ON TEXT STRUCTURES.   Study guides based on the text's structure are particularly effective because they direct students to use the text's structure to find the missing information. This type of study guide resembles a graphic organizer, but it has either questions or "fill-in-the-blanks." The students complete the guide while they are reading. A study guide based on the text structure of cause and effect is Appendix I.

(2) KEY QUESTIONS STUDY GUIDE. The simplest study guide is a set of questions based on the most important information in the text. For children who have difficulty reading content-area material, some teachers include the page number(s) where the answers can be found. A simple study guide like this would be as follows:

Study Guide—The Russians in California Pages 122–123

1. Where in Alaska had the Russians built a trading post?
2. Why did Nikolai Rezanov sail to San Francisco?
3. How long did the Russians stay at Fort Ross? Why did they leave?

---

(3) THREE-LEVEL STUDY GUIDE. This type of study guide, sometimes called an *interlocking guide*, typically defines three levels of comprehension: literal, interpretative, and applied. As originally conceived, the three-level guide consisted of statements written by the teacher; students check those that are true. Other three-level guides consist of two or three questions from each of the levels of comprehension. Here we will base our guide on RICA's three levels of comprehension: literal, inferential, and evaluative. The sample three-level guide below features a combination of true–false statements and questions:

Three-Level Study Guide—The Articles of Confederation Pages 77–80

Literal

Check each statement that is true:

_____ *The Articles of Confederation were the first "constitution" of the United States.*

_____ *The Articles provided for a Senate and House of Representatives.*

Inferential

Check each statement that is true:

_____ *Ambitious politicians who wanted to be president would be frustrated if we still used The Articles.*

_____ *It would have been difficult for the United States to become a world power while under The Articles.*

Evaluative

If you thought The Articles were a better set of rules than our current Constitution, what three arguments would you make?

(D) During and After Students Read: Data Retrieval Charts

Data retrieval charts allow students to record information in a framework provided by the teacher. They do not require a great deal of writing, and they focus students on the essential information in a selection. Below is a data retrieval chart for a chapter on the United States Congress.

Data Retrieval Chart The United States Congress		
	House of Reps	**Senate**
Number of legislators	_____	_____
Term of office	_____	_____
Minimum age	_____	_____
Presiding officer	_____	_____

(5) ORAL AND WRITTEN ACTIVITIES FOR EXPOSITORY TEXTS

There are many possibilities for oral and written activities for expository texts.

(A) Evaluating the Text

(1) "HOW-TO" TEXTS.   If the purpose of the text was to explain how to do something, such as the directions for assembling a product or a recipe for a meal, students could be asked to evaluate the text's clarity. Was each step easy to follow? Were the steps in the right sequence?

(2) PERSUASIVE TEXTS.   Moving away from social studies textbooks for a moment, some expository texts will be persuasive. These include editorials in newspapers and advertisements for goods and services. Students should be challenged to question the quality of the author's argument. In a persuasive text, the author will present a point of view, or thesis. Teachers should ask students to determine whether the author's thesis is well supported with relevant information. Is the supporting evidence factual? Does the supporting evidence seem reasonable? Students also should determine whether the author has distorted the competing perspectives.

(B) Similarities and Differences Between Texts on the Same Topic

One excellent stimulus for discussion or writing is to have students read two or three expository texts on the same topic. For example, third graders might read three different biographies of an historical figure. Do the texts all present the same information? Are there inconsistencies?

(C) Summarizing and Paraphrasing

Two important challenges for expository texts are summarizing and paraphrasing. Can students distill what they have read in a chapter into two or three paragraphs or five or six sentences? Those are summarizing challenges. Can students restate what they have learned in their own words? That is a paraphrasing challenge.

(D) Creating Graphic Organizers or Semantic Maps (or Webs)

One challenge for advanced learners would be for them to read a chapter from a textbook before the rest of the class will read it and ask them to create the graphic organizer that will be displayed before the chapter is read. Another powerful tool to help students organize what they have learned is to have them complete a semantic map (or "web") on what they have learned. Sometimes the teacher will start the semantic map by placing the key concept in the center of the diagram and providing students with "satellite" topics that key facts will fall under.

(6) PROMOTING STUDY AND RESEARCH SKILLS

(A) Specialized Reading Experiences: Skimming, Scanning, In-Depth Reading

(1) SKIMMING.   Skimming is a fast reading of a text, usually for purposes of preview or review. While skimming, the reader is looking for key words, subtitles, and important sentences. This type of reading develops only with practice. Teachers should model skimming and then challenge students to skim a page or two on their own.

(2) SCANNING.   Scanning, on the other hand, is a rapid reading to find specific information. The reader must swiftly sweep over the page, looking for a path to the correct details. As with skimming, this type of reading is learned with practice. The teacher should model scanning and then provide guided practice for children.

(3) IN-DEPTH READING.   Finally, some assignments require students to read a content-area selection very carefully, aiming for a full understanding of the information presented. There are many tools students could use to assist themselves with this type of reading.

SQ3R is an old technique, first proposed in 1946, for helping students become proficient at in-depth reading. SQ3R stands for *survey, question, read, recite, review*. First, students survey the chapter, looking at the title, subtitles, captions, and anything in bold type. Next, they write two or three questions they think the chapter will answer. Third, the students read the chapter, looking for answers to their questions. Fourth, students test themselves on the material presented in the chapter, stating aloud key points. Finally, students periodically review what they have learned, using their written questions and answers as a guide.

(B) Research Skills—Gathering Information From Encyclopedias

Study skills refer to locating and retrieving information from such reference materials as almanacs, atlases, encyclopedias, and, now, Internet websites. There are some things teachers should cover with their students.

(1) LESSONS ON THE ORGANIZATION OF AN ENCYCLOPEDIA. Teachers should help students understand that information is organized by topics, called entries, that are arranged in different volumes in alphabetical order. For example, a first lesson might involve showing students a full set of encyclopedias. Then, the teacher would present some sample entries (*archery, Wisconsin, insects*) and ask students to identify the volume where the entry would be located.

(2) LESSONS ON HOW TO USE THE INDEX, GUIDE WORDS, AND CROSS-REFERENCES. Once students understand the organization of an encyclopedia, the teacher should teach how to swiftly find information by using the index, the guide words on each page, and the cross-references within each entry. The essential task here is to give children topics, and then help them find the relevant pages as quickly as possible.

(3) HOW TO SCAN FOR SPECIFIC INFORMATION. Finally, once students have located the relevant page number for an entry, they need to practice scanning to find the information they need.

(C) Research Skills: Note Taking, Outlining, and Alternatives

Elementary school students will need a great deal of help in learning how to take notes and make outlines. Teachers must model both processes, but even then, most students will need a high level of scaffolding. For note taking, many teachers help students by providing a template with subtopics to organize each student's notes. For example, for students gathering information about Jackie Robinson's early life:

> *How Jackie Got His Name*
>
> *Brothers and Sisters*
>
> *From Georgia to Pasadena*
>
> *High School Sports Hero*

Likewise, few elementary school students will be able to create their own outlines. Teachers will usually have to provide the major topics. For students who struggle, the outline may need to be in the form of questions that the students answer.

(1) ALTERNATIVES TO NOTE TAKING. Most elementary school children find it very difficult to take notes while reading reference material. This is an important skill because it allows the reader to preserve important information he or she has found in an almanac, atlas, encyclopedia, or website. One alternative is the *I-Chart*.

The use of I-Charts (information charts) will help children retrieve and preserve information from reference sources. The I-Chart is a sheet of paper containing the following information: the student's name, the student's research topic, a subtopic of that topic, a section entitled, "what I already know," a place to write new information, a place to write the bibliographic information about the reference source, a space for "other related information," a space for "important words," and a space for new questions. Each time a student consults a reference source, he or she completes an I-Chart.

(D) Research Skills: Specific Process Skills

There are four important process skills students must be taught to help them write research reports.

(1) IDENTIFYING RESEARCH TOPICS. Teachers will set many different purposes when students read (e.g., build comprehension, vocabulary), but whatever the teacher's purpose, students should be allowed to use reading as a source of topics they personally want to learn more about. Many teachers encourage students to write down questions they have in their journals after they have read.

Once something from their reading experiences has sparked their interest, elementary school students will need help defining a researchable question. The key here is narrowing the focus. For example, a student who wants to know more about the Olympics will easily become frustrated; there is simply too much information to be gathered and analyzed. Working with the student, the teacher discovered that the student really wanted to know more about the Olympic flag. A researchable question was, "What does the Olympic flag look like and why were the symbols and colors chosen?" Eventually, of course, the goal is to have students define their own researchable questions.

To summarize, appropriate topics have the following characteristics: (a) they are neither too narrow nor too broad; (b) there are adequate, accessible resources on the topic; and (c) the topic is phrased as a question. For example, the topic of "ships" is too broad, whereas the topic of "sails" is probably too narrow. A more appropriate topic would be "Why do the sailboats in the America's Cup competition go so fast?"

(2) DEVELOPING AN ACADEMIC ARGUMENT. Some research reports completed by older students should be persuasive. For example, "No More Smog—A Solution." In this type of expository text, the student must learn how to identify a few strong advocacy points and support them with data.

(3) USING MULTIPLE SOURCES. This is essential—students need to learn how to use Internet websites, hard copy encyclopedias, information books, and other texts to find information. The real challenge is synthesizing information from multiple sources.

(4) USING TECHNOLOGY TO MANAGE INFORMATION. Older elementary school children should learn how to use computer-based resources to manage the information they collect. For example, instead of taking hard copy notes, notes could be entered into laptop computer. Students can learn how to cut and paste information from multiple sources into a single document.

(7) MEETING THE NEEDS OF ALL LEARNERS

(A) Struggling Readers and Students With Learning Disabilities

(1) ASSISTING THE STUDENTS WITH READING TEXTBOOKS. Although there will be basal readers at many grade levels, there will be only one social studies textbook and only one science textbook for your grade level. Struggling readers will have a great deal of difficulty with grade-level textbooks. There are a number of ways to help struggling readers access textbooks:

- Record a chapter on tape and let struggling readers listen to the tape before they are asked to read the chapter.
- The teacher reads aloud portions of a chapter either before, during, or after students are asked to read the chapter.
- Struggling readers are given additional instruction in key vocabulary before they are asked to read a chapter.

(2) FOCUSING ON KEY CONTENT/RETEACH. Another way of differentiating instruction for struggling readers would be to teach additional lessons on the key content of a chapter in a textbook. These additional lessons would reduce the information load on the students by focusing on a small number of key points.

(3) MORE SCAFFOLDING ON KEY PROCESSES.   When teaching processes such as using text features, gathering information, or taking notes, struggling readers will need a great deal of help. Teachers must do some of the task themselves, which will reduce the amount of work struggling readers need to complete.

(4) VOCABULARY INSTRUCTION WITH REAL OBJECTS, ILLUSTRATIONS, DIAGRAMS.   As noted in previous chapters, real objects, illustrations, and diagrams help struggling readers learn the meanings of words. Unfortunately, of course, not every word can be taught in this fashion (for example, the meaning of *peninsula* can be taught with an illustration; the meaning of *justice* cannot).

(B) English Learners and Speakers of Nonstandard English

(1) EXPLICIT MODELING.   English learners will need explicit modeling of the processes described in this chapter. For example, in a series of lessons on gathering information from an encyclopedia, the teacher should use think-alouds and use deliberate movements when selecting the correct volume, using the guide words, and using subtitles.

(2) USING ORAL LANGUAGE AND WRITING ACTIVITIES TO SUPPORT CONTENT-AREA KNOWLEDGE.   To help English learners acquire the key concepts presented in expository texts, teachers should plan oral language activities and writing experiences as follow-ups to reading assignments. English learners, working in groups that include their monolingual English-speaking peers, should talk about the concepts and facts presented in expository texts. Then, English learners should write about what they have learned. The combination of oral language activities and written experiences will strengthen their understanding of key concepts.

(3) BUILDING BACKGROUND KNOWLEDGE WITH L1 RESOURCES.   A lack of background knowledge makes comprehension difficult. If there are resources in an English learner's first language, then the English learner should read those to build background knowledge. For example, if a fifth-grade class is going to read about insect metamorphosis, then a Spanish-speaking English learner would benefit from reading a description of the topic in Spanish before reading the relevant chapter in English.

(4) VOCABULARY INSTRUCTION WITH REAL OBJECTS, ILLUSTRATIONS, AND DIAGRAMS, AND ASSISTING THE STUDENTS WITH READING TEXTBOOKS.   These two interventions described in the previous section work well with English learners.

(C) Advanced Learners

The same forms of differentiation mentioned in previous chapters can be used with advanced learners.

(1) INCREASE THE PACE.   Advanced learners will not take long to learn the processes described in the chapter. Only a few lessons will be necessary, for example, to teach advanced learners how to read some forms of charts, and this can be very difficult for most elementary school children.

(2) MORE ADVANCED TEXTS.   There are expository texts on almost all topics written at all reading levels. When doing research reports, advanced learners can be challenged to gather information from sources written for readers well beyond their grade level.

(3) EXTENDING DEPTH AND BREADTH.   Advanced learners won't have difficulty with the grade-level textbook. They will need some challenges. Advanced learners should be asked to explore topics beyond those that the rest of their classmates will study. For example, for a fourth-grade class learning about the California Gold Rush, advanced learners could research how the price of gold is determined.

(8) ASSESSMENT OF COMPREHENSION OF EXPOSITORY TEXTS AND RESEARCH/STUDY SKILLS

(A) Using Text Structures

Teachers can use text structures to assess student comprehension of a content-area text. The teacher provides a "skeleton" and the students complete the missing parts. For example, take another look at Appendix G. The Venn diagram is a good way to show a comparison. A test for a science textbook chapter on the planet Mars might use a Venn diagram, with one circle for Earth and the other for Mars. Students would be challenged to list three things unique to Earth (abundance of water), three things the planets share (polar caps), and three things unique to Mars (atmosphere almost entirely carbon dioxide).

(B) Multilevel Questions

In Chapter 13, I described how to use the QAR system to create simple tests of a child's mastery of comprehension skills, especially the higher order skills of inference and evaluation. Teachers should use the QAR hierarchy with social studies and science textbooks to assess their students' ability to answer all types of questions. Again, it is essential to see whether students can answer the think-and-search, author-and-you, and on-my-own types of questions.

(C) Teacher Observation/Anecdotal Records

Teachers can gather useful data about the content-area reading performance of their students by simply observing their behavior and taking notes. For example, when students are asked to read in their science textbook and retrieve information by completing a chart, a teacher should note who completes the task easily and who struggles. Likewise, if a student trying to find information in an encyclopedia is unable to use guide words to locate the appropriate entry, the teacher should make a note of that. Over the course of time, these informal notes begin to add up and can be used to support your conclusions. If, for example, you think that Fred has difficulty reading his social studies textbook, then it helps if you have anecdotal notes from September 11, October 2, and October 16 verifying that conclusion.

(D) Readability of Texts

One other evaluation concept needs to be explained here. Readability is a measure of the difficulty of a text. Several readability formulas exist that teachers can use to determine whether a child can read a specific book. Readability formulas are applied to a passage from a book. These formulas measure the difficulty of a text by calculating (1) word length and the number of syllables in the passage and (2) the number of words in sentences. Two well-known readability formulas are the Fry Graph Readability Formula and the Raygor Readability Estimate.

Your reading methods text will explain how to administer a readability formula. There have always been many questions about the validity of these formulas because they don't take into account the quality of the text's writing, nor do they measure a student's interest in the topic the text addresses. It is always easier to read something well written because information presented is more interesting. Finally, the utility of readability formulas is diminished by the time it takes the teacher to use them.

Once again, if a teacher has determined a child's independent, instructional, and frustration reading levels through an IRI, then a readability formula would tell the teacher how a textbook or an information book from the library "fits" a child's reading ability.

(E) Entry-Level, Progress-Monitoring, and Summative Purposes

The fact of the matter is that few teachers conduct a thorough assessment of either (1) students' ability to comprehend their social studies and science books or (2) students' ability to gather information from reference materials. When teaching a process, such as using an index, entry-level assessment is essential—some students will already have mastered the process and won't need any instruction. Progress-monitoring assessment requires skillful observation of students' behavior and careful analysis of their written work. Summative assessment should be standards-based and clearly indicate which students have met or exceeded which standards.

(F) How to Analyze, Interpret, and Use Results

(1) ANALYSIS AND INTERPRETATION SHOULD BE STANDARDS-BASED. Teachers need to know, for each standard, which students' level of performance is (a) below expectations, (b) at expectations, or (c) above expectations.

For example, for fourth grade, one of the *English–Language Arts Content Standards* is that students are able to "use a thesaurus to determine related words and concepts" (Vocabulary and Concept Development, 1.6). Students who are below expectations either can't locate target words in a thesaurus or don't understand the function of this reference source. On the other hand, a student who can use a thesaurus to find synonyms and antonyms has met expectations. Students who go beyond expectations are those who can distinguish which synonym is closest in meaning to a target word.

(2) ANALYSIS AND INTERPRETATION SHOULD REVEAL WHY CHILDREN ARE PERFORMING BELOW EXPECTATIONS. In many cases, this involves talking individually with children to determine why they are "not getting it." This is a difficult standard to meet, and many children will struggle with making good use of the information in a thesaurus.

(3) TEACHERS SHOULD USE RESULTS TO CREATE STANDARDS-BASED INDIVIDUAL PROFILES FOR EACH STUDENT. For this standard, the individual profiles might be even more specific. For example, Fred's individual profile shows that he quickly learned how to use a thesaurus and that he has used this resource on several occasions without being told to do so. He clearly has gone above expectations for the standard.

(4) TEACHERS SHOULD USE RESULTS TO CREATE STANDARDS-BASED CLASS PROFILES. As has been stated earlier, the class profile will tell the teacher how the class has performed as a group. If many children have failed to meet the standard, then a new set of lessons teaching the standard should be planned. If almost all of the children have met or exceeded the standard, then the teacher should move on and plan remedial lessons for those who continue to need help, either individually or in small groups.

CHAPTER 16

Study Guide: Key Points to Remember

The *RICA Content Specifications* present a huge amount of information. In this chapter, I provide a study guide covering the most important items in the *Content Specifications*. Please note that I am being selective here. You should read the entire book before you focus on the topics and items listed below.

(1) PLANNING, ORGANIZING, AND MANAGING READING INSTRUCTION (COMPETENCY 1, CHAPTER 1)

1.1 The role of the *English–Language Arts Content Standards*
1.2 The role of the *California Reading/Language Arts Framework* of 2007
1.3 Definition of *differentiated instruction*
1.4 Components of instructional delivery in the *California Reading/Language Arts Framework*

(2) INDEPENDENT READING (COMPETENCY 1, CHAPTER 1)

2.1 I + I strategy for reluctant readers
2.2 How to assess student independent reading: Individual conferences

(3) READING ASSESSMENT (COMPETENCY 2, CHAPTER 2)

3.1 Definitions of *entry-level assessment, progress-monitoring assessment*, and *summative assessment*
3.2 How to differentiate assessment of students with an IEP or Section 504 Plan: (1) break into smaller units, and (2) provide practice assessment
3.3 Contents and purpose of an IRI
3.4 Criteria to determine frustration, instructional, and independent reading levels
3.5 Purposes of standards-based individual profiles and group profiles

(4) PHONOLOGICAL AWARENESS AND PHONEMIC AWARENESS (COMPETENCY 3, CHAPTER 3)

4.1 Definitions

Phonological awareness versus *phonemic awareness*

Phonemic awareness versus *phonics*

4.2 Instruction

Phonemic awareness tasks: Sound isolation, sound identity, sound blending, sound segmentation

4.3 Assessment

Start with test of phonemic segmentation; if failed, test other tasks

4.4 Differentiation

Struggling readers: Focus on key skills of blending and segmenting

English learners: Teach phonemes that don't exist in first language (L1)

(5) CONCEPTS ABOUT PRINT (COMPETENCY 4, CHAPTER 4)

5.1 Definitions

What are the four concepts about print?

5.2 Instruction

The Shared Book Experience

5.3 Assessment

Informal assessment by teacher: Picture book, crayon, paper

5.4 Differentiation

Struggling readers: Reteach key concepts, such as directionality

English learners: Take advantage of transfer between L1 and English (e.g., directionality is the same from Spanish to English)

(6) LETTER RECOGNITION (COMPETENCY 4, CHAPTER 4)

6.1 Definitions

The differences among *letter recognition, letter naming, letter formation*

6.2 Instruction

Direct instruction with practice writing the letters

6.3 Assessment

Letter recognition: Teacher names letter, child points

Letter naming: Teacher points, child names letter

Letter formation: Isolation—teacher names, child writes; and Context— assessing a writing sample

6.4 Differentiation

Struggling readers: Tactile and kinesthetic methods

English learners: Take advantage of transfer between L1 and English (e.g., the similarities in the letters in Spanish and English)

(7) PHONICS AND SIGHT WORDS (COMPETENCIES 5 AND 6, CHAPTERS 5 AND 6)

7.1 Definitions

Definition of *phonics*

Which words are taught as sight words?

Definition of *decodable text*

7.2 Instruction

Direct instruction: Whole-to-part (both phonics and sight words)

7.3 Assessment

Decode in isolation: For both phonics and sight words, read a list of target words

Decode in context: Analyze the results of an oral reading

7.4 Differentiation

Struggling readers: (1) Phonics: Use concrete examples, use three-dimensional letter tiles; (2) Sight words: Additional practice with high-frequency words

English learners: Highlighting language differences: Explicitly teach letters that represent sounds that don't exist in L1

(8) SYLLABIC ANALYSIS AND STRUCTURAL ANALYSIS (COMPETENCY 7, CHAPTER 7)

8.1 Definitions

> Definition of *syllabic analysis*
>
> Definition of *structural analysis*
>
> Definition of *morpheme, affix, prefix*

8.2 Instruction

> Structural analysis: Whole-to-part lesson
>
> Syllabic analysis: Teach common syllable patterns (e.g., never divide compounds between the root words)

8.3 Assessment

> Structural analysis: Isolation—read aloud nonsense words; Context—oral reading of a specially written paragraph with many words with prefixes and suffixes

8.4 Differentiation

> Struggling readers: Key skills—how to spell and pronounce common prefixes, suffixes, and root words
>
> English learners: Key skills—same as above

(9) ORTHOGRAPHIC KNOWLEDGE/SPELLING (COMPETENCY 7, CHAPTER 7)

9.1 Definitions

> None

9.2 Instruction

> Multisensory techniques: visual—use of color, auditory, kinesthetic, tactile, mental imagery

9.3 Assessment

> Isolation—traditional spelling test; Context—analysis of writing samples

9.4 Differentiation

> Struggling readers: Increased use of tactile and auditory study activities
>
> English learners: Teach common English roots and affixes

(10) FLUENCY (COMPETENCIES 8 AND 9; CHAPTERS 8 AND 9)

10.1 Definitions

> Key indicators of fluency: *accuracy, rate, prosody*
>
> Definition of *automaticity theory*

10.2 Instruction

> Monitored oral reading with teacher: Model, practice, feedback

10.3 Assessment

> Accuracy: Oral reading, teacher records errors
>
> Rate: Timed oral readings to calculate words correct per minute (wcpm)
>
> Prosody: Oral reading—assess for appropriate pitch, response to punctuation, characterization

10.4 Differentiation

> Struggling readers: Additional practice—oral reading
>
> English learners: Phrase-cued reading

(11) VOCABULARY, ACADEMIC LANGUAGE, BACKGROUND KNOWLEDGE (COMPETENCIES 10 AND 11, CHAPTERS 10 AND 11)

11.1 Definitions

Differences among *listening, speaking, writing, sight,* and *meaning vocabularies*

Definition of *word consciousness*

Difference between *technical (or specific) academic language* and *nontechnical academic language*

Definition of *background knowledge*

11.2 Instruction

Small group of words: Contextual Redefinition

One important word: Semantic Map

Small group of related words: Semantic Feature Analysis

Importance of teaching nontechnical academic language

11.3 Assessment

Test: Each target word in a sentence, multiple choice definitions

11.4 Differentiation

Struggling readers: Focus on words absolutely necessary to understanding the text

English learners: Cognates

(12) COMPREHENSION: ANY TEXT (COMPETENCIES 12 AND 13, CHAPTERS 12 AND 13)

12.1 Definitions

Definitions of *literal, inferential,* and *evaluative comprehension*

Definition of *text structure*

12.2 Instruction

To build literal comprehension: Story Maps (see 13.2 below)

To build inferential and evaluative comprehension: Question Classification/Answer Verification

To build strategic reading: Gradual Release of Responsibility

12.3 Assessment

Determine reading levels: Reading passages in an IRI

Assess literal, inferential, evaluative comprehension: Ask questions using a taxonomy such as the QAR

12.4 Differentiation

Struggling readers: Reteaching reading strategies

English learners: Same

(13) COMPREHENSION OF NARRATIVE/LITERARY TEXTS (COMPETENCY 14, CHAPTER 14)

13.1 Definitions

Definition of *narrative text*

Definition of *genre*

Elements of a story grammar: Character, plot, setting, mood, theme, style

13.2 Instruction

Story elements, literal comprehension: Story Maps

13.3 Assessment

Analysis of discussion and writing: Text-to-self, text-to-text, text-to-world

13.4 Differentiation

> Struggling readers: Focus on key elements of story grammar

> English learners: Clarify the cultural context of a story

(14) COMPREHENSION OF EXPOSITORY/INFORMATIONAL TEXTS (COMPETENCY 15, CHAPTER 15)

14.1 Definitions

> Definition of *expository texts*

> Definition of *content-area literacy*

> Difference between *skimming* and *scanning*

14.2 Instruction

> Using text structures, prereading: Graphic Organizers

> Using text structures, during and after reading: Study Guides

14.3 Assessment

> Using text structures: Students complete a Graphic Organizer

14.4 Differentiation

> Struggling readers: Increase scaffolding on written assignments (e.g., provide page number location of answers)

> English learners: Build background knowledge with L1 resources

CHAPTER 17

The Case Study

In this chapter I will present a process for answering the case study. This method has been used successfully by hundreds of students I have taught at Cal State East Bay and in my one-day RICA preparation classes. It worked for the original RICA and I think it will work for the revised RICA.

In the case study section of the exam, you will be presented with background information about a student and samples of materials illustrating the student's reading performance. The hypothetical student could be in any grade, kindergarten through grade 8. The test will provide you with "raw" data, copies of between 5 and 10 assessments of reading performance. You write an essay, with three parts.

Don't forget how important the case study is. I am not sure how the revised RICA will be scored, but on the original RICA, it was possible to obtain 24 of the 81 points needed to pass on the case study alone!

My process for answering the RICA has three parts: (1) budget your time, (2) understand the examinee tasks, (3) use the major topics in the RICA *Content Specifications* as criteria for analyzing the data, and (4) organize your essay under clear subtitles.

BUDGET YOUR TIME

You must give yourself one hour to answer the case study. You will have one hour if you devote 90 minutes to the multiple choice section, 15 minutes each to the two short essays (total of 30 minutes), and 25 minutes each to the two long essays (50 minutes total). Should you answer the case study first? I will leave that up to you. Some of my students think it works well to answer the case study first, when you are freshest. Others students answer the case study last and do the rest of the test first. The multiple choice questions and essays then "activate their background knowledge" about reading instruction.

UNDERSTAND THE EXAMINEE TASKS

The Practice Test on the official RICA web has a sample case study (**www.rica.nesinc. com**). The examinee (that's you) is asked to write a three-part essay. It is important that you do exactly what is asked of you in each part. Your answer must fit on four pages and should be about 300 to 600 words.

Part One: Identify Strengths/Needs and Cite Evidence

In the first part of your answer you will be asked to identify three of the student's important reading strengths and/or needs. You must cite evidence from the documents to support each strength or need. Please note: you identify a *total* of three strengths and/or needs. That can be three strengths; or three needs; or two strengths and one need; or two needs and one strength. My guess is that your case study will focus on a student who has some clearly identifiable areas of need.

This part of your answer should have three paragraphs. In each paragraph you will (a) identify the strength or need and (b) cite the specific document that you used as evidence (which could be a test, or a worksheet, a teacher's anecdotal notes, etc.).

Part Two: Describe Two Instructional Strategies or Activities

In the second part of your answer, you will describe two instructional strategies or activities that either address a need or build on a strength. Please note: two means two. When I pose a case study-like question to my reading methods students, there is a tendency among some students to ignore the examine task and describe several instructional interventions. This is a mistake! Select *just two* instructional strategies or activities, each one must clearly help the student.

This part of your answer should have two long paragraphs, and should be longer than the first part. It is absolutely essential that you describe what both the teacher and the student will do in each activity. It is not enough to write that "the student needs to take part in Reciprocal Teaching lessons," or to write "I would implement direct, explicit lessons in phonics." You must go further and write about what happens during each activity. The section is purely descriptive, *don't* explain why you chose the strategy or activity (that's the next section).

Part Three: Explain

In the final part of your answer, you will explain how each strategy will help the student. This part of your answer should have two paragraphs, one for each instructional strategy/activity you described in the second section. There are two types of explanations you should provide here.

First, you could write about *the connection* between the student's area of need and the activity. Example:

> Reciprocal Teaching will work for the student because it focuses on summarizing, a strategy that the student clearly lacks. The results of both the comprehension test and individual conference showed that this student has a great deal of difficulty summarizing. Reciprocal Teaching follows a gradual release of responsibility model, so the student will have many opportunities to see me (the teacher) model summarization before trying these tasks under my guidance.

Second, you can also explain the *underlying rationale* for the activity. Example:

> Tactile spelling activities will help the student because they open up another sensory "channel," touch, that is not used in other spelling lessons. The tactile spelling activity described in the previous section allows the student to feel the letters in vowel digraphs at the same time she hears and sees them.

USING THE RICA TOPICS AS CRITERIA FOR ANALYSIS

The most logical way to organize your analysis of the data in the case study is by the major topics in the *RICA Content Specifications*:

Independent Reading (abbreviated as "INDRD")

Phonological Awareness and Phonemic Awareness (PA)

Concepts About Print (CAP)

Letter Recognition (LET)

Phonics and Sight Words (PHSW)

Syllabic and Structural Analysis (SYST)

Orthographic Knowledge/Spelling (SPL)

Fluency (FL)

Vocabulary, Academic Language, Background Knowledge (VOACBK)

Comprehension: Any Text (COANY)

Comprehension: Narrative/Literary Texts (CONAR)

Comprehension: Expository/Information Texts (COEXP)

I suggest that before you start reading the case study, you make a little chart in your test booklet (there will page for you to write notes). The chart would look like this:

INDRD

PA

CAP

LET

PHSW

SYST

SPL

FL

VOACBK

COANY

CONAR

COEXP

These are abbreviations for the topics listed previously.

Then, as you read each source of information, use the chart to record whether each area is a strength or area of need. No case study, of course, will address every topic. And if your case study presents more than three areas of strength and/or need, there will be many different possible correct answers.

I will use the case study that appears in the Practice Test on the RICA website as an example. The hypothetical third-grade student, Isabel, demonstrates strong phonics and word identification skills on an informal reading assessment. In a follow-up discussion with her teacher, however, she answers two literal questions correctly but misses an inferential question. Most of the sources in this case study show that Isabel does not read enough independently. The results of a student reading survey, her teacher's notes, an excerpt from a reading log, and a dialogue with her teacher about the reading log are all consistent. Isabel doesn't read independently, and, in fact, the only books she claims to have read are about her favorite television show. Finally, Isabel does poorly on a worksheet on multiple-meaning words.

For this case study, the RICA topic analysis would look like the following. *S* stands for "area of strength," *N* stands for "area of need," and *NO* stands for "no evidence about this topic."

INDRD	*N—only reads "sometimes" on survey fidgets during independent reading—from notes doesn't read at home—from notes Elmwood Kids—log, dialogue*
PA	*NO*
CAP	*NO*
LET	*NO*
PHSW	*S—only two errors or IRA 97% accuracy on ORF*
SYST	*NO*
SPL	*NO*
FL	*S—97% accuracy in ORF 70 wcpm—at 50th percentile*
VOACBK	*N—poor performance on multiple meanings worksheet*
COANY	*S—literal okay on questions after silent reading N—missed inference question*
CONAR	*NO*
COEXP	*NO*

ORGANIZE YOUR ESSAY WITH SUBTITLES

After you have completed your analysis, take a deep breath. Look at the chart and select the three strengths and/or needs you will address. Decide on the two instructional strategies or activities you will describe and explain. Then, it is time to write! I encourage my students to have their essays organized under clearly stated subtitles. The sample answer to the case study provided on the RICA website does not use subtitles, but I think you should. Why should the examiner reading your test "go fishing" to find answers to each examinee task? Subtitles will make the examiner's job easy.

Here is what my response to the case study on the RICA website looks like:

THREE STRENGTHS/NEEDS

1. ***Strength: Word Identification.*** Isabel has excellent word identification skills. On the informal reading assessment (IRA), she made only two errors (*little, Oregon*). Her short pauses were before difficult words. On the oral reading fluency test (ORF), she read with 97% accuracy and at a rate of 70 wcpm. It should be noted, however, that on both tests she paused before high-frequency, irregular words and low-frequency content words.

2. ***Need: Independent Reading.*** Isabel needs to read more independently at school and at home. The Teacher Notes reveal she was distracted during independent reading time and she did not finish her Pioneer Unit book on time. Her parents do not check to see if she reads at home. The books she claims to have read are about her favorite television show.

3. ***Need: Vocabulary, Multiple Meanings.*** Isabel needs to understand that many words have more than one meaning. On the Worksheet on Multiple-Meaning Words, Katie completed only two of the five exercises correctly.

TWO INSTRUCTIONAL STRATEGIES/ACTIVITIES

1. ***I + I for Independent Reading.*** To help Isabel read more, I would use the I (independent level) + I (interest) strategy. First, I would use an IRI to determine Isabel's independent reading level. Next, I would administer a reading interests survey to find out what type of books Isabel enjoys reading. Then, I would go the library and select two copies of a book that meets both criteria (at her independent level, on a topic of interest). We would read the first book together. Eventually, I would show Isabel how to select books that meet both criteria.

2. ***Sentence Sorts for Multiple Meanings.*** Sentence sorts will address this area of need. The words she missed on the worksheet are all both nouns and verbs (*rose, rock, play*). For each word, I would prepare six sentences, three with the word as a noun and three with the word as a verb. We would learn the definitions of nouns and verbs. Isabel would sort the sentences under the categories of "Word Used as a Noun," and "Word Used as a Verb." We would then do the same activity for other multiple-meaning words.

HOW EACH STRATEGY/ACTIVITY HELPS

1. ***I + I.*** The I + I strategy works because it removes two important reasons students do not read. Some children select books that are either far too easy or far too hard for them. Others do not know how to find books that fit their interests. I + I connects children with books they can read *and* want to read.

2. ***Sentence Sorts.*** Sentence sorts for words with multiple meanings will help Isabel because they show that words can have two "identities," as nouns and verbs. The categorization tasks highlight this feature and focus attention on the words' different meanings.

You definitely should look at the sample answer for the case study provided in the Practice Test on the RICA website. The answer provided there is different from mine. For one thing, it doesn't use subtitles, which I think is a mistake. The sample answer identifies word identification as a strength and the lack of knowledge of multiple meanings as an area of need, like I did. The sample answer, however, does not identify a lack of independent reading as an area of need, rather the sample answer notes Isabel's lack of inferential comprehension as an area of need. The instructional interventions in part two are different than the ones I described.

The important thing to remember is that there will be more than one right answer to the case study on the RICA. I think my answer is a good one and the one provided in Practice Test on the RICA website, though different, is also nicely done.

CHAPTER 18

Working With the Practice Test on the RICA Website

In previous editions of this book I created a sample RICA exam. I decided not to do so this time, because the practice test you should take is the one provided on the official RICA website (http://www.rica.nesinc.com). The Practice Test on the website looks almost exactly like the RICA you will take—with different questions, of course. The only difference between the Practice Test on the RICA website and the RICA you will take is that the Practice Test has only 60 multiple choice questions and the real test will have 70 multiple choice questions.

You should take the Practice Test in the same context as the real test. Give yourself 4 hours and do not refer to any sources for answers. What I have provided is an index explaining what parts of this book you should reread if you missed a question or an essay on the Practice Test.

MULTIPLE CHOICE QUESTIONS

1. Correct answer is C. If you missed this question, reread The Introduction, section on "Common Strategies for Meeting the Needs of All Learners."
2. Correct answer is B. Reread Chapter 1, section 2, "Key Factors in Differentiated Reading Instruction."
3. Correct answer is C. Reread Chapter 1, section 6, "Strategies for Promoting and Monitoring Independent Reading."
4. Correct answer is C. Reread Chapter 1, section 5, "Engaging and Motivating Students."
5. Correct answer is C. Reread Chapter 2, section 4, "Interpretation and Use of Assessment Results."
6. Correct answer is D. Reread Chapter 2, section 2, "Alternative Assessments for Students with an Individualized Education Program (IEP) or a Section 504 Plan."
7. Correct answer is A. Reread Chapter 2, section 2, "Alternative Assessments for Students with an Individualized Education Program (IEP) or a Section 504 Plan."
8. Correct answer is D. Reread Chapter 2, section 4, "Interpretation and Use of Assessment Results."
9. Correct answer is B. Reread Chapter 3, "Introduction" section.
10. Correct answer is A. Reread Chapter 3, section 5, "Assessment of Phonological Awareness, Including Phonemic Awareness."
11. Correct answer is C. Reread Chapter 3, section 2, "How to Teach Phonological Awareness, Including Phonemic Awareness."
12. Correct answer is C. Reread Chapter 3, section 2, "How to Teach Phonological Awareness, Including Phonemic Awareness."
13. Correct answer is A. Reread Chapter 4, section 2, "The Importance of Letter Recognition in Reading Development and Instructional Strategies."
14. Correct answer is B. Reread Chapter 4, section 1, "Concepts About Print: Their Role in Early Reading Development and Instructional Strategies."

15. Correct answer is A. Reread Chapter 4, section 3, "The Alphabetic Principle."
16. Correct answer is B. Reread Chapter 4, section 5, "Meeting the Needs of All Learners."
17. Correct answer is A. Reread Chapter 5, section 2, "The Sequence of Phonics and Sight Word Instruction."
18. Correct answer is A. Reread Chapter 5, section 3, "The Interrelationships Between Phonics Development and Stages of Spelling Development."
19. Correct answer is B. Reread Chapter 5, section 3, "The Interrelationships Between Phonics Development and Stages of Spelling Development."
20. Correct answer is D. Reread Chapter 5, section 2, "The Sequence of Phonics and Sight Word Instruction."
21. Correct answer is A. Reread Chapter 6, section 1, "The Fundamentals of Teaching Phonics."
22. Correct answer is D. Reread Chapter 6, section 6, "Assessment of Phonics and Sight Words."
23. Correct answer is D. Reread Chapter 6, section 1, "The Fundamentals of Teaching Phonics."
24. Correct answer is B. Reread Chapter 6, section 5, "Meeting the Needs of All Learners."
25. Correct answer is A. Reread Chapter 6, section 3, "Systematic, Explicit Instruction in Phonics at the More Advanced Stages."
26. Correct answer is C. Reread Chapter 7, section 2, "How to Teach Structural Analysis and Syllabic Analysis of Multisyllabic Words."
27. Correct answer is A. Reread Chapter 11, section 4, "Developing Word Consciousness in Students."
28. Correct answer is D. Reread Chapter 7, section 5, "Meeting the Needs of All Learners."
29. Correct answer is D. Reread Chapter 11, section 4, "Developing Word Consciousness in Students."
30. Correct answer is D. Reread Chapter 8, section 7, "Independent Silent Reading and the Development of Fluency."
31. Correct answer is B. Reread Chapter 8, section 4, "Factors That Can Disrupt Fluency."
32. Correct answer is C. Reread Chapter 9, section 5, "Meeting the Needs of All Learners."
33. Correct answer is A. Reread Chapter 9, section 3, "Strategies for Building Reading Rate."
34. Correct answer is B. Reread Chapter 9, section 3, "Strategies for Building Reading Rate."
35. Correct answer is B. Reread Chapter 9, section 2, "Specific Strategies for Building Accuracy."
36. Correct answer is D. Reread Chapter 7, section 2, "How to Teach Structural Analysis and Syllabic Analysis of Multisyllabic Words."
37. Correct answer is B. Reread Chapter 11, section 5, "How to Use Wide Reading to Increase Vocabulary, Academic Language, and Background Knowledge."
38. Correct answer is D. Reread Chapter 10, section 2, "Important Issues Related to the Development of Vocabulary, Academic Language, and Background Knowledge."
39. Correct answer is C. Reread Chapter 11, section 3, "Independent Word-Learning Strategies."
40. Correct answer is D. Reread Chapter 11, section 1, "Research-Based Principles of Vocabulary Instruction."
41. Correct answer is C. Reread Chapter 11, section 3, "Independent Word-Learning Strategies."
42. Correct answer is B. Reread Chapter 11, section 8, "Assessment of Vocabulary, Academic Language, and Background Knowledge."
43. Correct answer is D. Reread Chapter 11, section 6, "How to Use Listening, Speaking, Reading, and Writing Activities to Support What Students Have Learned."
44. Correct answer is A. Reread Chapter 11, section 6, "How to Use Listening, Speaking, Reading, and Writing Activities to Support What Students Have Learned."
45. Correct answer is A. Reread Chapter 7, section 2, "How to Teach Structural Analysis and Syllabic Analysis of Multisyllabic Words."
46. Correct answer is D. Reread Chapter 12, section 5, "The Role of Sentence Structure and Text Structures in Facilitating Comprehension."
47. Correct answer is C. Reread Chapter 11, section 4, "Developing Word Consciousness in Students."

48. Correct answer is B. Reread Chapter 7, section 2, "How to Teach Structural Analysis and Syllabic Analysis of Multisyllabic Words."
49. Correct answer is C. Reread Chapter 12, section 5, "The Role of Sentence Structure and Text Structures in Facilitating Comprehension."
50. Correct answer is B. Reread Chapter 11, section 6, "How to Use Listening, Speaking, Reading, and Writing Activities to Support What Students Have Learned."
51. Correct answer is D. Reread Chapter 12, section 5, "The Role of Sentence Structure and Text Structures in Facilitating Comprehension."
52. Correct answer is C. Reread Chapter 15, section 7, "Meeting the Needs of All Learners."
53. Correct answer is C. Reread Chapter 15, section 2, "Using Text Structures."
54. Correct answer is D. Reread Chapter 14, section 6, "Meeting the Needs of All Learners."
55. Correct answer is B. Reread Chapter 13, section 6, "Assessment of Comprehension."
56. Correct answer is B. Reread Chapter 14, section 2, "Instruction in the Elements of Story Grammar."
57. Correct answer is B. Reread Chapter 14, section 2, "Instruction in the Elements of Story Grammar."
58. Correct answer is A. Reread Chapter 15, section 5, "Oral and Written Activities for Expository Texts."
59. Correct answer is C. Reread Chapter 15, section 5, "Oral and Written Activities for Expository Texts."
60. Correct answer is A. Reread Chapter 15, section 5, "Oral and Written Activities for Expository Texts."

OPEN-ENDED ASSIGNMENTS

A. A correct answer is provided with the Practice Test on the RICA website. If your answer was not similar to the one provided there, then you need to review what you learned about reading fluency. Reread Chapters 8 and 9.
B. A correct answer is provided with the Practice Test on the RICA website. If your answer was not similar to the one provided there, then you need to review what you learned about differentiated vocabulary instruction for English learners. Reread Chapter 11, section 7, "Meeting the Needs of All Learners."
C. A correct answer is provided with the Practice Test on the RICA website. If your answer was not similar to the one provided there, then you need to review what you learned about using structural analysis to decode multisyllabic words. Reread Chapter 7.
D. A correct answer is provided with the Practice Test on the RICA website. If your answer was not similar to the one provided there, then you need to review what you learned about literal comprehension. Reread Chapter 12, section 2, "Literal Comprehension," and Chapter 13, section 2, "While Children Read: Question Classification/Answer Verification."

CASE STUDY

A correct answer is provided with the Practice Test on the RICA website. I provided another answer in Chapter 17. If your answer was not similar to the one provided at the end of the Practice Test, or it was not similar to the one I provided in Chapter 17, then reread the following sections of the book:

On word identification (decoding): Chapter 5

On fluency: Chapters 8 and 9

On inferential comprehension: Chapter 12, section 3, "Inferential Comprehension," and Chapter 13, section 2, "While Children Read: Question Classification/Answer Verification"

On vocabulary teaching: Chapter 11

On independent reading: Chapter 1, section 6, "Strategies for Promoting and Monitoring Independent Reading"

APPENDICES

APPENDIX A   Graded Word Lists   139

APPENDIX B   Scoring Sheet for Graded Word Lists   140

APPENDIX C   Graded Reading Passage—Grade 1   141

APPENDIX D   Graded Reading Passage—Grade 6   142

APPENDIX E   Scoring System for Oral Reading Miscue Analysis   143

APPENDIX F   Scoring Sheet—Graded Reading Passage   144

APPENDIX G   Diagrams of Expository Text Structures   145

APPENDIX H   Graphic Organizer   147

APPENDIX I   Study Guide Based on Text Structure   148

APPENDIX A

Graded Word Lists

Student Name ——————— **Highest instructional level (2w)** ———————

A (PP)	**B** (P)	**C** (1.0)	**D** (2.0)
_____the	_____come	_____today	_____biggest
_____am	_____vou	_____does	_____where
_____get	_____went	_____three	_____yourself
_____is	_____him	_____from	_____those
_____and	_____two	_____under	_____before
_____here	_____then	_____began	_____things
_____see	_____know	_____name	_____stopped
_____not	_____around	_____there	_____place
_____can	_____pet	_____could	_____always
_____will	_____house	_____again	_____everyone

E (3.0)	**F** (4.0)	**G** (5.0)	**H** (6.0)
_____morning	_____important	_____because	_____aircraft
_____since	_____airport	_____bridge	_____necessary
_____together	_____through	_____microscope	_____argument
_____begin	_____fifteen	_____curious	_____chemical
_____which	_____information	_____estimation	_____representative
_____near	_____ocean	_____reliable	_____terminal
_____should	_____preview	_____government	_____apology
_____yesterday	_____laughter	_____business	_____instruction
_____eight	_____preparation	_____direction	_____evidence
_____remember	_____building	_____avenue	_____consideration

From Lois A. Bader, *Bader Reading and Language Inventory* (3rd ed.), p. 13. Columbus, OH: Merrill/Prentice Hall, 1998. Reprinted with permission.

APPENDIX B

Scoring Sheet for Graded Word Lists

Student Name _____Valerie_____   **Highest instructional level (2w)** _____/_____
Grade : /

A	B	C	D
(PP)	(P)	(1.0)	(2.0)

A	B	C	D
✓ the	✓ come	✓ today	_BAGGEST_ biggest _C_
✓ am	✓ you	✓ does	✓ where
✓ get	✓ went	✓ three	✓ yourself
✓ is	_HIT_ him _C_	✓ from	✓✓ those
✓ and	✓ two	(under)	✓ before
✓ here	✓ then	✓ began	✓ things
✓ see	_KA-NO_ know	✓ name	_STEPPED_ stopped
✓✓ not	✓✓ around	✓ there	✓✓ place
✓ can	✓ pet	_COLD_ could	(always)
✓ will	✓ house	✓ again	_AIRYONE_ everyone

✓ CORRECT   ✓✓ HESITATES   C SELF-CORRECTION

(oval) COULDN'T SAY

E	F	G	H
(3.0)	(4.0)	(5.0)	(6.0)

E	F	G	H
morning	important	because	aircraft
since	airport	bridge	necessary
together	through	microscope	argument
begin	fifteen	curious	chemical
which	information	estimation	representative
near	ocean	reliable	terminal
should	preview	government	apology
yesterday	laughter	business	instruction
eight	preparation	direction	evidence
remember	building	avenue	consideration

APPENDIX C

Graded Reading Passage—Grade 1

TONY AND THE FLOWER SHOP

Tony lived in a big city. He ran a flower shop. Tony loved his flowers, for the flowers did not make any noise. Tony loved peace and quiet.

The city where Tony lived was noisy. The buses, trucks, and cars were very noisy. He did not like the noise of the city.

Without the quiet Tony found in the flower shop, he would have moved from the city. The flower shop was his only reason for staying in the city.

From Lois A Bader, *Reader's Passages to Accompany Bader Reading and Language Inventory* (3rd ed), p 8 Columbus, OH Merrill/Prentice Hall, 1998 Reprinted with permission.

APPENDIX D

Graded Reading Passage—Grade 6

CONSTELLATIONS

People all over the world have looked at the stars and have seen patterns that reminded them of everyday things. A group of stars that forms such a pattern is a constellation. A constellation lies within a definite region of the sky. By knowing the positions of the constellations, one can locate stars, planets, comets, and other galaxies. There are eighty-eight officially recognized constellations.

Many of the ancient names for certain constellations are still used today, though the things they were named for are no longer a part of our everyday experiences.

Almost anyone who grew up in the Northern Hemisphere can point out the Little Dipper. The Little Dipper is part of the constellation Ursa Minor, which means Little Bear.

Ursa Minor appears to circle the North Star. It is visible all year long. Some groups of stars are only visible during certain seasons of the year.

There are twelve seasonal constellations that are especially important because the sun and the moon always rise within one of their patterns. These are the constellations of the Zodiac.

Constellations are used in ship and airplane navigation. Astronauts use them to help orient spacecraft.

From Lois A. Bader, *Reader's Passages to Accompany Bader Reading and Language Inventory* (3rd ed.), p. 23. Columbus, OH: Merrill/Prentice Hall, 1998. Reprinted with permission.

APPENDIX E

Scoring System for Oral Reading Miscue Analysis

SUBSTITUTION AND MISPRONUNCIATIONS

Underline and write the student's response above the word

Example: they <u>*shall*/will</u> go to principal's office

REPEATED WORD

Underline and write "R" above the word or phrase that was repeated

Example: Fred decided to go <u>to the *R*/movies.</u>

INSERTIONS

Write the word the student inserted with a caret

Example: the ^*big*/ bear

OMISSIONS

Circle the word omitted

Example: and so the (grumpy) giant walked

WORDS PROVIDED BY THE PERSON GIVING THE TEST

Underline the word and write T above it

Example: was so heavy it took three <u>*T*/sailors</u> to lift it

SELF-CORRECTIONS BY THE STUDENT

Underline the word, write the word the student said first, then write a C

Example: the <u>*terrific C*/terrible</u> storm destroyed

APPENDIX F

Scoring Sheet—Graded Reading Passage

Student Name _____Debbie_____   **Date** _____11/21/00_____

Passage Level: 3

JAMES' CUT

     It was after lunch when James cut his finger on the playground. He was bleeding

and <u>he hurt</u> *[HURTING]* a little too.

     He went inside to find his teacher. He showed her his <u>cut finger</u> *[R]* and asked for

a Band-Aid. <u>She</u> *[R]* looked at it and said, "Well, its not too bad, James. I think we should

wash it before <u>we</u> *[you]* bandage it, don't you?" James did not want it washed because he

thought it would sting. But he was afraid to tell Miss Smith. He just <u>acted</u> *[ACT]* brave.

     When it was washed <u>and</u> *[a]* bandaged, he thanked Miss Smith. <u>Then</u> *[WHEN]* he rushed out to

the playground to show everyone his shiny new bandage.

Passage from Lois A. Bader, *Reader's Passages to Accompany Bader Reading and Language Inventory* (3rd ed.), p. 13. Columbus, Ohio: Merrill/Prentice Hall, 1998. Reprinted with permission.

APPENDIX G

Diagrams of Expository Text Structures

Cause and Effect

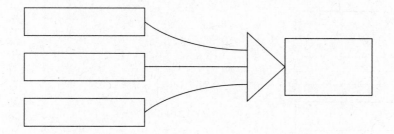

Problem and Solution

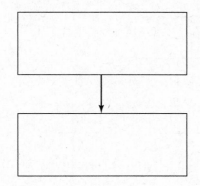

Comparison/Contrast

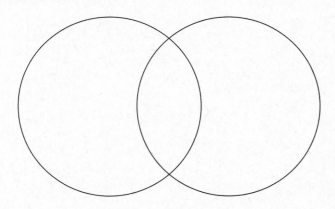

Sequence

1. ☐

2. ☐

3. ☐

4. ☐

5. ☐

Description

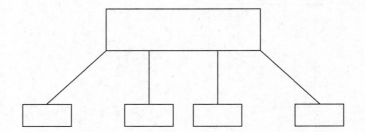

APPENDIX H

Graphic Organizer

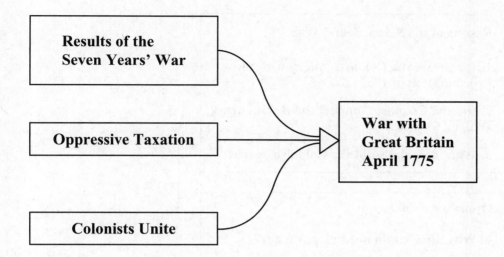

APPENDIX I

Study Guide Based on Text Structure

Results of the Seven Years' War

1. Why were the Colonists angry with the Proclamation of 1763?

2. Did the Colonists support the British army? Why or why not?

3. What new skills did the Colonists learn?

Oppressive Taxes

4. Why did Britain need more money?

5. Why were the Colonists opposed to new taxes?

6. How did the Colonists protest the Tea Act?

Colonists Unite

7. Why did the first Continental Congress meet in September 1774?

8. How had the Colonists' views of themselves and Britain changed in the 20 years from 1754 to 1774?

War with Great Britain April 1775

REFERENCE NOTES

This is a test preparation guide and books in this format do not usually include a reference list of the sort you would find in a methodology textbook. As I noted in the Introduction, the book is meant to be read after you have read a reading methods textbook. The relevant chapters in a methods text would both expand your knowledge of each topic and provide you with additional resources. I will mention relevant sources that you might want to look at for more information.

STATE OF CALIFORNIA DOCUMENTS

The revised *RICA Content Specifications* serve as the organizing framework for this book. They can be found at the RICA website: www.rica.nesinc.com. If you are taking the RICA, you should read the *Content Specifications*.

The *California English–Language Arts Content Standards* are referred to repeatedly in the book. The revised RICA is based on the *California English/Language Arts Framework for California Public Schools: Kindergarten through Grade Twelve* (2007). Both can be found on the State of California Department of Education website, www.cde.ca.gov. All future elementary teachers in California will need to work with these documents.

READING METHODS TEXTBOOKS

There are many excellent reading methods textbooks. I referred to the following three textbooks published by the publisher of this book:

Reutzel, D. R., & Cooter, R. B. (2008). *Teaching children to read: The teacher makes the difference* (5th ed.). Boston: Allyn & Bacon.

Temple, C., Ogle, D., Crawford, A., & Freppon, P. (2008). *All children read: Teaching for literacy in today's diverse classrooms* (2nd ed.). Boston: Allyn & Bacon.

Tompkins, G. E. (2010). *Literacy in the 21st century: A balanced approach* (5th ed.). Boston: Allyn & Bacon.

SUPPLEMENTAL BOOKS

Here are a few supplemental texts published by the publisher of this book that I found useful:

Bear, D. R., Invernizzi, M., Templeton, S., & Johnston, F. (2008). *Words their way: Word study for phonics, vocabulary, and spelling instruction.* Boston: Allyn & Bacon.

Eldredge, J. L. (2004). *Phonics for teachers: Self-instruction, methods and activities* (2nd ed.). Boston: Allyn & Bacon.

Hendricks, C., & Rinsky, L. A. (2007). *Teaching word recognition skills* (7th ed.). Boston: Allyn & Bacon.

Herrell, A. L., & Jordan, M. L. (2006). *Fifty strategies for improving vocabulary, comprehension, and fluency* (2nd ed.). Boston: Allyn & Bacon.

Rasinski, T., & Padak, N. (2004). *Effective reading strategies: Teaching children who find reading difficult.* Boston: Allyn & Bacon.

Yopp, R. H., & Yopp, H. K. (2010). *Literature-based reading activities* (5th ed.). Boston: Allyn & Bacon.

SUMMARIES OF READING RESEARCH

These works are appropriate for candidates for masters and doctoral degrees, but if you want to read summaries of the research on the topics presented in this book, then:

Farstrup, A. E., & Samuesl, S. J. (Eds.). (2002). *What research has to say about reading instruction*. Newark, DE: International Reading Association.

Kamil, M. L., Mosenthal, P. B., Pearson, P. D., & Barr, R. (Eds.). (2000). *Handbook of reading research (Vol. III)*. Mahwah, NJ: Lawrence Erlbaum.

National Institute of Child Health and Development (NICHD). (2000). *Report of the National Reading Panel. Teaching children to read: An evidence-based assessment of the scientific research literature on reading and its implication for reading instruction. Reports of the subgroups*. Washington, DC: National Institute of Child Health and Human Development/U.S. Department of Education/National Institute for Literacy. U.S. Government Printing Office, NIH Publication No. 00-04789. www.nationalreadingpanel.org

Snow, C. E., Burns, M. S., & Griffin, P. (Eds.). (1998). *Preventing reading difficulties in young children*. Washington, DC: National Academies Press.

JOURNALS

For any topic in this book, you can find relevant articles in two journals published by the International Reading Association, *The Reading Teacher* and *Reading Research Quarterly*.

INDEX

A

Abbreviations, 131–132
ABC books, 35
Academic argument, 121
Academic language
  assessment, 79, 87–88
  and comprehension, 76, 90, 91
  reading development, 76
  RICA study guides, 128
  teaching nontechnical, 78
  term, 75
Academic vocabulary tiers, 78
Accuracy
  assessment, 73
  fluency indicator, 65
  fluency strategies, 69, 70–71, 72
Acquainted words, 77
Advanced learners
  concepts about print, 38
  differentiated instruction, 29
  expository texts, 122–123
  fictional genres, 111
  language components, 62
  phonetics instruction, 54
  reading comprehension, 100–101
  reading fluency, 72
  vocabulary instruction, 87
Advanced stages, 47, 50–51
Affixes
  term, 57
  types of, 82
Alexander, Lloyd, 8
Alphabet principle
  assessment, 31, 39
  concepts about print, 31
  reading development, 31,
    35–36
  term, 24
Alphabet songs, 35
Alternate assessments, 14
Americans with Disabilities Act, 16
Analog phonetics, 48
Analogies, 87
Anecdotal records, 123
Animalia, 35
Answer verification, 95, 97
Antonym, 82
Application, 7
Assessment

academic language, 79, 87–88
background knowledge, 79
communicating results, 14, 22–23
concepts about print, 31, 38–40
expository texts' comprehension,
  123
IEP/Section 504 Plan, 14, 15–16
instructional decisions, 2
interpretation/uses, 14, 17–20
literary comprehension, 111–112
orthographic knowledge, 58, 62
phonemic awareness, 29–30
phonetics, 47
phonological awareness, 29–30
quality indicators, 14, 16–17
reading comprehension, 95, 101–103
reading fluency, 69, 72–74
sight words, 47
spelling, 63
structural analysis, 58, 62–63
student reading levels, 14, 20–22
syllabic analysis, 58, 63
term, 14
three purposes, 14–15
vocabulary, 79, 87–88
Association
  letter recognition strategies, 34
  reading comprehension, 96
At-home reading, 10–11
Auditory discrimination, 29
Auditory strategies/techniques
  challenged students, 62
  high frequency words, 52
  spelling, 61
Author and you
  QAR system, 97
  reading comprehension assessment,
    101–102
Author studies
  engaging/motivating students, 8
  fictional genres, 109
Autobiography, 105
Automaticity
  reading fluency, 66
  skills, 2
  word recognition, 42
Automaticity theory
  and comprehension, 90
  fluency indicator, 66

B

Backdrop, 106
Background knowledge
  assessment, 79
  and comprehension, 90, 91
  and expository texts, 122
  and reading comprehension, 95–96
  and reading development, 76
  and reading fluency, 65, 67
  RICA study guide, 128
  term, 75
Bader Graded Word Lists, 21
Bader, Lois A., 139, 141, 142, 144
*Bader Reading and Language
  Inventory*, 20, 21, 139
Balanced instruction, 2
Ballad, 105
Basal reading programs, 6
Base, Graeme, 35
Beginning stage phonetics instruction,
  47, 49–50
Benchmark groups, 6
Big books, 33
Biography, 105
Black Cauldron, The, 8
Blending, 49
Blending skills, 28
Book clubs
  engaging/motivating students, 8
  fictional genres, 109
Book-handling skills
  concepts about print, 32
  English learners, 37
Book reports, 11
Book selection, 9
Books, 32–33
Bound morphemes, 57, 82
Brown, Margaret Wise, 8, 112
Bud, Not Buddy, 8
Burton, Virginia Lee, 107

C

California Achievement Tests (CAT), 87
California Department of Education
  web site, 1
California Reading Association
  (CRA), 13
*California Reading/Language Arts
  Framework for California Public
  Schools, Kindergarten through
  Grade Twelve*
  assessment types, 14–15
  as blueprint, 2

instructional delivery model, 6–7
instructional profile, 4
California Reading/Language Arts
  Specialist Certificate/Credential, 12
California Standards Test (CST), state
  standards, 1
California State Board of Education
  (SBE), 6
Capitalization, 85
Case study
  RICA example, 130–134
  RICA practice test, 137
Cause and effect
  diagram, 145
  expository texts, 115
  sentences, 93
Character(s)
  literary analysis, 108
  literary genres, 106
  story grammar, 106
Characterization, 73
Charlotte's Web, 101–102, 105
Charts, 116
Clarifying, 98
Class profile
  assessment results, 18, 19–20
  concepts about print, 40
  expository texts, 124
  literary comprehension, 113
  reading comprehension, 103
  reading fluency, 74
  structural/syllabic analysis, 64
  vocabulary, 89
Classroom
  borrowed books, 10–11
  independent reading, 10
  print-rich, 33
Clay, Marie, 31, 38
Cleary, Beverly, 105
Closed syllable, 57
Cognates, 86
Compare/contrast
  diagram, 145
  expository texts, 115
  sentences, 93
Complex sentence, 92
Complexity factor, 5
Compound sentence, 92
Comprehension. *See also* Reading
  comprehension
  evaluative, 90, 92
  inferential, 90, 91
  language components, 90–91

literal, 90, 91
other activities, 90, 93–93
reading fluency, 65, 67
RICA study guide, 128
and sentence/text structure, 90, 92–93
term, 90
Comprehension skills, assessment, 101–102
Comprehensive instruction, 2
Concepts about print
alphabet principle, 31, 35–36
assessment, 31, 38–39
assessment results, 39–40
instructional strategies, 32–34
learners needs, 31, 36–38
reading development, 31, 32–34
recognition strategies, 31, 34–35
RICA study guide, 126
term, 31
writing strategies, 31, 36
Concepts about Print test, 38
Concrete examples
phonemic awareness difficulties, 28
phonics skills/sight words, 52–53
vocabulary instruction, 86
Consonant blends, instruction sequence, 43
Consonant- consonant-vowel-consonant (CCVC) patterns
advanced phonics instruction, 50
instruction sequence, 44
Consonant digraphs, instruction sequence, 43
Consonant instruction sequence, 42–43
Consonant-vowel-consonant (CVC) patterns
instruction sequence, 43–44
phonetics instruction, 49
Consonant-vowel-consonant-consonant (CVCC) patterns
advanced phonics instruction, 50
instruction sequence, 44
Consonant-vowel-consonant-e (CVCE) patterns
advanced phonics instruction, 50
instruction sequence, 44
Consonant-vowel-vowel-consonant (CVVC) patterns
advanced phonics instruction, 50
instruction sequence, 44
Consonants, 25

Contemporary realistic fiction, 105
Content-area literacy, 114
Content-area textbooks strategies, 114, 116–118
Context clues, 42
Contextual analysis, 81, 82
Contextual clues, 21
Contextual redefinition, 80
Conventional stage, 45
Coordinators, 92
Couplet, 105
Creech, Sharon, 105
Cross-references, 120
"Cubbies," 34
Cultural context, 110
Cumulative tales, 104
Curious George, 4

D

Data retrieval chart, 117, 118
DEAR (Drop Everything and Read), 10
Decodable text
phonetics instruction, 49–50, 51
reading fluency, 65, 67
Definition, 82
Delivery mode, 16
Denouement, 106
Dependent clause, 92
Description, 115
Description diagram, 146
Descriptive sentences, 93
Diagrams
cause and effect, 145
compare/contrast, 145
description, 146
expository texts, 145–146
graphic features, 116
problem and solution, 145
sequence, 146
Dictionary, 81, 82–83
Differentiated instruction
concepts about print, 36–37
instruction standards, 3–4
Diphthongs, 43
Direct/explicit instruction, 47
Direct instruction, 3
Direct teaching, 34
Directionality
concepts about print, 32
English learners, 37
Discussions
and comprehension, 90, 93, 94
reading comprehension, 99

Double-entry journals, 110
Dramatic plays, 104
*Dynamic Indicators of Basic Early
Literacy Skills* (DIBELS-ORF), 72

E

Ebert, Roger, 11
Ella Enchanted, 8
E-mail, 23
Embedded phonetics, 48
Encyclopedias, 120
English language structure, 85
English learners (EL)
  additional SBE materials, 6
  concepts about print, 37
  expository texts, 122
  fictional genres, 111
  language components, 62
  parental support, 11
  phonemic awareness difficulties, 29
  phonics interventions, 53
  reading comprehension, 100
  reading fluency, 72
  vocabulary instruction, 86
*English-Language Arts Content
Standards for California Public
Schools, Kindergarten through
Grade Twelve*
  communicating assessment
   results, 22
  compound sentences, 92
  concepts about print, 40
  establishment, 1
  goals/objectives, 4
  grade-level meetings, 12
  literary comprehension, 113
  phonemic awareness assessment, 30
  reading comprehension, 103
  student skills/knowledge, 3
  summative assessment, 17
  vocabulary assessment, 88
Entry-level assessment
  concepts about print, 39
  expository texts, 123–124
  literary comprehension, 112
  phonics/sight words, 55
  phonological/phonemic
   awareness, 30
  reading comprehension, 102, 103
  reading fluency, 73
  structural/syllabic analysis, 63
  term, 14
  vocabulary, 88

Environmental print, 33
Epic, 105
Essays, 110
Established words, 77
Etymology
  phonetic irregularity, 44
  word consciousness, 84
Evaluative comprehension, 90, 92
Evidence, 112
Example, 82
Explicit instruction, 3
Expository texts,
  activities, 114, 119
  assessment, 123
  assessment results, 124
  characteristics, 114–115
  content-area strategies, 114,
   116–118
  learners' needs, 121–123
  research skills, 114, 121
  RICA study guide, 129
  study skills, 114, 119–120
  term, 104
  text features, 114, 115–116
  text structures, 114, 115
  text structure diagrams, 145–146
Exposure, 79

F

Fables, 105
Fairy tales, 104
Families, phonograms, 25
Feedback, 69
Fictional stories
  assessment results, 112–113
  comprehension assessment, 104,
   111–112
  learners' difficulties, 104, 110–111
  major genres, 104–105
  narrative analysis/literary criticism,
   104, 108–109
  oral language activities, 104, 109–110
  story grammar, 104, 106–107
  teaching literary genres, 106
  writing activities, 104, 110
Fifth grade, 103
Figurative language, 109
First grade
  fluency standards, 74
  graded reading passage, 141
Flexible grouping, 5
Fluency. *See* Reading fluency
Folklore, 104–105

Folktales, 104
Foreshadowing, 109
Fourth grade, 92
Free morpheme, 57, 82
Free retelling, 102
Frequency, 78
Frustration reading level, 22
Fry, Edward, 51
Fry Graph Readability Formula, 123

G
Generating questions, 98
Glossary, 116
Goal(s), 4
Goodnight, Moon, 8
Grade equivalent scores, 17
Grade level
  fluency standards, 74
  reading instruction, 3
Grade-level content, 17–18
Grade-level meetings, 12
Graded reading passage
  grade 1, 141
  grade 6, 142
  reading levels, 21
  scoring sheet, 144
Graded word lists
  sample, 139
  scoring sheet sample, 140
Gradual release of responsibility
    model, 98
Graphemes, 24
Graphic features
  expository texts, 116
  reading comprehension, 96
Graphic organizer(s)
  diagram, 147
  expository text activity, 119
  text instruction strategies, 117
Graphophonemic errors, 21
Gray Oral Reading Test (GORT-4), 72
Groups, 61
Guardian, 22, 23
Guide words
  research skills, 120
  text features, 116
Guided practice, 7

H
*Harry Potter and the Sorcerer's
    Stone*, 110
Hesse, Karen, 107
Heterogeneous groups, 5

High fantasy genre, 105, 106
High frequency words, 51–52
Historical fiction, 105
Hoban, Tana, 35
Holdaway, Don, 32
Holes, 8, 112
Homogenous groups, 5
Homographs, 83
Homophones, 83
House That Jack Build, The, 33, 104
"How-to" texts, 119
Hyperbole, 109

I
I-Chart, 120
Idioms, 84
Illustrations, 116
Imagery, 109
In-depth reading, 119–120
Independent practice, 7
Independent reading
  advantages of, 9
  and comprehension, 90, 93, 94
  RICA study guide, 125
  term, 8
Independent reading level
  assessment results, 22
  book selection, 9
Index
  research skills, 120
  text features, 116
Individual conferences
  assessment results, 22
  and independent reading, 12
Individual profile
  assessment results, 18–19
  concepts about print, 40
  expository texts, 124
  literary comprehension, 113
  reading comprehension, 103
  reading fluency, 74
  structural/syllabic analysis, 64
  vocabulary, 89
Individualized Education Program
    (IEP), 14, 15–16
Individualized instruction
  organization, 5
  spelling, 61
Individuals with Disabilities Education
    Act (IDEA), 15–16
Inferential comprehension, 90, 91
Inflected suffixes, 51
Informal assessment, 38

Informal reading inventories (IRI),
20–21
Instructional reading level, 22
Integral element, 106
Intensive groups, 6
Interest, 9
Interest inventories, 9–10
International Reading Association
(IRA), 13
Invented spelling, 36
Irony, 109
Island of the Blue Dolphins, 8, 105

J

Judge, The, 33

K

Key questions study guide, 118
Kindergarten, 74
Kinesthetic
activities/lessons/techniques
letter recognition strategies, 35
spelling, 61
vocabulary instruction, 86
King's Fifth, The, 8
Knowledge, 4
Knowledge level, 78
KWL charts
reading comprehension, 96
text instruction strategies, 117

L

Labels/captions, 33
Language experience approach
(LEA), 33
Language structure
knowledge assessment, 88
teaching, 85
L-controlled vowels, 43
Learners with difficulties
expository texts, 121–122
fictional genres, 104, 110–111
phonetics teaching fundamentals, 47,
52–54
reading comprehension, 95, 99–101
reading development/instruction, 31
reading fluency interventions, 71–72
structural/syllabic analysis, 58,
61–62
vocabulary, 79, 85–87
Learning environment, 7
Learning objectives, 4
Letter formation
assessment, 38–39

and English learners, 37
and letter recognition strategies, 34
term, 31
Letter naming
assessment, 38–39
and English learners, 37
and letter recognition strategies, 34
term, 31
Letter production, 31
Letter recognition
assessment, 31, 38–39
and English learners, 37
reading development, 31, 34–35
RICA study guide, 126
term, 31
Letter/word representation, 37
Letter-sound correspondence
concepts about print, 31, 32
reading development, 31, 32, 36
Letters, similar, 35
Lewis, C. S., 105, 109
*Lion, the Witch and the Wardrobe,
The*, 105, 109, 110
Listening, 79, 84–85
Listening comprehension, 90, 93
Listening vocabulary, 75
Literacy coaches, 12
Literal comprehension, 90, 91
Literary analysis, 108
Literary criticism, 108
Literary elements, 112
Literary texts
RICA study guide, 128–129
term, 104
Literature circles
engaging/motivating students, 8
fictional genres, 109
Literature journals, 110
Literature logs, 110
Little House, The, 107
Little Island, The, 8
Long-term goal, 4
Lowercase writing, 35
Lyric, 105

M

Mailboxes, 34
Make Way for Ducklings, 48, 113
Making words activity, 54
Maps, 116
Matthew Effect, The," 77
Meaning (reading) vocabulary, 75
Mental imagery, 61

Metaphor, 09
Midwife's Apprentice, The, 112
Miscue analysis, 21
Missing May, 105
Modeling
  expository texts, 122
  fluency strategies, 69
Modern fantasy genre, 105
Monitoring of progress assessment. *See*
  Progress-monitoring assessment
Mood
  literary genres, 106
  story grammar, 107
Morning message, 33–34
Morpheme, 57, 82
Morphemes instruction, 86
Morphemic analysis
  assessment, 88
  term, 57
  word-learning strategies, 81–82
Morphological units, 43
Morphology, 41
Motivation, 7
Multidimensional Fluency Scale, 73
Multiple choice questions, 135–137
Myths, 105

N

Napping House, The, 33
Narrative analysis, 108
Narrative texts
  RICA study guide, 128–129
  term, 104
*National Assessment of Education
  Progress Fluency Scale* (NAEP-
  Fluency), 72
"New Instant Word List, The," 44,
  51, 52
No Child Left Behind Act, 13
Norm-referenced scores, 17
Note-taking, 120
Novels, 104

O

O'Dell, Scott, 8, 105
Observation, 123
On my own
  QAR system, 97
  reading comprehension assessment,
  102
Onset/rime blending, 26
Onsets, 25
Open-ended assignments, 137

Open syllables, 57
Oral analysis, 111
Oral language, 90, 93
Oral language activities, 109–110
Oral presentation(s)
  independent reading, 11
  learner difficulties, 110
  reading comprehension difficulties, 100
Oral reading
  fluency strategies, 69
  miscue analysis scoring system, 143
  reading fluency, 72
Oral think alouds, 102
Organization, 120
Organizing associations, 96
Orientation, 6–7
Orthographic knowledge
  assessment, 58, 62
  RICA study guide, 127
  term, 57
  using, 58, 61
Orthography, 46
Out of the Dust, 107, 112
Outlining, 120

P

Pacing, 5
Pacing guides, 4
Paired reading, 70
Paragraph structure, 92
Paraphrasing
  expository text activity, 119
  strategic reading, 97
Parent(s), 11, 22
Parent conferences, 23
Part-to-whole instruction/lessons
  phonetics fundamentals, 48
  structural analysis, 58, 59
Percentile score, 16
Personal perspective, 99
Personification, 109
Persuasive tests, 119
Peter Rabbit, 4
Phase-cue reading, 71
Phoneme, 24
Phonemic awareness
  assessment, 29–30
  and phonics, 27–28
  RICA study guide, 125–126
  role, 25
  struggling students, 28–29
  teaching, 26–27
  term, 24

Phonetic alphabet, 24
Phonetic irregularity, 44
Phonetic knowledge, 45–46
Phonetic spelling, 36
Phonetic stage, 45
Phonetics
  advanced stage instruction,
    50–51
  assessment, 47, 54–5
  assessment results, 55–56
  beginning stage instruction, 47,
    49–50
  differentiated teaching, 47,
    52–54
  sight words instruction, 47,
    51–52
  teaching fundamentals, 47–49
Phonics
  instruction sequence, 42–45
  and phonemic awareness, 27–28
  RICA study guide, 126
  spelling development, 42
  term, 24, 41
  word identification, 42
Phonograms, 25
Phonological awareness
  assessment, 29–30
  RICA study guide, 125
  role, 25
  teaching, 25–26
  term, 24
Picture walk, 96
Pitch, 73
"Placement" assessment, 101
Plays, 104
Plot
  literary analysis, 108
  literary genres, 106
  story grammar, 106
Poems, 104
Poetry
  fictional genre, 105
  word consciousness, 84
Polar Express, The, 111
Pourquoi tales, 104
Practice
  delivery components, 7
  fluency strategies, 69
  phonemic awareness difficulties, 28
  phonetics fundamentals, 49
  phonics skills/sight words, 52–53
  reading fluency, 72
Practice assessments, 16

Practice test, *RICA*, 135–137
Precommunication stage, 45
Predictable books, 33
Predicting, 98
Prefix, 58–59
Prefixes
  morphemes, 82
  term, 57
PreP, 96
Prerequisites, 4–5
Presentation, 7
Prevention, 3
Principals, 23
Print tracking, 37
Probed recall, 102
Problem and solution
  diagram, 145
  expository texts, 115
  sentences, 93
Professional organizations, 13
Progress-monitoring assessment
  assessment types, 15
  concepts about print, 39
  expository texts, 123–124
  literary comprehension, 112
  phonics/sight words, 55
  phonological/phonemic awareness, 30
  reading comprehension, 102, 103
  reading fluency, 73
  structural/syllabic analysis, 63
  vocabulary, 88
Pronunciation errors, 53–54
Prosody
  assessment, 73
  fluency indicator, 66
  phased-cued reading, 71
  term, 69
Public library, 11
Punctuation
  prosody assessment, 73
  vocabulary building, 85
Puns, 84
Purpose, 96

Q

QAR system
  reading comprehension, 97
  reading comprehension assessment,
    101
Question classification, 95, 97
Questioning the author, fictional
    genres, 109
Quotes and notes, 110

R

Rate
  assessment, 73
  fluency indicator, 65
  fluency strategies, 69, 71, 72
Raygor Readability Estimate, 123
R-controlled vowels, 43
Read aloud, 111
Readability, 123
Reader's workshop, 10
Reading
  standards, 1
  structural analysis, 58
  syllabic analysis, 58
  vocabulary instruction, 79, 85
Reading aloud
  concepts about print, 32
  engaging/motivating students, 8
Reading coaches, 12
Reading comprehension
  and academic language, 76
  after reading, 95, 99
  assessment, 95, 101–103
  assessment results, 103
  background knowledge, 76
  learners' needs, 95, 99–101
  prior to reading, 95–96
  question/answer, 95, 97
  strategic reading, 95, 97–98
  study guide, 128
  vocabulary, 76
Reading development
  academic language, 76, 78
  background knowledge, 76
  vocabulary, 76–77
Reading fluency
  assessment, 69, 72–73
  assessment results, 73–74
  and comprehension, 90
  decodable texts, 65, 67
  disruptive influences, 65, 66–67
  instructional strategies, 69–71
  key indicators, 65–66
  orthographic knowledge, 58
  and reading development, 65, 66
  reading instruction, 65, 67
  reading skills, 65, 66
  RICA study guide, 127
  silent reading, 65, 68
  and vocabulary, 76
  word recognition, 42
Reading guides, 117
Reading instruction

alphabet principle, 31, 35–36
concepts about print, 31, 32–34
differentiated key factors, 1, 4–5
effectiveness components, 1, 6–7
engaging/motivating students, 1, 7–8
fluency strategies, 69
Framework standards, 2
independent reading, 1, 8–12
learners needs, 31, 36–38
letter recognition, 31, 34–35
letter-sound correspondence, 31,
  32, 36
organization, 1, 5–6
phonetics fundamentals, 47, 48–49
phonic/sight words sequence, 42–45
principles, 1–4
and reading fluency, 65, 67
RICA study guide, 125
sight words, 51–52
support systems, 1, 12–13
writing, 31, 36
*Reading Instruction Competence
  Assessment* (RICA). *See RICA
  Content Specifications*
Reading level determination, 101
Reading logs
  fictional genres, 110
  independent reading, 11
Reading rate adjustment, 98
Reciprocal teaching, 98–99
Reference texts, 114
Reflection, 96
Reliability, 16
Remediation, 3
Repeated readings, 70
Rereading, 117
Research skills, 120–121
Reteach(ing)
  expository texts, 121–122
  fictional genres, 111
  phonemic awareness, 28
  phonics skills/sight words, 52–53
  reading comprehension, 100
  vocabulary instruction, 86
Retelling, 102
RICA Content Specifications
  advanced learners, 38, 54, 62,
    72, 87
  advanced stage phonics, 50, 51
  beginning stage phonics, 49
  case study, 130, 131–132, 134
  case study analysis criteria, 131–132
  concepts about print, 31

decodable sight words, 44–45
differentiated instruction, 36
EL vocabulary instruction, 86
English learners, 37, 53
literary analysis, 108
phonic difficulties, 52
poetic genres, 105
practice test, 135–137
reading comprehension, 99
word identification/word
  recognition, 41
Right there
  QAR system, 97
  reading comprehension assessment,
  101
Rimes, 25
Roll of Thunder, Here My Cry, 105
Roots, 58–59
Rowling, J. K., 105
Runaway Bunny, The, 8
"Running record," 21
Rylant, Cynthia, 105

S
Sachar, Louis, 112
Scaffolding
  expository texts, 122
  key factors, 5
Scanning
  research skills, 120
  study skills, 119
School district, 23
School library, 10–11
Science fiction genre, 105
Science textbooks, 114
Second grade
  fluency standards, 74
  vocabulary assessment, 88
Section 504 Plan, 14, 16
Self-paced, 8–9
Self-selected, 8–9
Self-study, 60
Semantic errors, 21
Semantic feature analysis, 80, 81
Semantic maps (webs)
  expository text activity, 119
  vocabulary instruction, 80, 81
Semiphonetic stage, 45
Sentence, 93
Sentence representation, 32
Sentence structure
  and comprehension, 90, 92
  vocabulary building, 85

Sequence
  diagram, 146
  expository texts, 115
  sentences, 93
Setting
  literary analysis, 108
  literary genres, 106
  story grammar, 106
Shared book experience, 32–33
Short stories, 104
Short-term goal, 4
Sight (reading) vocabulary, 75
Sight words
  assessment, 47, 54–55
  assessment results, 55–56
  and decodable words, 44–45
  English learners, 53
  instruction sequence, 42–45, 52
  reading fluency, 72
  study guide, 126
  teaching fundamentals, 47, 51–52
  word identification, 41, 42
Silent reading, 65, 68, 72
Simile, 109
Simple sentence, 92
Simplification, 16
Sing Down the Moon, 8
Siskel, Gene, 11
Sixth grade, 142
"Skeletal" map, 107
Skill, 2
Skills
  grade level mastery, 3
  key factors, 4
Skimming, 119
Social studies textbooks, 114, 115
Sonnet, 105
Sound blending, 27
Sound deletion, 27
Sound identity, 26–27
Sound isolation, 26
Sound substitution, 27
Sounding out, 49
Sounds
  consonant, 42
  English learners, 53
  stop, 43
Sources, 121
Speaking, 79, 84–85
Speaking vocabulary, 75
Spelling
  advanced phonetics instruction, 51
  high frequency words, 52

and phonics, 42, 45–46
  RICA study guide, 127
  teaching techniques, 58, 60
  VC/CVC words, 50
SQ3R, study skills, 120
Standardized Testing and Reporting
    (STAR)
  communicating assessment
    results, 23
  state standards, 1
Standardized tests
  interpretation, 17
  quality indicators, 16–17
  term, 16
Stanford Achievement Tests (SAT), 87
Stanine scores, 17
Star diagram, 107
Story grammar
  learner difficulties, 110
  literary elements, 106
  outlines, 107
Story maps
  learner difficulties, 110
  story grammar, 107
Stow, Jenny, 33
Strategic groups, 6
Strategic read-alouds, 94
Strategic reading, 95, 97–98
Strategy, 2
Strengths, 130–131
Structural analysis
  assessment, 58, 62–63
  reading/writing use, 58, 61
  RICA study guide, 127
  teaching, 58–59
  term, 41, 57
Structural overview, 117
Structured independent reading, 10
Structured practice, 7
Student engagement, 7
Student
  with concepts about print difficulties,
    36–37
  with expository text difficulties,
    121–122
  with fictional genres difficulties, 104,
    110–111
  with phonemic awareness difficulties,
    28–29
  with phonic difficulties, 52–53
  with reading difficulties, 61–62
  with reading comprehension
    difficulties, 95, 99–101

with reading fluency difficulties,
    71–72
  reading logs, 11
  strengths/needs, 130–131
Study guide
  RICA key points, 125–129
  text instruction strategies, 117–118
  text structure diagram, 148
Study skills, 119–120
Style
  literary analysis, 108–109
  story grammar, 107
Subordinators, 92
Subtitles, 133
Suffixes
  morphemes, 82
  structural analysis, 58–59
  term, 57
Summaries of progress, 22, 23
Summarizing
  expository text activity, 119
  reading comprehension, 99
  strategic reading, 98
Summative assessment
  assessment results, 17
  concepts about print, 39
  expository texts, 123–124
  literary comprehension, 112
  phonics/sight words, 55
  phonological/phonemic awareness,
    30
  reading comprehension, 102, 103
  reading fluency, 73
  structural/syllabic analysis, 63
  term, 15
  vocabulary, 88
Support systems, 12–13
Sustained silent reading (SSR), 10
Syllabic analysis
  assessment, 58, 63
  reading/writing use, 58, 61
  study guide, 127
  teaching, 58, 59–60
  term, 41, 57
Syllable(s)
  awareness, 26
  blending, 26
  division rules, 44
  term, 57
Symbol, 109
Synonym(s)
  contextual clue, 82
  vocabulary assessment, 87

Syntactic errors, 21
Syntax, 85, 86–87
Systematic instruction
 phonetics, 47
 term, 3

T

Table of content, 116
Tactile activities/techniques
 spelling, 61
 vocabulary, 86
Tactile lessons, 35
Tactile strategies
 challenged students, 62
 high frequency words, 52
"Talk written down," 32
Tall tales, 104–105
Tape-assisted reading, 70
Target words
 vocabulary, 77
 vocabulary instruction, 79
Taylor, Mildred, 105
Technology, 121
Telephone, 23
Temporary spelling, 36
Tests, 38. *See also* Assessment
Text
 complexity, 77
 and reading fluency, 72
 term, 8
Text features, 114
Text structure(s)
 and comprehension, 90, 93
 diagrams, 145–146, 148
 patterns, 115
 textbooks, 114
Text-to-self, 112
Text-to-self connections, 99
Text-to-text, 112
Text-to-text connections, 99
Text-to-world, 112
Text-to-world connections, 99
Textbooks, state standards, 1
Theme(s)
 literary analysis, 108
 literary genres, 106
 story grammar, 107
Think and search
 QAR system, 97
 reading comprehension
  assessment, 101
Think-alouds, 116
Think-pair-share, 109–110

Third grade, 74
Three-level study guide, 118
Time, 16
Timed-readings, 70
Topic identification, 121
Topics
 fictional genres, 110
 RICA abbreviations, 131–132
Traditional literature, 104
Transitional stage, 45
Trickster tales, 104
26 Letters and 99 Cents, 35

U

Unaided retelling, 102
Units, 16
Unknown words, 77
Uppercase writing, 35
Utility, 78

V

Validity, 16–17
van Allsburg, Chris, 111
Venn diagram, 123
Verbal irony, 109
Visual activities/techniques/strategies
 high frequency words, 52
 spelling, 60
 vocabulary instruction, 86
Visual/graphic representations, 99
Visualizing, 97
Vocabulary
 assessment, 79, 87–88
 and comprehension, 90
 expository texts difficulties, 122
 fictional genres, 111
 and spelling, 46
 "The Matthew Effect," 77
 reading development, 76
 reading fluency, 67
 study guide, 128
 term, 75
Vocabulary instruction**
 assessment results, 88–89
 consideration factors, 78
 and reading, 79, 84
 and reading comprehension, 96
 research-based, 79–80
 specific words, 79, 80–81
 student with difficulties, 85–87
 support activities, 79, 84–85
 target words, 77
 word consciousness, 79, 83–84
 word-learning strategies, 79, 81–83

Vowel digraphs, 43
Vowel-consonant (VC) patterns
  beginning phonetics instruction, 49
  instruction sequence, 43
Vowels
  instruction sequence, 43
  term, 24–25

W

Walk Two Moons, 105
Where the Wild Things Are, 40
Whole-class instruction, 5–6
Whole-to-part instruction/lessons
  phonetics fundamentals, 48
  structural analysis, 58
*Why Mosquitoes Buzz in People's
  Ears*, 104
Wood, Audrey, 33
Word analysis, 90
Word analysis skills, 65, 66–67
Word awareness, 25–26
Word blending, 26
Word consciousness, 79, 83–84
Word identification
  components, 58, 100
  instruction sequence, 42–45
  phonics/sight words, 42, 44–45
  and spelling stages, 42, 45–46
  term, 41
Word identification lessons, 49, 50
"Word of the day," 83–84

Word recognition
  concepts about print, 32
  term, 41
  and word identification, 42
Word recognition lists, 20–21
Word sorts, 80, 81
Word-learning strategies, 79, 81–83
Writing
  as applied phonics, 46
  and comprehension, 90, 93, 94
  fictional genre activities, 110
  letter recognition strategies, 35
  and orthographic knowledge, 58
  and reading comprehension, 99
  reading development/instruction, 31
  structural analysis, 58
  syllabic analysis, 58
  vocabulary instruction, 79, 85
Writing vocabulary, 75
Written analysis, 111
Written assessment, 102
Written summaries of progress, 22, 23

Y

*Yopp-Singer Test of Phoneme
  Segmentation*, 29

Z

Zemach, Harve, 33
Zia, 8